THE OPEN DOOR AT HOME

THE OPEN DOOR
AT HOME

A TRIAL PHILOSOPHY
OF NATIONAL INTEREST

BY

CHARLES A. BEARD

With the collaboration of
G. H. E. SMITH

GREENWOOD PRESS, PUBLISHERS
WESTPORT, CONNECTICUT

The Library of Congress has catalogued this publication as follows:

Library of Congress Cataloging in Publication Data

Beard, Charles Austin, 1874-1948.
  The open door at home.

    1. Economic policy. 2. United States--Economic
policy--1933-1945. 3. United States--Foreign relations.
4. United States--Commercial policy. I. Smith, George
Howard Edward, 1898-1962, joint author. II. Title.
HC106.3.B43 1972   330.9'73'09   76-140650
ISBN 0-8371-5811-7

Originally published in 1934
by The Macmillan Company, New York

Reprinted with the permission
of William Beard and Mrs. Miriam B. Vagts

First Greenwood Reprinting 1972

Library of Congress Catalogue Card Number 76-140650

ISBN 0-8371-5811-7

Printed in the United States of America

PREFACE

IN a previous volume, *The Idea of National Interest*, an effort was made to set forth, in systematic form, professions and actions of American statesmen coming under the head of "national interest." That work was the result of an inquiry: What is the meaning of this term so generally employed to guide and justify the foreign policies of the United States? In those pages the design was to present theories and facts without criticism, as far as humanly possible; not all the theories and facts, as was explained in the Preface (p. vi), but *relevant* theories and facts.

The upshot of the inquiry into the idea of national interest as manifested by professions and practices of American statesmen was a revelation of confusions and contradictions. Self-cancelling operations were found to be approved by statesmen of the same political school. For example, under Republican administrations, it was supposed to be in the national interest to promote the sale of cigarettes to China, and at the same moment to promote the sale of cigarette-making machinery which almost destroyed the Chinese market for American cigarettes. As a result it proved to be impossible to arrange even the major portion of the facts unearthed by the investigation in any consistent pattern, and secure a uniform meaning for the idea of national interest. At best the facts collected seemed to acquire a certain congruity only when classified under two schemes of thought, characterized as Hamiltonian and Jeffersonian respectively. Even then the border line between them appeared uncertain; as time went on the Jeffersonian system seemed to merge into the Hamiltonian system, with some variations and discordances.

After studying thousands of actions justified by the appellation "national interest," I was tempted to conclude that the conception was simply a telling formula which politicians and private interests employed whenever they wished to accom-

plish any particular designs in the field of foreign affairs. At
all events, it has been widely used for just such purposes and
with no additional significance. But there is something in the
idea, difficult as it is to discover the nature of that something.
There are a few common denominators, such as American
nationality, defense, security, and economic advantage, varying as the interpretations of these words have been in the long
course of American history. Furthermore, although past practices justified by the use of the formula of national interest
have eventuated in a ruinous crisis in economy, new policy is
being sought under the same covering maxim.

Finding it impossible to construct a consistent system of
national interest by adding particular interests often irrecon-
cilable as pursued and equally impossible to escape from the
exigency of certain realities covered by the formula, I then
sought to work out a conception of national interest free from
gross contradictions and unattainable ambitions. In this operation things deemed inexorable in the American scene were
taken into account and changes in policy designed to effect
consistency and security were drawn under consideration.
Hence the structure of the present volume is enclosed in what
may be called an ideal conception of national interest and
takes, for that reason, the form of an argument.

In other words, I have sought to separate, to the best of my
ability, the fact statement given in *The Idea of National Interest* from my personal views submitted here to the judgment of
the reader. Although it is impossible to draw an absolute line
between descriptions of things said and done by others, on the
one side, and statements of personal opinions, on the other, this
ideal has been kept constantly in mind in the preparation of the
two volumes.

The effort to distinguish between knowledge that can be
verified by research, and thought or opinion hazarded, difficult
as it may be, is especially useful in the discussion of public
questions. As a rule fact and fancy, things actually known
and things merely desired, are hopelessly confused in contemporary thinking, whether by scholars, scientists, politicians,
businessmen, or casual bystanders. Indeed, it is an almost
universal practice to mix facts and fancies, and to imagine that

pure personal opinions, not subject at all to verification by knowledge, if stated passionately and vociferously enough, are facts established beyond debate.

For practical as well as theoretical reasons, therefore, I have striven to maintain the distinction in these two volumes. The operation is frankly confessed in advance. This is my interpretation of history and policy, my presentation of a program. No attempt is made to slip up on the reader silently, throw a snare of alleged or indubitable facts over his head, and bring him to earth in a net of inexorable logic or historical necessity. The following pages are, avowedly, an expression of my conception of national interest as a guide to future policy. They are presented to the reader as such and in no other guise. Time will pass upon their validity and upon his judgment. Since any formulation of a large public policy is at bottom an interpretation of all history, it follows that a judgment upon such a policy is also an interpretation of all history—frightful as the thought is to contemplate.

Perhaps a few words should be said about the title, *The Open Door at Home*. It is borrowed in part from a misleading formula of that diplomacy which ostensibly seeks the welfare of the United States by pushing and holding doors open in all parts of the world with all engines of government, ranging from polite coercion to the use of arms. As employed here the title means the most efficient use of the natural resources and industrial arts of the nation at home in a quest for security and a high standard of living. Thus it is a direct antithesis of the historic policy which has eventuated in the present economic calamity. It implies a reversal of reliance on imprudent risks and invites the American nation to open doors at home, to substitute an intensive cultivation of its own garden for a wasteful, quixotic, and ineffectual extension of interests beyond the reach of competent military and naval defense.

Like *The Idea of National Interest*, this volume has been prepared under the auspices of the Social Science Research Council, with the aid of a grant from the Carnegie Corporation; but, since both institutions gave me an absolutely free hand, I must assume full responsibility for all that follows. It was originally my purpose to include supporting materials for the text in an appendix containing about two hundred pages of bibliography, notes, and statistical tables; but, since the volume is really directed to the general reader rather than the specialist, I have finally decided to omit this display of "scholarly apparatus."

CHARLES A. BEARD.

New Milford, Conn.,
Autumn, 1934.

CONTENTS

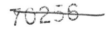

THE OPEN DOOR AT HOME

CHAPTER I

THE CRISIS IN MODERN THOUGHT

THE predicament in which the nations of the earth are now floundering is a crisis in thought as well as economy. Any attempt to comprehend and escape from either dilemma involves an effort to grasp and resolve the other emergency. Nevertheless, this simple fact, though plain—at least on second consideration—is generally neglected in public discussions of the present contingency, especially by commentators who take pride in their practical sense. For such default in attention, however, some reasons appear on the surface of things.

So evident is the crisis in economy that even illiterate persons admit its existence and call for no proof. From every angle of vision its signs thrust themselves into the range of observation. Stark before us stand millions of man's machines, idle and rusting—engines silent, locomotives weather-beaten on grass-grown sidings, ships falling into ruin at rotting docks, tractors mouldering in deserted fields. On all sides are signs of decay in that province assigned by tradition to woman: empty cupboards, ragged clothes, unpainted houses, hideous tenements, and stinking jungles of tin and wood in the very shadows of our centers of culture. In the field of human manifestations equally striking symbols of the calamity appear: wandering men and women, stranded boys and girls, broken homes, deserted families, leaders of finance and affairs poring over balance-sheets revealing defeated calculations, and, on the slabs of city morgues, bodies of suicides finding in death a security against want denied in life. At the capitals of great nations, bewildered governments devise measures of relief, pour out doles to save themselves, drill soldiers and police for impending disorders, provide decorations for the graves of ten million men slaughtered in the last war, and at the same moment forge in feverish haste weapons for another armed conflict on a scale more vast and with instruments more deadly.

On the other hand, the crisis in thought preceding and accompanying the disruption of economy is not obvious to the eye. It is evident only to contemporary knowledge. Yet not much knowledge is required to show a relationship between the two dilemmas, which are in truth parts of the same thing, and to suggest an exploration of the critical situation in thought to its very periphery. Surely all will concede that thought was mingled with the activities which eventuated in the economic conjuncture, and that thought is still operative in the making of decisions amid the collapse. It must be granted, also, that thought of some kind will and must precede actions designed to relieve the tension and attain economic equilibrium and abundance, or, at least, sufficiency.

Indeed, none of the evidences of the crisis in economy which may be described superficially as things standing outside the human mind, such as idle factories and bread lines, is wholly separated from the operation of thinking. All will admit that these outward signs of the emergency are, in certain respects at least, the outcome of thought. Bankers *thought* that foreign loans now in default were "good" at the time they were floated and that transfers of credit would redound to the interest of the American nation. Businessmen *thought* that the plant extensions which they were building a few years ago would be profitably employed in the manufacture of commodities. Farmers *thought* that markets would be found for the produce of additional acres brought under cultivation. And most leading citizens of the United States *thought* that the country had reached a high plateau of permanent prosperity and could find ever-expanding markets for the goods which flowed from factory and farm. With the outward signs of the crisis in economy today, thought is also combined. What men and women do in the present situation depends to some degree upon what they think they can do and the amount of effort they think they can make to give effect to their thought. In other words, those immediately and directly involved in practice—even the hardest of pretended realists—base their actions on intellectual assumptions of some kind, right or wrong as tested by outcome. The most stiff-necked practitioner, who pours scorn on theorists and denies that he operates on theory, will not confess, at least, that he has no *idea* of what he is trying to do.

Equally real to common sense, but open only to special knowledge, are evidences of the crisis in thought somewhat removed from the economic emergency and yet linked with it by invisible ties. Shading off gradually from the thought immediately entwined in practice, there is a realm of thought not intimately and continuously concerned with practice—a realm of thought reaching outward in abstractness to ethical and esthetic theory and occupied by various schools of adepts. At no point along the radius of outward extension, to be sure, can a sharp line be drawn between "pure theory" and "pure practice." Even those who indulge in sheer contemplation, in art for art's sake, are not timeless and placeless spirits; they are always associated with and sustained by some scheme of economic practice and are more or less affiliated with practitioners. But it so happens that, owing to its economy of abundance and system of distribution, Western civilization has long sustained various élites engaged in research and speculation somewhat remote from practical concerns. Money drawn from railways and steel has supported large armies of scholars, given them physical security, released them from the necessity of intense concern with immediate utility, and allowed them to wander hither and yon in a wide kingdom of inquiry.

Although less subjected to the material stresses and strains in which practice operates, the thought of these thinkers has long been suffering from a crisis growing in part out of intellectual development itself and in part out of the conflicts in surrounding economy. For more than a quarter of a century the crisis has been gathering in intensity and spreading to the uttermost limits of every division or category of thought. Evidences of this emergency are not open to simple observation, like rusting engines, bread lines, and smokeless chimneys; they cannot be described in the language of weight and measurement; nor in their higher abstractness are they apparent to untutored understanding. Indeed, so wide-reaching and complicated are the manifestations of the tensions in thought that no single human being is competent to grasp their fullness and interrelations. They appear in thousands of books, pamphlets, and fugitive articles, written in many languages, and published in places as far apart as New York and Tokyo. They lurk in the formulas and dissertations offered by the intellectual élite of all lands, in universities and outside, among professionals and amateurs. They thrust themselves upward in such broad subjects as general philosophy and in such specialties as economics, politics, sociology, geography, and history. Everywhere the learned world is split into "schools" and rare indeed is the savant who does not appear to be at war even with himself in his own bosom.

To make a swift summation, the crisis in Western thought may be said to spring from the disconcerting recognition of the fact that science cannot of itself provide the certainty, understanding, and unequivocal direction to policy and practice profoundly expected after theological supremacy and assurance were disrupted in a conflict extending through several centuries. During its own period of unquestioned dominance over the mind of Europe, the theological élite felt competent to make an *a priori* explanation of the world, and its competence was generally accepted by the laity in profound belief. Occurrences in astronomy, biology, geology, physics, chemistry, and history were brought within the single formula of God's providence, and the most perplexing and insistent questions of theory and practice could be referred to authority.

As long as the theological élite was unchallenged by any other élite, and the masses were generally excluded from learning, this certainty and assurance gave a peace of mind and a complacency almost universal, in that small region of the world called Europe. In the worst of calamities and tragedies, faith in the validity of theological explanation and guidance gave solace and contentment of spirit. And when this faith was shaken, when thought became secularized as the manufacturing era opened, the quest for certainty, assurance, and unequivocal guidance was renewed under the leadership of a secular and scientific élite, employing new methods.

The procedure of the new élite was to take nothing for granted, to observe, to assemble facts, to derive inferences and conclusions from observations, and to establish, whenever possible, laws invariable and beyond human or providential intervention. Truth was to be ascertained by research and observation, as distinguished from meditation or logical deduction from premises, and out of positive truth were to come understanding and certain guidance.

Such secular methods and operations were, of course, fundamentally different from those employed by the theological élite; and, despite efforts to effect compromises, there developed the conflict called "the warfare between science and theology." In this struggle practical interests, ideas, and methods were all involved. The clerical élite had an enormous vested interest in landed property, tithes, and fees, all fortified by the assumed validity of its thought and its *a priori* explanations; so the maintenance of the one involved the defense of the other. On its side, the scientific élite became increasingly affiliated with the rising commercial and industrial interests, especially after the first mechanical revolution. Since its methods were immediately useful to merchants and manufacturers, its base of economic support was rapidly widened and steadily shifted into the commercial and industrial realm.

Thus the conflict opening in the sixteenth century was a conflict of ideas and interests—thought and economy—so intertwined that knowledge could not separate them. Protestant theologians assailed Catholic theologians; counter attacks ensued; and eventually the unity and certitude of theology were dissolved by inner dissension and skepticism. To inner corrosion was added the sapping and mining of science in every branch of divinity. At the same time the bourgeois, as merchants and manufacturers, made war on the clergy as landed proprietors. And in the course of events, the clerical élite was largely stripped of its landed property and its compulsory fees, deprived of its unquestioned dominion over the human mind, and forced more and more to rely for new sources of support on revenues from commercial and industrial enterprises, so intimately affiliated with science. Thus it took over, more or less, the ideology of its patrons.

While theological unity was being disintegrated by dissensions in divinity itself and the historic Church was being shorn of its estates, the *a priori* explanations of the clerical élite in the fields of astronomy, biology, geology, physics, and history were rudely challenged and its huge errors of fact and assertion ruthlessly exposed. At the close of the battle, the theologians in their rôles as astronomers, geologists, biologists, economists, and historians were so thoroughly routed and so completely deprived of authority that neither statecraft nor economy looked to them any longer for certain direction in practical affairs.

By the middle of the nineteenth century, the victory of the scientific élite over the theological élite was substantially complete. And above the shattered ramparts of theological assurance was raised the banner of scientific assurance; for an old faith in the possibilities of human understanding was substituted a new faith conceived in the same spirit of certitude and dedicated in its higher manifestations to the same quest for dogma. With increasing vigor, and sustained by state appropriations and swelling endowments, a secular élite, imagining itself on the right track, applied the scientific method to human affairs on the wholly unwarranted assumption that, like physical occurrences, they could be brought within the scope of law, explanation, and determinism; that the certainty and assurance of astronomy, for example, could be won for such subjects as economics, sociology, and history; and that unequivocal guidance could be provided for human conduct and policy, to guarantee positive, predictive, and apparently "desirable" outcomes. Impetus was given to this hope by the widespread belief that Darwin had actually explained the origin and development of the species, including mankind, by reference to the struggle for existence, natural selection, and the survival of the fittest. At last it was thought that the scientific élite was about to substitute a real or "natural" explanation for the false or "divine" explanation offered by the theological élite— a guaranteed guidance for an illusory guidance.

Concerning the fruitfulness of the scientific method in the field of physical phenomena there could be no doubt. Its triumphs in all divisions of technology, such as mechanical engineering, naval architecture, and hydraulics, for example, were beyond question. Natural science had cut knots, solved problems, accomplished ends in the domain of physical phe-

nomena; and, what was more, it had provided canons of verification and authentication which could demonstrate that its
solutions were real solutions, beyond reasonable doubt—solutions clothed in the precision of mathematics. Moreover, as a
crowning triumph, it had taken millions of heavenly bodies in
motion, so long confusing and mystifying to astrologers and
astronomers, reduced them to a system of celestial mechanics
controlled by a single law, and created a scheme of verifiable
prediction, beyond debate or conjecture, in innumerable relations.

Into the world of human affairs, torn by political and economic controversies, natural science came with a healing promise to mankind. In this world there existed doubt, uncertainty,
and mystification, such as once characterized astronomy; and it
seemed perfectly reasonable to suppose that the method of natural science—observe facts and draw rules—would solve social
"problems" just as it had solved mechanical problems. In due
course, under the influence of the scientific method, "positive"
history, economics, sociology, and politics were announced as
forthcoming—to be created presumably by the collection of
facts and the establishment of classifications and firm laws.
With the variables of love, joy, admiration, hate, ideas, and
delusions ruled out, it was believed that problems of economics
and politics could be solved, like those in engineering; and,
by the more ambitious, that even human history, including
every form of particularity in politics, economics, esthetics,
ethics, and theology, could be reduced to a kind of terrestrial
mechanics like the celestial mechanics of Newton. On such
assumptions parliamentary commissions without number were
established, universities lavishly equipped, research institutions created, investigations and inquiries carried on in the
spirit of empirical positivism, and innumerable volumes,
pamphlets, and studies produced for the enlightenment of
mankind.

The simple and engaging faith in the power of the mind,
equipped with the scientific or positive method, to bring human occurrences under law and discover mandates to thought
and conduct more certain than those furnished by the theological élite, appeared early among those who came to be called

economists. Indeed, in the opening decades of the nineteenth century, writers in this field began openly to boast that within a short time the "principles" of economic science would be as positively established as those of astronomy; in fact, Ricardo was proclaimed by admirers "the Newton" of economics. For many years these positivists, who concentrated on what they called economic data and embroidered the classical system, were almost unchallenged, except by moralists, such as John Ruskin, and revolutionary thinkers, notably Karl Marx. Works on economics took on the confident tone of an engineer's handbook. The right thing to think and to do was made manifest, and the sponsors of this way of thought, with the old assurance of the theologians, pronounced their work good and final—almost, at least.

Behind the firm façade of assurance, however, this system of economy was beset by difficulties in practice and theory. The tendency toward *laissez faire* in public policies, domestic and international—so marked near the middle of the nineteenth century—was checked and reversed. Beginning, roughly speaking, in 1873, a great panic swept with devastating results through the Western world, raising grave doubts respecting the validity and permanence of the prevailing scheme of economy itself. France, Germany, and the United States, after indicating sympathy with free trade, veered swiftly in the direction of protection. About the same time the theory of English economy was countered on the Continent by the national systems of political economy and the state socialism of German thinkers. It was also shaken by the sapping and mining of the historical school which rejected its timeless validity, and treated it as a passing phase of ideology to be explained by reference to the historical conditions in which it arose. Indeed, so badly damaged was the great "science" of economics by the middle of the seventies that the editor of the *Encyclopædia Britannica,* in preparing the ninth edition, decided that economics was in a troubled state, that no unequivocal treatment of the subject was possible, and that an article on the history of the science was preferable in the circumstances.

But the new spurt in business which followed the panic and

the new lease of life given to expanding capitalism by imperialistic activities eased many of the pains of practice for a long time, and were followed by efforts to reëstablish the science of economics on another basis, especially the psychological conceptions of the marginal utility school. For many years the new economists managed to be fairly well satisfied with themselves and their "discipline."

Nevertheless, disintegration of thought was going on rapidly under the surface. At length the vast dislocations of the World War produced reverberations in economic speculation. Shortly after that general disaster many Continental thinkers came to the conclusion that economics had been too narrow in the range of its data, and they sought to widen its reach to include other occurrences—indeed, to the very borders of culture—in an attempt to discover foundations more satisfactory to themselves and more secure. Economy was either a smooth-running and independent machine inside society or it was not. If it was, why did it break down periodically?

Efforts of economists to answer this question did credit to their ingenuity but failed to establish the authenticity of their alleged Newtonian system. Unable to devise means for preventing breakdowns, they sought to explain the fact by regarding each calamity as part of the "normal" or "mechanical" functioning of economy (theory of "business cycles"), just as physicists treat reaction as part of the same process that produces action, or as engineers regard periodic machine breakdowns as a part of the functioning of their mechanical equipment. This, however, was merely using another analogy of physics to cover up a hole in the original conception of economics as mechanics. If economists knew enough to know that economic occurrences in society were events in a deterministic sequence, why were they unable to discover the causes of occasional breakdowns and indicate measures of prevention and repair, as the engineer can and does in operating his mechanisms? The real difficulty lay in the fact that the application of the analogy of physics to human affairs was utterly indefensible as either science or logic and that economists did not *know* economic occurrences as determined events.

While trying to hold fast to the false analogy of physics,

economists also introduced an extraneous force, a kind of *Deus ex machina*, the State, motivated by irrationality, to help explain the faulty functioning and periodical collapses of their perfect machine. All would be well for the economic engineer if the State would not interfere with domestic or international economy and would refrain from injecting the disturbing element of war. Thus another manifestation of animism—the scapegoat—was brought into economic reasoning. Of course it was obvious that the nature and functioning of the State bore some relation to the structure and movements of economic affairs, which could have been partly uncovered by a little research, but this central fact was generally ignored by the Newtons of economic mechanics, and the State was treated as a willful and irrational disturber of economic peace. This conclusion, however, merely led to an intellectual disaster equally ruinous: If the operation of the economic machine is conditioned by and subject to the ruinous interpositions of non-economic realities or forces—beyond description, calculation, and measurement—then no true science of economics is possible. In either case the assurance of mechanistic economics was positively destroyed.[1]

By 1930 dissolution had proceeded so far that the editors of the *Encyclopaedia of the Social Sciences* gave up the case of systematic economics as hopeless. Instead of providing for either a systematic or a purely historical treatment, they described the inner turmoil of the "science" and then presented ten different articles on as many schools and methods of economics. By way of preface, the chief editor, E. R. A. Seligman, frankly confessed that economics had long been the battleground for rationalizations of group and class interests and that no end of the conflict was in sight. In other words, so far as anything approaching a science is concerned, this was a timely and appropriate confession of utter intellectual confusion, made before the crash in practice had revealed its height and depth.

As the panic which opened in 1929 ran its course and as efforts were made to find, in economic thought and knowledge,

[1] Jostock, *Der Ausgang des Kapitalismus*, and Mueller-Armack, *Die Entwicklungsgesetze des Kapitalismus.*

ways of escape from the distresses and sufferings of business defeat and unemployment, the utter bewilderment of economics, already evident to thought, became apparent to practitioners who sought guidance in this branch of learning. Those individual economists who ventured to put forward new proposals for practice generally received scant respect or support from their professional colleagues. On the whole, timidity, uncertainty, and skepticism characterized economists as an élite, revealing to the public the crisis in their thought which had long been known to those concerned with the history of thought.

In the field of "political science," the emergency in thought had appeared during the early years of the twentieth century in the writings of Schaeffle, Benoist, Duguit, Prins, Sorel, Bentley, and a handful of workers who sought to unite politics and economics, which had been so violently put asunder by the older generation. In the course of the nineteenth century, after the economists had made their artificial system based on the economic man, writers on politics turned mainly to the description of the forms of government and administration. Ignoring almost entirely underlying economic and cultural realities, they treated government as if it were an independent political mechanism running inside a legal framework under its own momentum, or they concentrated on minute political occurrences without much reference to any ends, purposes, or expectations. Following the general trend of practice, they usually assumed that political democracy and representative government were destined to spread throughout the world and that, very likely, these institutions were the ultimate political forms. To be sure, there were some skeptics who kept referring to economic and other considerations in politics, but in the main the mere describers of institutions long dominated thought in political science. Although they produced no "Newton of political science," they were fairly well satisfied with themselves, the world, and their works.

But a few who widened their range to include technology, war, imperialism, labor, and other powerful interests in Western societies began to spread doubts about the validity, utility, and significance of mere institutional descriptions, before the twentieth century had advanced very far on its way. The contradiction between political equality and economic inequality and the possibilities of war and social revolution disturbed the thought of political science in certain areas. The challenge offered by the dictatorship of the proletariat and by counter-thrusts of power raised insistent questions about the reality and meaning of writings which had long passed as "political science" in the academic world. This crisis in thought was already developing when the crash in economy (1929) was followed by the downfall of political democracies in Central and Eastern Europe. In such circumstances, political science, so-called, appears to be as confused as economics. It can offer no positive commands to policy and statecraft; indeed it has been so long indifferent to the problems of policy and statecraft that the heritage of thought bequeathed by Aristotle, Machiavelli, Hobbes, Locke, and Adam Smith, for example, has fallen into disuse and is almost covered with dust.

That division of the humanities known as sociology is in no better case. Many times during the nineteenth century a powerful mind—Comte, Herbert Spencer, Gumplowicz, for instance, sought to grasp the scheme of human affairs entire, reduce it to system, and reveal its "laws." By enthusiastic devotees, each delivery was hailed as providing "the science"; and yet within a few years corroding criticism undermined the perfect structure of the new offering and left it in intellectual ruins. Now, as a kind of memento of that dead past, the vast pile of fact, classification, opinion, and conjecture by Pareto, called *General Sociology,* appears in an English dress and is greeted by his satellites as "the real science" of society at last. But already it is sicklied over with the pale cast of doubt and is on its way into the muniment room of huge works which attempt to explain man, society, and social development—and fail, of necessity, owing to the very nature of things and the limitations of the human mind. Sociology, as a "science" of society, was riddled with skepticism before the crisis in social practice revealed its ineptitude.

The hope for a "science" of history was likewise exploded in the first decades of the twentieth century. When the old theological explanation of events by reference to God's provi-

dence was rejected and the method of explaining them by reference to preceding events was substituted, historical thought
in turn became positive and scientific in emphasis. With an
avidity truly remarkable, historians began to collect documents, papers, and other sources bearing upon the history of
the past. They put aside, or rather imagined that they were
putting aside, all assumptions and presuppositions, and proceeded to get "the facts" and describe the past as it "actually"
was. They became "scientific" also, in the heavy scientific
climate of the nineteenth century, and the boldest spirits
among them dared to hope that in due course the law or laws
of history would be revealed, as the law of the heavens had
been revealed by Newton and the laws of biological evolution
had been disclosed by Darwin (it was imagined). Even those
historians who had no such large ambitions were quite sure
that they were "telling the truth" about history, as they compiled, documented, selected, and wrote treatises on history.
If a volume on the subject was dry, heavy with footnotes, and
painfully accurate as to dates and details, it was believed to be
"scientific."

Yet discontent with this kind of historiography appeared
among historians who eventually stopped to ponder their work,
and it slowly crept around in obscure circles. At length in
1916 Benedetto Croce openly announced that scientific history had come to the close of its epoch and no longer satisfied
the human spirit. After all, historians had been human beings,
belonging to certain nations, classes, and times; and, despite
their claims to utter detachment and "objectivity," their writings betrayed their underlying interests and preconceptions.
They asserted that they were concerned only with "facts" but
they selected and organized facts; and their selection and organization revealed their own intellectual structure in its time
and place. Poignant consciousness of this operation at length
dismayed them, or at least those who took the trouble to inquire into their own mentality and its fruits. And at last historical skepticism reached its climax in the doctrine of relativity: all schemes of historical construction are relative to
time and place and are destined to pass with the passing of the
circumstances—ideas and interests—in which they originate.

History as it actually was and is cannot be known or explained, in short, and those who imagine that it can are deluding themselves.

After suffering defeats in every direction, adepts in the application of the scientific method to human affairs, except perhaps the least sophisticated, fell into a state of bewilderment. Slowly it dawned upon them that the human mind and the method employed were not competent to the appointed task, that omniscience was not vouchsafed to mortals. Moreover, it was finally realized that if all human affairs were reduced to law, to a kind of terrestrial mechanics, a chief end of the quest, that is, human control over human occurrences and actions, would itself become meaningless. Should mankind discover the law of its total historical unfolding, then it would be imprisoned in its own fate and powerless to change it; the past, present, and future would be revealed as fixed and beyond the reach of human choice and will. Men and women would be chained to their destiny as the stars and tides are to their routine. The difference between human beings and purely physical objects would lie in their poignant knowledge of their doom and of their helplessness in its presence.

The relevance of this crisis in thought to the crisis in economy must now be apparent. The final blow to the hope of finding an escape from the economic dilemma by the scientific method is given when an effort is made to conceive the nature of the solution for the problem in hand, which is possible to that method. The only kind of occurrences or events which the natural scientist can bring under law is a deterministic sequence actually under law and susceptible of expression in mathematical terms.[2] Now the occurrences of things, thoughts, and actions coming within the scope of the crisis in economy are scattered over a long period of time and over widely separated parts of the earth, embracing such "data" as commercial routes, naval zones, the movements of intangible capital and tangible steamships, and the "stake abroad." If these occurrences did in fact constitute a fixed order, with which the natural scientist is competent to deal, and could be brought into a fixed scheme of corresponding rationality, then the past,

[2] E. W. Hobson, *The Domain of Natural Science,* pp. 84-90.

present, and future of American economy as a phase of world economy would be subdued to certain inexorable formulas enclosed, perhaps, in one inexorable formula. The policies and actions of statecraft in relation to the crisis, as they inevitably will occur, would be predicted and human effort could not change them. All so-called choices among measures designed to relieve the economic tension would be foreseen and their outcomes in practice at different periods in the future would become apparent in human knowledge.

The very dilemma or crisis in thought and economy would itself disappear, for it grows out of the assumption that something better or more satisfactory than the present disarray of things is possible, as well as desirable, and that a choice of new lines of action, positive or negative, is possible and desirable. A crash among stars is no crisis, but a fulfillment of predetermined relations. So if politics, policies, and efforts to avoid calamities or gain advantages were reduced to the order of causal sequences, they would become as meaningless as the foam that arises on waves as they break on the seashore. The statesman would see today the line of action he will take tomorrow, despite all tossing about in present uncertainty; the only possible action would be taken; and the use of adepts for advice and counsel would become a mere phase of a mechanical puppet show.

It may be that all human affairs are determined; certainly the contrary cannot be *proved*, any more than the proposition itself. But the law of that determinism has not been disclosed; and no efforts of the positivists, no matter how prolonged, assiduous, and eager, can establish it, because it is known that untold numbers of events in the past, which must be included as relevant parts of any alleged deterministic sequence, are unknown and cannot be known on account of the fragmentary character of the historical data available. Hence the conclusion: The scientific method has been defeated and must be defeated in the effort to reach its supreme goal—the reduction of large areas of human affairs to isolated groupings subject to unequivocal law; and were it to reach its impossible goal, victory would be defeat for mankind, that is, imprisonment in a doom actually foreknown.

In any event, the triumph of science over human thought could not provide direction to policy, for the very essence of science is neutrality, the kind of neutrality that observes without emotion a tide rolling in upon a shore. Knowledge of the nature of materials, human beings, and forces does not dictate the uses to which such knowledge may or must be put. Knowledge of chemicals may be employed in destroying a city, or it may be devoted to healing the sick. That one use is preferable to the other cannot be demonstrated by the scientific method—cannot be demonstrated at all. It can be asserted only as a value cherished, believed in, or hoped for, by those who present it.

Associated with, indeed underlying, the crisis in thought growing out of the dissolution of theological and scientific assurance is another dilemma. It arises from the tragic sense of the conflict between the ideal and the real—between a positive knowledge of the possibility of a good and abundant life demonstrated by physical science and human industry on the one side, and an equally positive knowledge of the miseries, sufferings, cruelties, and ugliness of the world as it actually exists, on the other. Freedom from the long servitude to material things, from such calamities as the one through which we are now passing, rises before mankind like a haunting dream, inviting, urging thought and action directed to realization through the use of knowledge and methods already available. In the presence of a veritable Aladdin's lamp, that offers to banish degrading toil, gnawing poverty, demoralizing insecurity, and distressing ugliness, humanity feels a call to the exercise of great energies, intellectual, ethical, and esthetic.

Already these energies beat against the artificial barriers of thought erected by the élite of positivism. Members of that élite, pursuing the scientific method in the domain of the humanities, either insisted on ignoring the tragic sense of the conflict between the ideal and the real—the rôle of ethical and esthetic ideas in the movement of thought and action, or they treated it as incidental, almost as if it were a trivial mannerism belonging to the sphere of *politesse*. Indeed, by its very presuppositions, scientific procedure in the humanities was compelled to exclude ethical and esthetic manifestations from its operations. Committed to describing actual occurrences, weighing, measuring, enumerating, and assigning mathematical symbols to its data (as far as possible), to dealing with things "as they are," scientific procedure was inclined to rule out intangibles, imponderables, and immeasurables. Indeed, the climax of its assumptions may be expressed in the following formulation: Everything that exists, even knowledge and the affections, exists in some *quantity,* is therefore measurable and can be reduced to system. The existence of intangibles was not always denied by the positive élite, to be sure, but they were regarded as matters largely irrelevant for practical purposes, or as minor factors to be mentioned casually, perhaps with a patronizing air. When scientific thinkers were asked to turn from "what is" (as it appeared to them) and consider what "ought to be," they generally treated the request as a vagary of a sentimentalist. Many did this honestly, and others, no doubt, because they knew that an effort to face the question of values would reveal the bankruptcy of their thought and call for the assumption of a perilous ethical responsibility.

The spell is now broken. The tragic sense of the conflict between the ideal and the real becomes the center of worldwide interest. The utter incapacity of the scientific method, or any other *method,* to cope with it, or to provide, from the "data" with which the positive élite insists upon working, unequivocal directions for policy, is now openly acknowledged. War upon its tyranny has begun on all fronts. Frankly posited human values now become fundamentals, and science is being treated correctly as instrumental, as a servant of human purposes. The obvious is being discovered, namely, that a creature of the human mind must in the nature of things be a servant of the mind. And the fate of the scientific élite, including its seats of authority in the press, universities, and educational systems, like that of the theological élite in its former domains, will depend upon its capacity to recognize the imperatives of the transformation in thought, to admit that its empirical operations alone cannot untie the knot of the crisis in economy and thought, to adapt itself, and to assume leadership. What has happened to this élite in Russia, Italy, and Germany, where its numbers must either conceal their knowledge or serve openly as the lackeys of governments founded on sheer force, may well symbolize its task, if not its future, in other parts of the world.

As might have been expected, this growing recognition of the incompetence of the empirical method to make a science out of any aspect of human affairs has led many to assume that a restoration of the *a priori* method and authority of theology is inevitable. Countenance is lent to this assumption by the fact that in the teachings of Christ, on whose life and work Western theology is a commentary often prolix and remote, ethical considerations are primordial. Moreover, in their days of supremacy, the greatest of the theologians, such as Thomas Aquinas, for example, included within the scope of their contemplation some ideal arrangements of economy (below, Chapter VII). They sought not only a rational ordering of thought within the limits of their presuppositions, but also an ideal way of life in its most material manifestations. That the faithful did not always conform to their prescriptions, that the movement of ideas and interests in history dissipated the order of things they once idealized, that they did, in part, merely rationalize interests actually dominant, can be admitted, without in the least invalidating the fact that ethical considerations occupied a central position in their thought.

Conceding all this, there are reasons for believing that a restoration of theological supremacy is out of the question. That supremacy, while it endured, was made possible by conditions of knowledge and thought prevailing among the masses of people, as well as within the élite itself. A restoration of these conditions is, according to all signs, utterly beyond human power. It would mean a reversal in the process of history. It would call for a revolution in knowledge, the inner spirit, and outward relations, which could give to a theological élite and its system of thought the sanctions and convictions necessary to its functioning—a revolution now inconceivable. Such a restoration would also mean the utter destruction of immense bodies of positive knowledge developed by astronomy, anthropology, economics, history, politics, and sociology, and a limitation of learning once more to theological adepts. It would mean the re-creation of the intellectual climate and the social conditions in which mankind could be-lieve in the power of theology to prescribe the right and work-able things to think and do, even in the most complicated crisis of economy and thought. If anything is known, then the futility of any such hope is known.

Moreover, even within each of the several schools of the theological élite, there is, despite unity of abstract symbols, thought, and belief, a bewildering diversity of opinion as to actual ways and means of bringing any ideal arrangement of human affairs into being. When practice is touched—taxation, the distribution of wealth, the ownership of capital, the proc-esses of production, labor legislation, the position of women in industry and social economy, hours of labor, actual wages, to cite a few instances among hundreds—the theological élite of no school, Catholic or Protestant, is able to deliver an agreement or an unequivocal mandate guaranteed to work in the world of objective things and human relations.

Far from meaning defeat to mankind, however, the crisis in thought has opened the way to emancipation from two delu-sions of certainty respecting human affairs—the theological and the scientific. It means an escape of humanity unto itself, an imperative call of life for the deliberate assumption of ethi-cal and esthetic responsibility, a freedom to dare and experi-ment—to experiment and correct miscalculations with the aid of such knowledge and physical power as was never before vouchsafed to human mind, will, and purpose. Any overarch-ing and all-embracing symbols or abstractions which particu-lar theologians and particular men of science may find satis-factory to themselves as "explanations" and "guarantees" may be left to the sifting of time, when work is begun under the new conception of things that *may* be thought and done in the age now opening.

Herein, then, lies the substance of the crisis in thought. The contrast between the ideal that seems possible and the real that oppresses us is painfully evident to contemporary knowl-edge; and it is increasingly understood that science, which once supplanted theological assurance, can furnish no un-equivocal prescriptions for national policy and action—pre-scriptions guaranteed to work as promised in human affairs—

especially in bringing the ideal and the real into that degree of harmony which will relax the tension and resolve the crisis. Despite all the sayings, declarations, and prognostications of practitioners, interpreters, editors, politicians, professors, researchers, investigators, commissions of inquiry, and agitators who speak as men having authority, unequivocal explanations and guidance are denied to us. Deprived of the certainty which it was once believed science would ultimately deliver, and of the very hope that it can in the nature of things disclose certainty, human beings must now concede their own fallibility and accept the world as a place of trial and error, where only those who dare to assume ethical and esthetic responsibility, and to exercise intuitive judgment, while seeking the widest possible command of realistic knowledge, can hope to divine the future and mould in some measure the shape of things to come.

CHAPTER II

THE WORLD IN CONTEMPORARY THOUGHT

How then does the world present itself in contemporary thought emancipated from the mechanism and scientific certainty prevalent in the nineteenth century? Since all plans for overcoming the crisis in economy involve some conception of the nature of things, this question must be asked and answered before these several programs are examined and subjected to appraisal as workable schemes. In other words, it is self-deception to assume that no assumptions precede a consideration of human affairs and that an inquiry into assumptions is unnecessary to procedure. Some view of the world as appearances lies behind and inheres in every choice and declaration of fact and policy, whether large or small in range.

TRENDS OF INTERESTS AND IDEAS [1]

To all except those who still cling to mechanist determinism, whether theological or materialistic, the world presents itself in contemporary thought as necessity and ideal, as interests and ideas, inextricably interwoven, and developing in time; not the one or the other exclusively, but both interlocked; not a static complication of ideas and interests, but forward movement of both in time.[2] Wherever ideas appear, interests are attached; wherever interests appear, ideas are associated with them. Even the cult of the irrational, sheer force, clothes itself in ideas and draws interests into its train.

The inner nature of the interwoven movement of ideas and interests in time is not known, but some of its manifestations

---

[1] The conception of interests, subjective and objective, and its relation to ideas is examined more closely below, Chapter VIII.

[2] Kurt Riezler, "Idee und Interesse in der politischen Geschichte," *Die Dioskuren* (1924), pp. 1 ff.

are grasped by thought. Ideas change, exfoliate, under the internal drives or compulsions of thinkers and exponents; they divide, running to the right or left (Platonism and Neo-Platonism); they draw in new content and drop old content; they grow richer or thinner in the substance covered. Ideas also change under the impacts of changes external to the thinker —changes in objective interests—things (machines), conduct, and relations connected with human existence and the struggle for existence. They dissolve into fragments and sometimes disappear, entirely or almost entirely (for example, the divine right of kings).

Interests as things, conduct, and relationships also change under the propulsions of inner forces and under the impacts of ideas. The tool exfoliates into the simple machine, the simple machine into the complex machine, and the complex machine into a vast technological configuration under the hand and brain of the thinker. One mechanical step "leads" to another, as one idea "leads" to another. Then mechanism as idea or cluster of ideas also exfoliates as thought in the brain of the thinker, and is carried back into practice, developing the mechanism as thing. Here, as in the domain of ideas, the process of construction, dissolution, and creation goes on. Old forms of interests (handicrafts) decline and dissolve, as new forms of work (*e.g.* the factory system) appear; the new forms flower, develop, change, and are transformed.

At times ideas run far ahead of, or break away from conformity to, interests. For example, the immense exfoliation of ideas in the brains of the French *philosophes* in the eighteenth century digressed from the configuration of practices enclosed in the absolute monarchy, and presented another view of interests emerging, interests which the thinkers thought "ought to be." Again, interests sometimes run far ahead of ideas, that is, take other forms than those of the interests already mirrored in ideas. For example, the swift development of the factory system under the impact of inventions in steam power and machinery quickly escaped from conformity to the ideas of economy formulated under the handicraft system of manufacturing once generally dominant. This uneven growth of ideas and interests, this "lag" between them, makes tensions in the thought and life of society. If such tensions can be adjusted by the informed coöperation of practitioners and thinkers, can be relaxed by appropriate adaptations, then social development, the unfolding of ideas and interests, proceeds peacefully. If, on the other hand, the tension becomes too great, it snaps, and a revolution of violence occurs and continues until some working correlation of ideas and interests is effected.

In this unfolding of ideas and interests in time, certain tendencies appear and can be observed and described (with a high degree of scholarly accuracy), thus presenting apparent necessities for the thinker and the practitioner. Some of these tendencies seem to be inexorable, even though their projection into future time cannot be made with mechanical certainty, and they force thinkers and practitioners to adjust themselves to the inevitable or to drop out of sight as influences in the world. For example, the growth of machine industry in the United States and its increasing predominance over agriculture seems to have had the characteristics of fatality; at all events, it was a marked feature of American history in the nineteenth century. It came about in spite of the fact that the political party (Jeffersonian) which ruled the country during a large part of that century cherished in the beginning an agricultural conception of policy. Again, the concentration of industrial control in the United States has continued almost unabated, despite the *laissez faire* and anti-trust ideas appropriate to handicrafts, corner stores, single factories, free land, and "independent" farming. In other words, there appear to be movements of interests which escape the control of inherited ideas, defy them, and compel consideration in other terms, if at all.

This is no place to present world history, or even the history of the past fifty years as movement of ideas and interests, but certain tendencies are vitally relevant to the problem in hand —the crisis in economy and thought—and may be concisely described. Some of them are essentially domestic, and others pertain particularly to international relations:

1. Multiplying functions of government in the domain of economy, health, safety, education, and cultural development.[2]

2. Growing centralization of industrial control, bringing ever larger areas of individual enterprise, interest, activities, and chaos in order and plan.[3]

3. The intensifying quest for social and economic security, through organization, private and public—association and legislation.

4. Growing nationalism, that is, increasing reliance of each nation on its own resources and powers for the attainment of social security, and diminishing reliance on the "natural" course or free play of private interests in international commerce as a guarantee of social security.

5. Expanding industrialization of great commercial nations —shift from agriculture to industrial base—and hence tendency of these nations to form a common industrial pattern, to manufacture substantially identical machine commodities by substantially identical processes, with difference in wages or cultural standards only.

6. Intensification of the struggle among industrial nations to find outlets for the sale of goods substantially identical in character.

7. Increasing control of international trade by the respective governments through tariffs, subsidies, bounties, licenses, and quotas, in efforts to attain a larger degree of domestic security.

8. Swelling armaments, under special propulsions of munition makers and military and naval bureaucracies, in the quest for markets and security of domestic life and economy.

THE COMPETENCE OF INTELLIGENCE IN CONTEMPORARY THOUGHT

The world thus presents itself as movement of ideas and interests to the contemporary thought which has thrown off theological and scientific determinism. In this thought ideas and interests are held in a common continuum. Some things

[2] Wooddy, *Growth of the Federal Government.*
[3] Berle and Means, *The Modern Corporation and Private Property.*

are known and more may be known by inquiry, but it does not follow that all things may be known. The great tendencies of interests undoubtedly have been discovered and are described with a high degree of accuracy. Idea pictures of the world of nations as they seem to appear in the minds of the generation passed or passing are likewise known and are set forth in numerous empirical treatises. But facing the future, on the verge of the unknown, dark and shadowy, what competence for dealing with that future does contemporary thought ascribe to science, scholarship, or realistic inquiry?

There is a consensus of opinion to the effect that historical scholarship can trace with a high degree of accuracy the course of ideas and interests in the past, without pretending to "explain" the world we live in and to forecast the future. This scholarship has abandoned the conception of history as an all-embracing and fated chain of "causes," but in so doing it does not regard the world as wholly unintelligible chaos. On the contrary, it presents positive knowledge of innumerable necessities and treats them as limiting, deflecting, or conditioning, not determining, the choices and actions of private and public persons. It can describe some, not all, of the conditions which made possible what has happened.

In so doing it clears away whole collections of traditional mythologies concerning phases of the past and provides in their stead positive knowledge. A concrete example illustrates the operations for which such scholarship is competent. It can describe, with a high degree of accuracy, the ideas and interests prevailing in the United States at the time the Constitution was framed—the geographical situation, the posture of the several states, the commercial, agricultural, and financial situation, and the political ideas widely cherished. It treats these as facts, as necessities actually appearing in the scene, as necessities limiting and conditioning the policies and choices of the delegates who drafted the Constitution. From the records of the convention held at Philadelphia historical scholarship can describe the delegates tossing to and fro within the constricting influences of facts, making now one choice and now another and arriving finally at conclusions of will, purpose, and policy incorporated in the Constitution as a plan to control, within certain limits, future policies and actions.

But historical scholarship does not and cannot show that all particular choices in the convention were determined unequivocally by any set of circumstances or chain of previous events. It can, for instance, describe the conditions which made possible the decision against erecting a monarchy, but it cannot present determinants which unequivocally "caused" the delegates to choose an executive department headed by a single person instead of a triumvirate, or to choose the election of President by presidential electors instead of by Congress, as proposed.

Thus, while scholarship in history can and does furnish a large amount of accurate knowledge respecting the past, distant and immediate—knowledge indispensable to those who would propose and determine policy designed to work—it is forced to concede that no mere empirical inquiry into past facts or occurrences can possibly yield irrefragable rules for the determination of policy, present or future.

There is only one conceivable set of circumstances in which past experience could furnish indubitable direction: that is a fixed set of circumstances guaranteed to continue over a long stretch of time undisturbed by changes and tensions in economy and thought. Such a relatively stable order existed for centuries in the agricultural arrangements of Western Europe. The policy associated with it was historic conservatism, passed on from generation to generation. Things had worked and were working in a manner fairly satisfactory to all classes; no radical changes, such as those accompanying the introduction of technology, intruded disorders and dilemmas into the heritage; and a study of the past yielded workable knowledge for the future—as long as the future continued the general patterns of conduct and things prevalent in the past. In handicraft industries and guilds, also, a fairly stable scheme of human arrangements long perdured substantially unaltered; and policy secured from the past workable guidance for the oncoming future. In other words, where there is a fairly settled order of economy and life and a general correspondence of ideas and interests, no distressing tensions arise, and out of such a past come effective directions for the present and the future.

In the course of American history for more than a hundred years no such fixed order of economy and life has obtained, except perhaps for a brief period in the plantation regions of the Old South. Swift movements of ideas and interests, kaleidoscopic changes, have characterized the past century. Various choices have been made. Numerous modifications and adaptations in policy have occurred. Indeed, past events coming under the head of domestic and foreign affairs have been in a considerable measure the results of conscious policy; for example, the movement of imports has been controlled by tariff laws deliberately made.

Inasmuch as these occurrences, flowing at least in part out of policies, eventuated in the crisis from which escape is now sought, how could a mere study of the occurrences themselves yield constructive mandates as to ways and means of escaping and avoiding a repetition of such calamities? The very existence of the dilemma is evidence that there has been a certain degree of defeat, a partial failure of past policies; for had the past policies followed by statecraft produced satisfactory results, no crisis in economy and thought would have arisen. Only on one hypothesis, then, could faith in the power of scientific research to deliver constructive mandates to contemporary policy be justified, namely, on the hypothesis that knowledge of the failure of one policy or set of policies to produce satisfaction will yield the policy or set of policies that will work, will produce satisfaction. In other words, out of the rules of a past defeat will come the rules for winning a future victory. The assumption is untenable. A study of past failures may indicate some things that ought not to be repeated *if* similar failures are to be avoided, but it cannot reveal unequivocally the things that must be done to prevent a repetition of failure and to escape into a more stable and desirable order of things.

Since those divisions of knowledge and thought which deal primarily with contemporary affairs, such as economics, politics, and sociology, are embraced within the wide reach of history, it follows that none of these divisions can make out of its fragments of history an isolated science in its arbitrarily delimited area. This, too, is recognized by contemporary thought in economics, politics, and sociology, and must be taken into the reckoning by those who would formulate plans and policies for the future.

The state of thought in economics deserves especial consideration. It is widely and superficially held that the crisis in which Western nations are floundering is essentially an economic crisis, and that out of economic data a mechanism of release can be devised. But in reconstructing its world after the dissolution of its solid assurance proclaimed in the nineteenth century, contemporary scholarship in economic affairs has moderated its claims and is considering the things that are possible to knowledge and thought. It is aware that various schools of policy exist within its field—ranging from *laissez faire* individualism at one end to planned communism at the other, with state socialism and interventionist policy somewhere along the line. It openly acknowledges that assumptions derived from one or the other of these rationalizations are likely to control a consideration of single economic items and the formulation of large policies. It has abandoned all hope of constructing out of economic data, so-called, a smooth-running economic mechanism within the limits of society, and in its search for all appropriate relevances has widened the range of its inquiry to cover the whole of culture. Thus in escaping the absolutism of mechanics, it gains in realism.

Yet in casting off the shackles of mechanism, contemporary thought in economics does not surrender to chaos. Like historical thought, it takes note of things which it is actually competent to treat. Many occurrences and patterns of occurrences which may be called economic for convenience are open to accurate superficial description, often in mathematical terms. Hence economics can set forth innumerable necessities which must condition the choices made by private and public persons in the name of policy. In some areas it can present axioms that partake of the nature of laws. For example, it can plot with a fair degree of predictive accuracy the number of accidents and deaths in an industrial society of a given type and the amount of money requisite to meet compensation charges, *if* the government adopts a policy of workmen's insurance. It can see by observation that in the long run the export of commodities and services must be balanced by an import of commodities and services, *unless* credit is to be extended indefinitely, or defaults and repudiations are to intervene. But all such predicted repetitions of events are predicated upon the continuance of the cultural policy in which they have occurred and do now occur, and the perdurance of that cultural polity cannot be predicted beyond the peradventure of a doubt. Contemporary thought in economics, therefore, constrains itself to the possibility of presenting competing economic ideals and accurate knowledge of facts which condition the projection, execution, and realization of ideals. This service to statecraft is enormous, even when the omniscience of determinism is discarded.

Thus we are led to a consideration of just what it is that positive thought can offer to the formulation of policy and then what other intellectual operations falling within the realm of imaginative or humanistic thought are necessary to the formulation of policy. The élite of positive thought can point to an immense body of exact knowledge, already acquired by the use of the scientific method, and to areas of inquiries in which additional stores of knowledge may be acquired by research. It can offer the scientific or empirical method as an instrument for ascertaining facts relevant to any given situation—facts which condition operations in that situation—and indicate probable outcomes of specific actions taken in conformity with policies formulated. It can collect, describe, and present alternative policies and furnish some indications respecting the nature and limits of choices and the probable sequences of particular actions decided upon. Finally, it can aid in the invention of institutions and practices designed to give effect to policies after they have been determined.

In fine, on the side of observation and performance, the scientific method is the chief, if not the only, instrument available to statecraft. This cannot be stated too often or with too much stress. Moreover, the inquiring and judicial spirit of science is absolutely necessary to the protection of society against the senseless routine of bureaucracy and the brutal acts of sheer power arising from irrational emotions.

The desirability of cherishing deeply the accumulated knowledge of the sciences and the method of science, and of providing lavishly for the promotion of science in every department, is particularly emphasized by the fact that technology and its high potentials are at the very center of the crisis from which emergence is sought. Any approximation of a solution calls for the socially efficient use of technology, the material endowment, and the industrial arts of the nation. Such use must, in the nature of things, proceed along the lines indicated by the laws of materials and forces with which technology deals. And when the purposes of that utmost efficient use are clarified, posited, and adopted, science may prescribe the most appropriate and promising ways and means of realizing them. Science, therefore, is in a large measure responsible for the crisis, is involved in every phase of it, offers knowledge of realities which must condition every attempt at escape, and provides methods and instrumentalities absolutely necessary to the projection of workable plans and to their execution in practice. A knowledge of the nature of science, including its limitations, emphasizes rather than diminishes its importance and clarifies the mind for its effective use.

But standing upon the edge of coming things—things unknown because the scientific method and positive knowledge cannot provide a map of them, contemporary thought concerned with mitigating the crisis, effecting a relaxation of the tension, must perform other intellectual operations besides inquiry and research in things past and present. Owing to the nature of the problem something *new* must be attempted, if emergency is to be resolved, and that something new does not now exist on land or sea; it exists only in the realm of the ideal, the imagination. Of necessity, also, it must be conceived of as desirable, at least more desirable than the present disarray of things, and the very introduction of desirability brings ethics and esthetics into the web of thought. An action or thing can be desirable only with reference to some posited or assumed standard of good or beauty. From this conception of the world of matter and action, contemporary thought can find no release in dealing with private or public affairs. Suicide is the only exit; for whoever lives has preferences and operates on canons of ethical and esthetic assumptions, grand or petty, however vociferously he may repudiate them as irrelevant and odious.

This conclusion emerging in contemporary thought draws ethics and esthetics out of the corner of obscurity and neglect into which they have been thrust by the scientific élite, and brings them to the very center of contemplation and action. Nay, more; it means that every thinker, large or small, even when using the scientific method in dealing with human affairs, has in his own mind a scheme of ethical and esthetic values, or frame of reference, which controls more or less his selection of problems to be studied, facts to be gathered, and policies of action to be determined upon. Thus the assertion of ethical and esthetic values is made by all human beings, in choosing their centers of attention, objects of desire, and policies among alternatives. It is made in humble life, in scientific life, in business and economy, and in the field of statecraft. The conscious, living mind inquires what is possible and what is desirable, and applies ethical and esthetic canons to the consideration of actions.

THE PLACE OF ETHICS AND ESTHETICS

This conception of the world in contemporary thought and of the competence of intelligence to deal with human affairs in a positive manner brings into a central place of consideration ethics and esthetics, once discarded, or at least neglected by science and empiricism. No longer can they be regarded as irrelevant or incidental. Nor are they to be treated as mere abstractions for debate in polite circles. They appear as ideas and interests, along with the other phenomena of history—as conceptions of the good and beautiful and as concrete embodiments of the good and beautiful in things—such as buildings and commodities—in institutions, conduct, and relationships. Conceptions of ethics and esthetics exfoliate, under inner compulsions and external impacts, and their embodiment in things and conduct changes under the pressures of inner forces and the impacts of ethical and esthetic ideas in development.

It is posited and asserted ethical and esthetic standards which furnish points of reference for the triangulation of policy (below, Chapter VII). Physical facts and the past facts of human history give no unequivocal instructions respecting policy to observers and knowers. This is as true of the physical sciences as of the social sciences. Facts may disclose whether a given measure of policy can be realized; for example, whether it is possible to have a system of social insurance. But facts do not disclose policy itself. Empirical inquiry may show that fifty per cent of the school children of a given age are subnormal according to preëstablished norms; but such a finding of fact does not reveal anything thàt *must* be done in the premises. Whether less effort or more effort should be devoted to their education is a matter to be determined by reference to some preconceptions of desirability and purpose. And in ethics and esthetics, as distinguished from morality (*mores*) and from crude utility, there are ideal elements—elements transcending in some degree things and practices already prevalent. These can only be posited and asserted; they cannot be proved.

Contemporary thought in ethics and esthetics tends to reject the absolutism of both "nature" and theology. Man is not regarded as condemned to remain forever "either a gluttonous brute offending the deity that flickers through his aspirations or a fallen angel struggling with his brute nature through the heroic failure of successive renunciations."[4] These conceptions of man are dissolving, with the dissolution of scientific and theological certainty and assurance. In their place comes another conception of ethics and esthetics, controlled by neither the compulsions of brute nature nor the fears of everlasting hell-fire. At its very center is *knowledge* of good and beautiful things and conduct which have been brought to realization, if only here and there and in fragmentary form; around this knowledge the imagination of the artist and ethical thinker creates new goods and beauties which effort can bring

[4] T. V. Smith, *Encyclopaedia of the Social Sciences*, Vol. V., p. 606.

into being. And when this knowledge respecting the nature of ethics and esthetics, and especially their precedence, consciously or unconsciously, as determinants in all formulations of policy, is made central to all thought about policy, the creative force of ethics and esthetics can be accelerated. In other words, when the idea of mechanistic necessity is abandoned and it is universally recognized that all who act, teach, and lead in any capacity, large or small, do operate on some conception of good and beauty, then the clarification of ethical and esthetic purpose will precede efforts to formulate and to apply policy. This recognition is now swiftly taking place and its widening and deepening in the consciousness of mankind constitutes the chief revolution wrought in contemporary thought. Such is the operating synthesis for the oncoming future.

§

The conclusions to which we are led are clear and positive. The conception of human affairs as constituting a mechanism operating according to fixed laws discoverable by the human mind is abandoned. The conceit which underlay the assumption is utterly disintegrated by contemporary criticism and observation. For this conception another is substituted. There are in human affairs intermittent if not continuous changes—a movement of ideas and interests, breaking temporary patterns of policy and performance. Only in very limited areas of human affairs, if anywhere, are fixed routines of conduct maintained for long periods of time. An effort to reduce the whole national economy to a sequential order would embrace a wide range of human history, past, present, and future, and the probability of effecting such a reduction is so dubious as to be little more than a fantastic chimera. Although many areas of human affairs can be brought within the scope of tentative laws or axioms, these areas are interrelated and are surrounded by larger areas which cannot be so ordered; hence the validity of any so-called laws or axioms of economy must always be conditional—must depend on the perdurance of surrounding circumstances that are beyond control and prediction. So we are driven to a formula which seems to strike bottom: in human affairs are to be found *necessity* or things inescapable, *fortune* or the appearances of choice, and *virtue* or the capacity for choice and action.

To the American statesman some necessities are presented, such as territory, the cultural heritage, the use of the English language, the state of the arts and economy, and diversity of natural resources, for example. Likewise he faces certain possible choices respecting the use of this heritage. Then within the necessities and possibilities of the situation he confronts the problem of making his choices: and this fact introduces into the operation ethical and esthetic values—one possible choice is more desirable than another with reference to some posited canon of valuation. Inevitably this procedure of valuation implies the establishment of an ideal conception of the American nation in its world relations to be realized by policy and action—a positive clarification of social purpose. At all events, decisions and actions are predicated on this conception of human affairs and no other operating hypothesis of life is possible, whatever pure contemplation may have to say in the case.

The human situation embracing the crisis in economy and thought thus presents to the mind: (1) necessities, or probabilities of such a high degree as to constitute necessities for practical purposes; (2) the possibility of choosing among alternative ways and means; and (3) ideas or conceptions of desirabilities, ethical and esthetic, within the limits of necessity and possibility. For example, the American nation and interests called American are here; their existence and the necessities associated with them are stubborn realities in the scene; to deny their fatefulness is to flee to utopianism. But the American nation and the world in which it operates are changing, throwing up occurrences having the signs of contingencies. To all appearances there are possibilities of resorting to war, to tariff modifications, to alterations in domestic wealth distribution, and to other alternatives of choice; these possibilities are assumed in all debates over policies, for debates over things necessary and determined are absurdities; people do not quarrel with one another over the fact that water normally runs down hill. Ideas respecting desirability are so numerous as scarcely to call for illustration: personal and national security is more desirable than disaster and defeat; decent and beautiful cities are more desirable than dirty and hideous cities; individual and national well-being is more desirable than poverty, misery, and wretchedness.

What then can those who pretend to seek a way out of the crisis in economy and thought actually do? They can collect and analyze the schemes of thought and action now presented as proposed exits from the dilemma. They can examine the instrumentalities of mind now available for a consideration of the problem and its solution. They can clarify their own social thought and purpose, take account of the stubborn necessities which seem to condition the realization of any program, distinguish between things known or subject to verification and things merely guessed or hazarded, and at the end submit their own scheme of conjecture—which will be an interpretation of history past and in the making—to the judgment of that ultimate tribunal for human causes: history in the process of making. The wider their realistic knowledge of history, including thought and social relationships, and the more certain their intuitive insight into the shape of things to come, the more likely they are to forecast accurately the policies that will be commanded by the necessity of things and the policies that will prove workable in the accomplishment of ideal ends.

Such are the assumptions and the knowledge, real or alleged, by which historic and proposed policies for the United States are here tested and an effort to formulate a consistent and workable policy is controlled.

CHAPTER III

INDUSTRIALIST STATECRAFT

AN examination of many professions, declarations, practices, and actions of American statesmen directed to a solution of the crisis in economy reveals two broad conceptions of policy, both pursued under the head of national interest. The first of these may be called, for convenience, the industrialist thesis. Although not without consideration for agriculture, it has its center of attention and affection in industry, commerce, and finance. The second, here characterized as agrarian, originally had its center of attention and affection in agriculture; and, despite the fact that it has materially widened its social base, it is still especially concerned with outlets for farm produce.[1] A third conception of policy, outlined by President Franklin D. Roosevelt in 1933, is now in process of formulation and is as yet too fragmentary to be characterized by a single word or phrase. Moreover, on account of its newness and indefinite nature, it cannot be subjected to the criticism drawn from the test of long experience.

STATEMENT OF THE INDUSTRIALIST THESIS

In order that the industrialist way of escape from the dilemma in economy and thought may be clearly in mind when criticism is undertaken, its main features may be recalled.[2]

---

[1] It should be emphasized that the titles "industrialist" and "agrarian" are not treated here as accurately descriptive. They are only rough approximations drawn from history. The future may invalidate them. American industrialism may turn to freer trade in its efforts to escape from the jam of overproduction and let down the bars to a flood of agricultural produce in an attempt to reduce the cost of production, after the fashion of British industrialists in 1840. Such a tendency to reversal is possible. Hence the use of the title here is to be considered as a matter of provisional convenience.

[2] For historical development and greater detail, see *The Idea of National Interest* (1934).

Materials for such an epitome are the professions and records of American statesmen attached to the industrialist school from the inauguration of President McKinley in 1897 to the close of President Hoover's term in 1933. Not many of these statesmen, to be sure, presented the creed with the precision of Senator Albert Jeremiah Beveridge, President Taft, or Secretary Philander C. Knox. Nor can it be truly said that the identical pattern of thought, in every detail, existed in the minds of all the leaders in public affairs associated with the conception. Indeed, some of them dissented here and there from particular items in the program, and declined to follow other items to their logical outcome. President Coolidge, for example, discarded a portion of the McKinley thesis when he signed the Kellogg Pact tying the hands of the United States Government, verbally at least, with respect to the effective prosecution of national interest in the seven seas; and President Hoover rejected certain naval doctrines espoused by President Theodore Roosevelt. Moreover, many Democrats, especially in the East, have been more wholeheartedly attached to the industrialist creed than have the left-wing members of the Republican party, which officially pressed it upon the country. But, as the shots of many marksmen, fired from different angles, tend to group themselves around the center of the target, so the professions, declarations, practices, and actions of Republican statesmen, during the years under review, conformed with fair exactness to the system of industrialist thought outlined in the following pages.

The industrialist conception of the only possible escape from the crisis in economy and thought, through activities clothed in the formula of national interest, rests upon an interpretation of American economic life—upon an economic theory supposed to be practical. The elements of this conception are simple. American industry, under the régime of technology, is producing more commodities than the American people can use or consume, and the "surplus" must be exported. The accumulations of capital in private hands in the United States are larger than can be employed advantageously at home, that is, profitably, so that there is a "surplus" for exportation. American agriculture likewise is producing more than the

American people can use or consume and the "surplus" must be sold in foreign markets. Outlets for these increasing "surpluses" of goods and capital must and can be found abroad, through the channels of commerce; otherwise the development of American industry and agriculture, with corresponding opportunities for gains and profits, will be slowed down, and brought, perhaps, to an impasse or deadlock which cannot be broken. It is, therefore, a question of commercial expansion or stagnation and decay; world power or economic decline. There is no other escape: the expansion of outlets for growing surpluses of commodities, produce, and capital must come; it is necessary, it is possible, it is desirable—all in the national interest.

The thesis just described runs like a powerful motif through state papers from the inauguration of President McKinley to the retirement of President Hoover, with variants and modifications. It was summed up with brevity and precision by Senator Albert Jeremiah Beveridge in a single paragraph of an address to American business men delivered at Boston in 1898. "American factories are making more than the American people can use; American soil is producing more than they can consume. Fate has written our policy for us; the trade of the world must and shall be ours. And we will get it as our mother [England] has told us how. We will establish trading-posts thoughout the world as distributing-points for American products. We will cover the ocean with our merchant marine. We will build a navy to the measure of our greatness. Great colonies governing themselves, flying our flag and trading with us, will grow about our posts of trade. Our institutions will follow our flag on the wings of our commerce. And American law, American order, American civilization, and the American flag will plant themselves on shores hitherto bloody and benighted, but by those agencies of God henceforth to be made beautiful and bright." [3]

In other words, the continuous expansion of foreign markets for American manufactures, capital, and agricultural produce is necessary, possible, desirable, and a part of the process of destiny and Almighty God. The economies of other nations

[3] Bowers, *Beveridge and the Progressive Era,* p. 69.

and of backward places, yet to be developed, can absorb the ever-swelling output of American industry and agriculture—goods and accumulating capital. If they will not or cannot of their own motion provide the widening markets for American goods and capital, then force, ranging from diplomatic pressure to war, will be applied to make them do it. A condition of domestic necessity as inexorable as the law of gravitation compels this expansion and determines the policy of the Government of the United States. To challenge the validity of the thesis is to question "the stars in their courses" as Senator Beveridge characterized the movement of American economic life. Only "mollycoddles," "mugwumps," and "simpletons" can refuse to see the determinism of the law, and reject its implications for the foreign policy of the Government of the United States.

Under this conception of national interest, it would seem, all exports of "surplus" goods and capital redound to the national advantage and by adequate government pressure sufficient outlets can be obtained to resolve the crisis created by the unlimited potentials of technology. No discrimination is made among the goods exported and the uses to which exported capital may be put. The manufacturer who sells cotton goods abroad serves the national interest and helps to relieve the strain; so does the manufacturer who exports the latest textile machinery which, in China or Japan for instance, cuts down the Oriental markets of American cotton-goods manufacturers. The American farmer who finds an outlet abroad for his wheat advances the national interest and aids in relaxing the tension; the same cause is served by the manufacturer of farm machinery who exports machines and implements which increase wheat production in foreign countries and curtail the market for American wheat. Capital exported to build branch factories and expand competing industries in foreign lands operates to the same ends as exported capital which develops industries in the Orient or in Latin America to supply the United States with necessary raw materials. American capital invested in foreign corporations, intensifying the competition which American enterprise must meet everywhere, promotes the national interest and reduces the domestic tension; capital invested in the rubber plantations of Liberia or the Dutch East Indies is to be set down on the same side of the ledger to the credit of the national interest and domestic peace in economy and thought.

According to similar reasoning, the entire "stake abroad" represents a genuine national interest and its exploitation is a part of the process necessary to resolve the domestic crisis. All the stocks and bonds of foreign governments and corporations held by American citizens, all the properties, rights, titles, privileges, and concessions in foreign countries and dependencies owned by American citizens are parts of the national interest and the ownership contributes to the reduction of the domestic tension. No discrimination is made between American properties abroad which intensify the competition encountered by American citizens in seeking expanding outlets for the growing "surpluses" and other properties which represent the development of non-competitive raw materials for import—raw materials necessary to the operations of domestic industries. Although doubts on this score are occasionally expressed, the industrialist thesis, as practiced, allows for no classification of goods and capital exported and for no restraints on the one or the other in respect of competition among domestic enterprises. It assumes a perfect harmony of interests.

The national interest, so conceived as embracing instrumentalities and processes for resolving the crisis in economy and thought, includes more than securities, rights, titles, and properties now in existence and held by American citizens. It also includes trade opportunities, concessions, and privileges *in posse,* which may be won, gained, and held in all parts of the world by American citizens. In the partition of the world's total commerce and the distribution of its undeveloped opportunities, citizens of the United States are entitled to, and are to have, "their share"—a quantity limited only by the power of American private enterprise and the support which it receives from the Government of the United States. Whatever *may* be won by ingenuity, by the influence of wealth, negotiation, and permissible intrigue, by diplomacy and naval pressure, belongs of right to American citizens and corporations, and comes within the scope of the national interest. Thus the potential achievements of the future as well as the accomplishments of the past and present are embraced by the formula and included in the operations deemed necessary and effective in escaping from the jam of domestic production.

Since the crisis in economy is exigent and these operations in the national interest are necessary to an escape from the dilemma, the responsibilities, duties, and foreign policies of the Government of the United States are clearly and unequivocally fixed. The business of the Government is to promote and protect all such economic activities, clothed in the formula of national interest. It acts as the "advance agent" and "attorney" for all exporters of commodities engaged in draining off the threatening "surpluses." It searches out at public expense trade opportunities in all parts of the world, brings pressure to bear upon foreign governments to induce them to buy American goods, and lends diplomatic and naval protection to citizens engaged in mercantile operations in other countries. With an even hand and as an all-around representation of interests, it favors, for example, the American manufacturer who exports commodities for consumption in Germany and the manufacturer who establishes a branch factory in Germany, or exports machinery to that country, for the purpose of making goods that come into competition with American products in the German market, in other countries, and perhaps even in the United States. With the same zeal it promotes the interests of the textile manufacturer seeking foreign outlets for his goods and the manufacturer of textile machinery who exports the latest improved spinning and weaving devices which help to curtail the sale of American cotton goods abroad. Likewise, in theory at least, it makes no discrimination between agriculture and manufacturing. It energetically pushes the sale of wheat, cotton, and meats and also the sale of agricultural machinery which will enable foreign farmers to cut their operating costs and compete more effectively with their American rivals at home and abroad.

In a similar manner the Federal Government comes to the aid of capital export. Pursuing uniform benevolence, it looks with approval on all export bankers, whether the capital which they send abroad is wasted by corrupt and inefficient governments, is applied to armaments which may be used against the United States or to found peaceful industries, is devoted to enterprises which ultimately expand foreign markets for American goods or is used in undertakings that curtail foreign markets for American commodities. Even though the Department of Commerce may have grounds for believing that a particular foreign State is on the verge of bankruptcy, the Government of the United States cannot move, on its own initiative, to protect American investors against losing their money. While proponents of the industrialist thesis probably would not now claim that capital exported and sunk in the bottomless pit of default promotes the national interest and relieves the domestic tension, they refused for years to assume the responsibility for preventing such business transactions. All exports of capital, with minor exceptions, are good and help to ease congestion at home.

Under the industrialist thesis, the Government of the United States must also regard diplomatic intervention on behalf of American citizens and enterprises to secure concessions in foreign countries as contributing to a relaxation of the domestic crisis in the national interest. Whether it is a question of a banking consortium in China, oil in Mesopotamia, Sumatra or Colombia, mineral resources in Chile, cable rights in South America generally, or any other operation involving action on the part of foreign governments, the assumption seems to be that the national interest, conceived as relief from the strain of "overproduction," is served by inventing and supporting American demands and claims. Indeed in many cases the Government of the United States has made a point of searching for opportunities and drawing private enterprise into its own projects, thus developing a public competition that goes beyond private competition.

Besides promoting the extension of interests and activities abroad which drain off domestic "surpluses" and permit the continuous expansion of technology at home—resolve the crisis—the Government of the United States, according to the industrialist thesis, must defend these interests and activities against the adverse pressures and discriminations of foreign persons, corporations, and governments, and, if need be, against disorders, threats of force, and open violence abroad. The things thus to be defended consist of goods and ships upon the high seas; commodities in warehouses and shops abroad; capital invested; mines, factories, and other plants owned in part or wholly by American citizens or corporations; concessions already won and in process of winning; lands, forests, houses, and other property owned in foreign places by American citizens or corporations; overseas possessions, protectorates, and spheres of influence and penetration; claims filed by American citizens and corporations against foreign governments; and similar rights, titles, and privileges *in esse* or *in posse*. Extending beyond corporeal things, national interest embraces intangible rights to be asserted by the Government of the United States against foreign governments, such as the right to the open door and to the same treatment as the most favored nation.

Thus pursuit of national interest, officially regarded as a forceful quest for an escape from "overproduction," traverses the seven seas and plunges into the territories and institutions of other countries, far and near. It was with reference to authoritative tradition that Curtis Wilbur, speaking as Secretary of the Navy, declared in effect that the American flag—naval defense—covers every dollar afloat on the high seas and invested abroad and every American citizen no matter where he may be or what "lawful" activity he is pursuing.

In promoting and defending the national interest so conceived, it is the duty of the Government of the United States to employ all the engines of state—diplomatic representation and pressures, discriminating legislation at home, the resources of official soliciting agents, a subsidized merchant marine, marines and soldiers upon occasion, the coercive force of the Navy, measures short of war, and, ultimately, war. Despite various verbal concessions to peace, the final sanction of American activities abroad in the pursuit of interests is the Navy. Its duty, according to repeated official declarations, is to protect the foreign commerce of the United States, to defend the overseas possessions, and to exert economic pressure on the course of trade. American gunboats lie off the coasts of Turkey offering the suggestion that the rights and property of American merchants on shore are to be respected by the aliens with whom they are dealing. American ships shell Nanking when local Chinese troops out of hand endanger American life and property in the city. Throughout the Caribbean region American vessels of war are stationed to suppress disturbances likely to disrupt American business or threaten American lives. If war is renounced as an instrument of national policy, thus outlawing such excursions as the war on Spain in 1898, limited war remains a fact and preparations are made, in the national interest, for the possibilities of unlimited war.

While the *export* of goods and capital is to be free from government restraints, in the main, and is to be promoted and defended, as offering an escape from the domestic crisis of "overproduction," the *import* of goods—manufactured and agricultural—is to be restrained, managed, and controlled by elaborate tariff legislation and administrative practices, with sharp discrimination between imports of raw materials and imports of manufactures. By the establishment of such government barriers, the import of goods likely to increase the domestic glut is reduced, the expansion of domestic industries to absorb the growing potentialities of technology is encouraged, with a view, it is said, to assuring legitimate profits to capital, a high standard of life to labor, and a large home market to agriculture—the utopia into which entrance is sought. And as domestic industries expand under this tariff protection, more outlets for "surpluses" of goods and capital must be found by private and public enterprise. Foreign policy thus becomes a servant of national interest conceived in such terms, and the operations of economy and Government multiply as they intensify.

Regarded as inexorable, the industrialist thesis imposes itself upon thought, economy, and government as the supreme law of the land. When its magic is evoked all citizens must automatically obey. According to a ruling of President Taft the country is bound to present a "united front" in dealing with foreign governments. President Coolidge once went so far as to declare that when the national interest is at stake in international affairs, in the form of American lives and property, executive action must be accepted as beyond criticism, as binding upon citizens, newspapers, and officials, without respect to party or private opinions. In this view national interest is the national faith, its law is unequivocal—beyond question, and the President of the United States as head of foreign affairs, if true to the industrialist thesis, is the infallible interpreter of the creed in theory and action. Foreign policy thus becomes an absolute which can be applied unerringly by a bureaucracy.

APPRAISAL OF THE INDUSTRIAL THESIS

Is the industrialist thesis a statement of unequivocal fact and law? When a hydraulic engineer declares that a given set of machines and a scheme of human actions in connection with a waterfall, let us say, will produce ten thousand horse power in electric current, he makes a statement of fact and law which can be verified by reference to hydro-electric plants already in existence or by a test to be made in accordance with the hypothesis advanced. In other words, the truth of the statement can be authenticated in terms of positive sequence and outcome. Does the industrialist thesis for providing an escape from the jam of domestic "overproduction" belong to such an order of data and thought? On its face it appears to be a deterministic sequence open to scientific verification.

Stripped of all irrelevancies, this thesis of national interest takes the form of a theorem:

1. American factories and farms are producing more goods than the American people can use or consume.[4]

2. The accumulations of capital in private hands exceed the amount which can be advantageously, that is, profitably, employed at home.

[4] This sweeping statement was less true in 1898 than it was in 1928. At the former date there were few American manufacturing industries that had completely saturated the domestic market and were prepared to compete effectively in the world market with older industrial countries. As a general rule, therefore, it was not an accurate characterization of the economic situation at the time it was made, even assuming the inexorability and perpetuity of the capitalist system.

3. Outlets must and can be found abroad for these surpluses of goods and capital.

4. In the processes of functioning the American economic machine requires large amounts of raw materials, absolutely essential to domestic production, which must come from foreign countries or colonial possessions, and to secure these materials it is necessary to sell abroad or export capital or acquire territories in which these requisites are found.

5. In such circumstances the American economic machine requires a large volume of foreign trade as a condition absolutely indispensable to its domestic functioning, that is, employment for labor and profits for capital.

6. Diplomacy and force can and will be employed to establish "trading posts" for the United States and create trade opportunities which will provide the requisite outlets, given a navy equal to "our greatness."

7. In expanding foreign trade and supporting it by national power, the United States comes of age and discharges a solemn "duty" which it owes to world order, enlightenment, and progress.

8. Protective tariffs can and will restrict the import of goods that might come into competition with domestic industry and agriculture, that is, might add to the surpluses in the domestic market.

Q.E.D. The problem of the economic surplus is solved and continuity of expanding operations—unbroken and ascending prosperity—is assured to domestic industry and agriculture.

When the intrinsic nature of this thesis is subjected to scrutiny it is found to comprise:

1. A statement of alleged fact describing an objective and independent sequence, that is, American industry and agriculture are producing more commodities and capital accumulations than the American people can use—a statement of fact presumably susceptible of positive verification.

2. An allegation of possibility: outlets *can* be found for the surpluses of goods and capital.

3. A prophecy (made as early as 1898): diplomatic and naval force *will* secure the necessary outlets.

4. A theological assertion: American law, order, civilization, and flag (force) *are* agencies of God.

5. An interpretation of history: this is the *fate* of the United States.

Let us look first at the statement of alleged fact: "American factories are making more than the American people can use; American soil is producing more than they can consume." Is this alleged fact an actual fact and is its existence independent of human will? When an architect says that a certain tower can stand at a certain angle to the surface of the earth and at no angle more acute, he is stating a fact that is beyond human power to change. His verb "can" describes something that has fixed mathematical limits, not a flexible array of probabilities; and human effort cannot alter these limits. When it is said that American industry and agriculture are producing more than the American people *can* use or consume, is the statement a description of inexorable and mechanical limitations, the lines of which are fixed by a law akin to that of gravitation and cannot be shifted by human effort and arrangement? Or is the statement founded on the assumption that a given set of human arrangements in the United States—the product of human will and effort—is fixed and permanent?

If anything is known, then the answer to this question is known. The first proposition presented in the thesis of national interest is not one in mathematical physics; it falls within the domain of the humanities. The statement that American industry and agriculture are producing more than the American people *can* consume or use is not a description of an isolated deterministic sequence independent of human will, purpose, power, policy, or arrangements. The amount which the American people *can* use or consume is not a fixed quantity, open to mathematical measurement, and beyond the power of human will to alter.

Fundamental assumptions enter into the structure of the

proposition in question. First of all, the assertion assumes the private ownership and manipulation of the means of production and, consequently, the distribution of wealth, or buying and consuming power, associated with a high degree of concentration in the ownership and management of the means of production.[5] This is an assumption of the first magnitude which vitiates the thesis as a description of an independent sequence at the very outset. The distribution of wealth, that is, buying and consuming power, is not determined for all time by a force, like that of gravity, outside the control of human will and policy. Within some limits of necessity, which cannot be exactly determined, the distribution of wealth has been, is being, and can be, altered by collective action, as the taxation and expenditure measures of every government budget demonstrate. If the distribution of wealth or consuming power is fixed, like the courses of the planets, why the endless struggle of capital and labor over wages, hours, and profits?

The statement of alleged fact in the industrialist thesis of national interest is, therefore, not a statement of inexorable fact, but of fact resting upon assumptions respecting the prevailing system of ownership and wealth distribution. To be accurately descriptive the statement should run as follows: American industry and agriculture are producing more than the owners of the industries and farms can sell, at a profit, to the American people under the current system of wealth distribution. Or to put the matter in another form: Given the present distribution of wealth or buying power, American industry and agriculture are producing *in various lines* more than the American people can buy for use or consumption, and the accumulations of capital in private hands make for plant extensions that outrun the buying power of the American people.

The amount that the American people *can* use or consume is a variable, and has limits difficult to disclose by any methods of research and construction open to contemporary knowledge. It is probably true that in some branches American industry and agriculture are equipped to produce more than

[5] Berle and Means, *The Modern Corporation and Private Property.*

the American people could or would use, even if a high standard of rational living were posited. It is certain also that under
any system of ownership and distribution some quantities of
given commodities would have to be reserved from domestic
consumption in order to pay for imports deemed necessary
and desirable for the maintenance of domestic industries and
the American standard of life. But can it be truthfully said
that the American people have all the food they need for
physical and moral strength, all the shoes they need, all the
furniture they can utilize, the kind of homes required for
comfort and decency? Can it be truthfully said that the
American people have full access to all the goods which their
labor and intelligence applied to the utmost potentiality of
technology entitle them?

In summation, the major premise of the thesis is not a
statement of objective, inexorable fact, beyond the reach of
human will, but is a statement based on assumptions as to
social policy open to challenge. These assumptions are relative to a given set of human arrangements in the United States,
which is in process of change, and they are now disintegrating
under theoretical criticism and actual practice. In any case,
the "surpluses" of American industry and agriculture over and
above the quantities that could or would be used or consumed
at home under any conceivable system of wealth distribution
are limited to certain branches of industry and agriculture, and
to lump them together as a "surplus" is to create a fictitious
abstraction.

Passing from the opening premise of the thesis, the statement of alleged fact, we now come to the second proposition
in the thesis—the alleged possibility: Outlets *can* be found
abroad for the sale of the surplus commodities and the export
of surplus capital produced by American industry and agriculture. Assuming even that the opening premise is sound,
namely, that there is an inescapable surplus, is this statement
of alleged possibility susceptible of authentication and verification? When an engineer says that a suspension bridge *can*
be built across this stream or that a given system of electrical
distribution *can* furnish outlets for a given amount of energy,
he advances a proposition which can be verified by reference

to, or by making, an actual demonstration in outward and visible reality. Does the alleged possibility of finding foreign outlets for the sale of the surplus of American industry and agriculture and export of surplus capital come within any such category of engineering knowledge? It does not. The source of verification and authentication is contemporary knowledge of historical experience.

The assertion that outlets *can* and *will* be found abroad for the surpluses of American industry and agriculture was made years ago—clearly and emphatically by Senator Beveridge in 1898, to go no further back in time. What conclusions on this point does authentic knowledge of historical experience since that date bring to bear? The first is that outlets for all the "surpluses," either on a rising scale or a continuous level, have not been found by the processes of private and public enterprise employed during the years intervening since the allegation of possibility, although large outlets have been found for certain quantities of certain commodities for certain periods of time, by no means synchronous. Second, the proportion of the total exportable production of the United States for which outlets have been found has not materially increased during the past forty years but has remained fairly constant, whatever the methods of promotion, public or private, employed in the meantime. Third, ever-expanding outlets for the growing surpluses of industry and agriculture, promised long ago by the proponents of the thesis, have not been found in fact; instead of continuous expansion, there has been a fairly constant level in the proportion of exportable production sent abroad and there have been periods of violent contraction in the absolute quantities of commodities exported; even during the boom period of 1923-1929, outlets for the agricultural surplus were not found; and after long practice, under the thesis here considered, the problem of the surplus for American industry remains unsolved; is more exigent in 1934 than it was during the closing years of the nineteenth century. Fourth, the proportion of agricultural produce for which foreign outlets have been found has been steadily declining over a long period of years despite the acuteness of the surplus problem in this field of American enterprise. Fifth, the maintenance of the fairly constant level in the proportion of exportable production for which outlets have been found has been largely due to the development in the United States of special technological devices, machines, and processes the export of which has filled the vacuum caused by the relative decline in the export of agricultural produce and older commodities; hence it would seem that the maintenance of even the fairly constant level of proportionate export in the future will depend in a considerable measure upon the ingenuity of technology in making new devices, rather than on the promotional and pressure measures and policies of the United States Government.

Likewise inexorable is another finding from experience; the pressure for the export of goods and capital, under the industrialist thesis, by creating the so-called "stake abroad," has altered fundamentally the conditions under which the future export business must be carried on. A substantial portion of the "stake" has been lost by defaults and by sale at depreciated prices, to the account of foreign governments and private parties, thus putting a damper on enthusiasm for renewed lending on a large scale. A considerable part of the money lent abroad has been applied in foreign countries to the more efficient production of goods which are identical with those entering into the American surpluses that seek outlets, and hence compete with American enterprise in other markets of the world, intensifying the rivalry for trade opportunities long prevailing. The export of manufacturing and agricultural machinery to foreign countries has had the same effect: the development of a competition checking the export of the surpluses of American industry and agriculture. A substantial part of the raw materials produced under American auspices in foreign countries adds to the flood of raw materials pouring into the world market, including the American market, in competition with American agriculture, particularly. The imperial stake—Cuba, the Philippines, Porto Rico—has increased the agricultural produce, especially sugar, tobacco, and vegetable oils, which enters into direct competition with American agriculture. The widening of the area of the stake abroad by the export pressure has contributed to the increase in naval and military expenditures now mounting in the direction of a billion a year, and national security has been put in jeopardy by expanding the American naval zone beyond the competence of the American Navy to defend in a major war in the eastern Atlantic or the western Pacific.

Such are the hard conclusions based upon a survey of past economic experiences under the practice of the industrialst thesis. What of the possibility of finding ever-expanding outlets for the growing surpluses of American industry and agriculture in the future, assuming the continuance of the prevailing productive and distributive arrangements and the reality of the surpluses? By what knowledge and methods of thought can this question of possibility be answered, if at all?

Here enters an axiom of international exchange that is open to objective and statistical verification: in the long run exports and imports must balance in pecuniary values, assuming no extensive repudiations of, and defaults on, debts. Even under the commercial régime contemplated in the thesis, a continuous expansion of exports would be possible only in case the exports were balanced by a continuous expansion of imports which the American people could use or consume; and this would mean, under present policy, imports of raw materials on the free list and other commodities which do not compete with the branches of American industry and agriculture in which surpluses exist. The statement of the issue disposes of it: a continuous expansion of exports cannot be effected under the system of closely restricted imports prevailing in the United States. A temporary stimulus, in the form of lavish foreign loans, may be administered to the export business, but in the long run the balance of payments must operate, unless defaults, scaling, and repudiation intervene. If any demonstration from experience is needed to settle the issue, the course of American industry and trade from 1920 to 1934, under the régime of feverish export promotion and high tariffs, surely supplies it. Those who are not convinced by the sequence of events during the years 1920-1934 are certainly beyond reach of knowledge and logic.

But the fact that American industry and agriculture failed to secure a continuous expansion of exports between 1920 and 1934 under the régime of export promotion and high tariffs does not lead, as some of our logicians would have us believe, to the demonstration that "lower trade barriers," or even free trade, would guarantee that continuous expansion of exports. This issue, which rises like a ghost whenever the defeat of the industrialist program is mentioned, will be treated later (pp. 74 ff.), but a warning should be entered now against resorting to the prevalent and inveterate American habit of jumping to the conclusion that, because one method of manipulating foreign trade has failed to secure the continuous expansion of exports, another method of manipulation *can* accomplish the end.

Besides purporting to be in part a statement of irreducible fact, the industrialist thesis is in part a prophecy. "Fate has written our policy for us; the trade of the world must and shall be ours." The United States *will* expand, *will* wrest colonies from other nations, *will* build a navy "to the measure of our greatness," by implication large enough to impose victory on any country that stands in the way of our acquiring colonies and extending trade. Commerce *will* expand in this process and *will* absorb the surplus goods which the American people cannot use or consume. This policy *will* find the widening outlets, *will* produce the results anticipated in the form of profits for American industries and agriculture and of employment and wages for workers. The operations *will* continue. The opposition *will* be crushed. This well-rounded prophecy was made in the spring of 1898.

The test of that part of the industrialist thesis which is prophecy is simple. Has the prophecy been realized? Has the projected policy written by fate actually worked? To some extent the prophecy of 1898 has been fulfilled. Hawaii, the Philippines, Porto Rico, the Panama Zone, and protectorates in the Caribbean have been acquired. Trade with these possessions has increased. To some extent the imports from these regions have consisted of goods which do not compete with domestic production, but supplement the wealth produced within the continental domain.

In the main, however, the prophecy has failed. These "trading posts" have not provided adequate outlets for the surpluses of American industry and agriculture; the burden of the "surpluses" remains. Moreover, the import of agricultural produce from these possessions into the United· States has added to the domestic surpluses against which American farmers complain. The United States has not continued the acquisition of trading posts and colonies; it might have claimed all Germany's colonies as the price of participation in the World War. As a matter of fact, it did not do this. Instead of continuing the acquisition of colonies, the United States has even reversed the process and tendered independence to the Philippines upon certain conditions. Under President Wilson it renounced all intention of making additional annexations. The Government of the United States, by solemn treaty obligations, has renounced the possibility of building a navy adequate to the purposes of the proposed thesis and has renounced war as an instrument of national policy; that is, war for the acquisition of more territories by force to serve the ends of commerce. In part, accordingly, events have belied the prophecy. In fundamentals it was a false prophecy—at least up to the present hour. What the future holds anyone may guess.

That part of the industrialist thesis, borrowed from British imperial ideology of the nineties, which maintains that American law, order, civilization, and flag (force) are agencies of God bringing enlightenment to benighted peoples, stated in this form, falls, strictly speaking, in the domain of eschatology and transcends rational and statistical analysis. In such a form it may properly be left to theologians and *Machtpolitiker*. Considered, however, from the standpoint of the American nation, the question properly arises whether the alleged passion for doing good to "benighted" peoples should not be turned into domestic channels. That the United States has moral obligations to the various races and mixtures already under its dominion goes without saying, and the state of welfare in Hawaii, Porto Rico, Cuba, and the Caribbean generally indicates that some of these obligations have not been fully discharged. But whether it should insist on bringing additional areas occupied by "benighted" peoples under its jurisdiction raises other considerations.

First of all, these areas are now either independent States

or the possessions of imperial powers. That any of them will voluntarily transfer their affections and property to the United States, or that any associate in the World War will pay debts in colonies may be regarded as highly unlikely. Very probably nothing except war, controlled by a policy of annexation, can add more "backward peoples" to the American dominion, and the outcome of a war involving other imperialist powers is so problematical that the quest for new opportunities to "civilize" and "Christianize" might end in defeat or, at all events, do material and moral damages to the participants which would more than offset any benefits bestowed upon the "benighted." Given the present distribution of colonies, possessions, and protectorates occupied by "backward" races, the present treaty restraints on American naval power, and the probable unwillingness of Great Britain, France, and Japan to give the United States a free hand in making an unlimited naval expansion, it seems reasonable to suppose that the United States cannot safely seek more opportunities to do good to backward peoples by conquering and annexing the territories they occupy.

A second consideration lies in the fact that there are numerous opportunities to do good at home which could supply outlets for swelling passions of sacrificial virtue. There are millions of illiterate and degraded people, young and old, now living in the continental United States. There are millions of American people, even in prosperous times, who are lacking the security, sanitary conveniences, medical services, educational opportunities, and habits of industry which American statesmen of the industrialist school are eager to supply to the "benighted" in distant and foreign places. It would seem in the *national* interest, therefore, to lay more emphasis on eliminating backwardness from the American *nation* than to make plans for wresting new "benighted" areas from Great Britain, France, or Japan for the purpose of securing more moral obligations to other races. Those who are deeply moved in the virtuous sense implied by "the white man's burden" can, in view of the condition of several million Negroes in the United States, probably find extensive outlets for their moral urges at home, in any case for a number of years, thus postponing for a considerable time the necessity for acquiring by force additional congeries of "brown brothers."

Should these domestic opportunities for the exercise of sacrificial virtues be deemed insufficient, it is possible to discover other opportunities for improving "benighted" peoples without going to war with some imperial power for the purpose of bringing them under the legal jurisdiction of the United States. Great Britain, France, Holland, Belgium, and Italy are Christian nations, in the accepted sense of the term, and their missionary enterprises would doubtless welcome American gifts of money and goods for use among the "benighted." Again, the United States could join the League of Nations and acquire a voice in the administrative supervision of the "mandates," thus aiding powerfully, if indirectly, in the process of spreading "order, civilization, and Christianity." Accordingly, in surrendering the thesis that outlets for the continuous expansion of American industry and agriculture can be found by acquiring new possessions in "benighted" areas, it is not necessary for the American people to deny themselves the privilege of doing any good "to them that sit in darkness," which they feel morally obligated to undertake. The defeat incurred in the effort to realize the economic part of the industrialist program does not involve blocking all outlets for the moral urge, should there be a vigorous resurgence of that passion after the abandonment of the Philippines.

So, as a statement of alleged fact, the major premise of the thesis will not stand the test of empirical analysis; as a prophecy it has not been fulfilled in essentials. Practice under it has not supplied the actual outlets for the goods and capital which the American people "cannot use." Thus far the thesis has been invalidated by events—events so indubitable that no one can successfully deny them. Yet the possibility of an indefinite increase in the output of American commodities under the prevailing system of technology and capital accumulation is also indubitable, and at the present hour we face the future. Is there any ground or reason for renewing the prophecy now, for urging the policy implicit in it, for believing that it is physically and morally possible, for supposing that the results predicted by it would flow from the unremitting and vigorous pursuit of the ends proposed, by the means proposed? That is a supreme issue of policy at the present moment.

Here, too, we confront stubborn realities. The backward places, islands of the seas, and naval bases to be acquired as "trading posts," as just indicated, are all organized as independent countries or as the possessions of great powers. There are no more vacant lands or weak races to be taken, without violently disturbing the claims and interests of other governments. Hence additional expansion by the United States must be at the expense of some rival or competitor. That much seems settled at least.

If deemed desirable, with a view to trade expansion, would it be possible for the United States to break the present distribution of imperial possessions and annex immense areas and various subject peoples now dominated by other powers, for the purpose of obtaining markets? Certainly not under the arms-limitation treaties which restrict the naval power of the United States to parity with Great Britain and a 5-3 ratio with Japan. It might be possible if the United States achieved the kind of naval supremacy which Great Britain once enjoyed, and lost in 1923-1930. Even then there would be perils calling for careful consideration. Should the United States embark upon a building program leading to unquestioned naval supremacy, how long would it be before Great Britain, France, and Japan, would enter into a protective, "balancing" combination, either secret or open? There is as much reason for believing that they would form a union against the United States as for accepting the history of their combination against Germany at the opening of the twentieth century. At all events the risks of an effort to expand trade by military and naval conquests are so high as to make impossible an exact calculation of outcome. Perhaps it was this fact, more than a moral revulsion, that led the great sea powers to consent to naval limitations in 1923, to accept the existing distribution of the spoils of empire, and to renounce war as an instrument of policy.

Nor is the way of trade expansion by conquest and annexation the same today as it was in the beginning of the system.

It now carries with it countervailing tendencies. It introduces capitalistic modes of exploitation and operation into primitive and backward societies, disrupting their ancient institutions.[6] It establishes railways, factories, and forced-labor economies. It tears up tribal and customary habits by the roots and substitutes competitive methods. It places Western science and contrivances at the disposal of races that might otherwise have lived undisturbed for indefinite periods as through the thousands of years of the past. It enables Western capitalists to take their machines and their managerial skill into undeveloped countries, reap the advantages of cheap labor, and curtail or destroy the markets which their compatriots have built up in the regions affected. It inoculates the simple minds of colonial peoples with the equalitarian ideas of the Western world, thus preparing the way for the spread of still more revolutionary conceptions under the inspiration, if not the direction, of Soviet Russia. Already, new and disruptive thoughts are in circulation among the laborers in the harbors and on the plantations along the west coast of Africa, on the plantations of Java, among the peasants toiling in the narrow valleys and on the hills of Korea.

If, from a study of the general setting for the expansion of outlets, we turn to consider specific areas of possible operations, the opposing realities of the situation become even more apparent. There are undoubtedly substantial possibilities for economic expansion in the Caribbean region and Latin America generally, which may absorb a part of the energies of expanding capitalism for half a century or more, but the conditions of that expansion are changing and are throwing up perils to such commercial enterprise. The very transformation wrought by industrialism in Latin America generates forces of resistance—revolutionary movements such as those reflected in the Mexican constitution of 1917 and the proposals advanced during the upheaval in Chile in 1932. It multiplies the risks of adventure for the investor, though not for the promoter. The enormous losses of American investors in Mexican railways, land, and mineral exploitation, in the defaulted bonds of South

[6] R. L. Buell, *The Native Problem in Africa.*

American countries, and in local enterprises scattered from the Rio Grande to Terra del Fuego indicate the probable price of trade promotion and suggest that hopes for ever expanding outlets are illusory. In any event, the growth of standardized industries in Latin America, under the leadership of American and European capitalists, will, in the course of time, curtail rather than extend the markets of the United States for manufactures.[7]

Even less inviting prospects are offered for penetration into the Orient, and higher risks. Since the age of Marco Polo, Western countries have been fascinated by dreams of riches to be won in the Far East, and visions of unlimited expansion have been dangled before enterprising leaders of industry, despite the low buying power of Orientals. For years the Department of Commerce of the United States issued propaganda portraying the "boundless opportunities" for trade and investment in China particularly, representing it as a land rich in resources and offering the possibilities of exhaustless markets. It was once a favorite device of the Department to say that when the people of China use as many of the leading commodities per capita as the people of the United States use, then the demands upon American mines and factories will keep American capital and labor fully employed.

Undoubtedly the trade with China is important in itself, but its significance to American economy as a whole is and must ever be relatively trivial. China is not a country possessing extraordinary wealth in natural resources, and her frightful excess of population bears down the standard of life until it is a fortunate laborer who receives as much as twenty cents a day on the average throughout the year. Approximately eighty per cent of the kerosene oil imported into China is retailed in quantities of a gill or less, revealing a buying power too low to sustain an immense foreign trade. If China had an orderly government, and could develop certain regions now backward, an increase of population, unless national habits were changed, would swamp and submerge the economic gains thus effected. In the very best presentation of the case for large increases in

[7] Normano, *The Struggle for South America.*

the China trade, calculations respecting outcomes are highly speculative. It is probable also that a well-organized China would dump huge amounts of cheap manufactures on the crowded world market, as Japan now does.

But there is no likelihood of a strong, unified government in China in the immediate future. For the present, the possibility of securing important railway, canal, mineral, and public-works concessions has utterly disappeared. If they were obtained, a powerful military force would be necessary to their execution and the collection of returns on the capital. The only way that large scale operations can be carried on in China, if at all, today, is the way chosen by Japan—frank conquest and subjugation, whatever may be the diplomatic formulas employed. In McKinley's day, John Hay thought that public opinion in the United States would not support any such operations on the part of his Government. Whatever may be the state of that opinion now, the undertaking is out of the question under the 5-3 ratio established for the navies of the United States and Japan, for Japan would not stand idly by while the United States carved out protectorates and spheres in China. Perhaps Great Britain and France also would take advantage of the occasion and support Japan in exchange for their share.

In any case, were the American Navy twice as large, the risks of operations in Chinese waters, especially without a fortified naval base in the Philippines, would be extremely hazardous, and the cost of a war, as Admiral Bristol has said, would run into the billions. Whatever the probabilities of the outcome, there is no way of making sure that the pecuniary gains would equal the economic cost of such operations. A certain moral fervor might be aroused by a military effort to protect China against Japan but even victory over the latter would be futile unless the transaction were accompanied by the organization of American authority over distracted China, including assumption of all political responsibilities associated with it. Such an operation may be justified by a theoretical moral obligation but not by any national interests conceived in terms of American economy and civilization.

In the remaining great theater of capitalist expansion—

Africa—the possibilities for the United States are not attractive. Most of the continent is now divided among the competing imperialist powers of Europe. It is separated from this country by thousands of miles of water, and major naval operations off its coasts would involve immense risks—indeed victory would be impossible, given the relative strength of France, Italy, and Great Britain as measured against American forces. The only foothold which the United States possesses is in Liberia, with its Firestone Rubber plantations, and this promises no large outlets for American commodities. The resources of Liberia are relatively insignificant and the country affords no base for extension except through collisions with France and Great Britain. It may be that the whole continent of Africa will some day be occupied by highly civilized nations, using telephones, bath tubs, and radios, but the time is far removed and European powers would resent the intrusion of the United States as an occupying participant in "the process of civilization" there. Economic penetration of Africa on a large scale, accompanied by political control, therefore, seems out of the question. By no stretch of the imagination could it be defended as promoting national interest, and offering large opportunities for the expansion of trade.

Such is the present distribution of the spoils of empire and the present state of those important parts of the world which seem to be open to the process of conquest, penetration, organization, and exploitation. Any move to expand American possessions outside the Caribbean region for the purpose of providing outlets for American commodities would mean war. Do the capitalists and farmers of the United States have the faith and will requisite to support war for this end? Do they believe that even a victorious war would in fact enlarge the outlets sufficiently to take care of "surplus production"? Is there anything in the experience of history to justify such a conviction? Would the possibilities of gain offset in their minds the risks of domestic and foreign turmoil certain to accompany such a high imperialist adventure even if successful? Is there any ground whatever for thinking that the outcome would be any less disappointing than the outcome of the Spanish war, which has been followed by at least three depressions and collapses of the market? Is there any reasoning, are there any facts, to support the contention that such a procedure is either the easiest way or a real way out of the periodical jams of "overproduction" in which the people of the United States have found themselves since 1898? Assuming a will to war for the conquest of market outlets, would it be possible to abolish all naval limitations, return to unrestricted naval rivalry, denounce the Kellogg-Briand Peace Pact, and resume the policy of the industrialist thesis—*Machtpolitik*—in its pristine form? And, granting that it were possible to go back to the unrestricted naval rivalry which marked the beginning of the twentieth century and to embark again on unlimited operations in trade promotion, do not the World War and the losses, dislocations, revolutions, and assassinations which accompanied it suggest a pause before taking the leap?

If the practice and thought of great nations—England, France, and Germany—lent sanction to the prophecy of the industrialist thesis when it was presented by Senator Beveridge and his colleagues, the times are less propitious for a renewal of the prophecy now. It is true that neither England nor France has renounced officially the theory and practice of imperialism and that German leaders speak of winning back their lost colonies and finding a place in the sun; it is true that Italy under the Fascist régime seems about to break out at any moment with imperialist zeal; it is true that Japan pursues in China with ruthless might imperial projects long nourished and cherished; but the posture and thought of the world in 1934 are not the posture and thought of 1898.

The Hohenzollerns and Hapsburgs have passed from the scene, and by no stretch of the imagination can the German Empire of William II and the Austria-Hungary of Francis Joseph be restored. Tsarist Russia has collapsed and a Russia of different ideas, methods, and ambitions has arisen from the Baltic to the Pacific. It is not Nicholas II and his entourage that face Japan across the narrow seas; it is Stalin and his communist army. If the "dangerous thoughts" of socialism and communism seem to be suppressed in Germany and Italy, if the Labor Party seems prostrate in England under a Nationalist Government, if Japanese imperialism rides high in

China, it is by no means certain that the explosive forces of revolution—the immeasurable forces which accompany imperialist rivalries and wars—are extinguished in these countries. To assume that they are is to suppose that the experience of the past is without meaning for the future. China of 1934 is not the sleeping China of 1898. The India of Ramsay MacDonald is not the India of Lord Curzon. Hence, to renew now the prophecy of the industrialist thesis offered in 1898 without respect to the movement of ideas during the intervening years is to forget nothing and to learn nothing.

It is not only necessary to record changes in the "backward places" of the earth where outlets for surpluses may be sought and in the conditions under which pressures for markets must now be exerted. It is equally imperative to take into account changes in the economic structures of the various powers engaged in the quest for markets. The United States has become predominantly industrial, as measured in terms of capital and labor employed; it can no longer take from the industrial countries of the Old World vast quantities of manufactures for which it once paid in agricultural produce. Germany has become highly industrialized and has rationalized her industries with the aid of American methods and capital. Japan is on the way to high industrialization and competes vigorously with all the industrial powers of the West in the world markets. Under the communist dictatorship, agrarian Russia is being transformed into a manufacturing nation, supplying herself with commodities for which she once exchanged wheat, timber, and other raw materials. And even the minor powers of Europe, with the aid of tariffs and subventions, seek to establish a balance between agriculture and industry.

Indeed, it may be said that nearly every independent nation is developing industries for producing at home the chief standardized products of the machine, thus constricting rapidly the areas that are content to supply raw materials in exchange for manufactures. Moreover, agriculture everywhere, under the stimulus of chemistry and machinery, is augmenting its output and capacity for output, thus narrowing the range for the export of agricultural produce by the United States. Trends plotted statistically show a decline in the proportion of American agricultural produce in the total export of the United States, and a decline in the proportion of American export which goes to Great Britain and the Continent of Europe. Certainly the industrial nations of the world cannot live by exchanging the standardized products of the machine among themselves; nor can they find adequate outlets in the raw-material regions for the almost unlimited output which modern technology can supply through machine industries. The issue, therefore, seems to be closed: the escape from domestic "over-production," present or potential, does not lie in the channels of foreign trade to be opened, widened, and protected by the diplomacy and force of the United States Government in the old style, while imports are restricted by high tariffs.

That this inexorable fact is dimly recognized by some leaders of the industrialist school has been made evident in recent pronouncements, especially by Ogden Mills and Henry L. Stimson, indicating the desirability of modifying historic tariff policies. Since 1898 many changes have taken place in the configuration of American manufacturing, although the interests supporting industrialist statecraft have been enlarged and consolidated. In other words, the interests are still powerful and active, but their posture and the lines of their activity have altered.

Most of the great industries have grown out of the "infant" stage and are prepared by perfection of technique and strength of capital to compete effectively with their rivals abroad. Several of the largest have developed into exporting industries and have branch offices or factories, or both, in the leading countries of the world. Among them may be mentioned steel, electrical, petroleum, automobile, telegraph, and telephone concerns. Although there are many thousand industrial corporations in the United States, a large portion of industrial business is concentrated under the control of about two hundred corporations. In this small group are included the "mature" industries heavily engaged in exporting and eager to increase their foreign markets.

Aware at last that they cannot increase export outlets under historic policies, leaders in this special group, tossing to and fro in an effort to escape from the impasse, are turning to the hope of enlarging their outlets by reducing the tariff here and there on imports. The best informed among them are acquainted with the significance of the branch factory movement and see that, in case competition became too fierce in the foreign market, arrangements could be made with international competitors. They know that cartels can be formed, markets divided, and price controls effected—despite difficulties and periodical disruptions. In other words, there are leaders in the industrialist school who are seeking new methods of handling their foreign economic relations without incurring the risk of disrupting their profitable operations within the United States, and are already welcoming proposals for revising the tariff downward. The key industries could hold their own and leave the smaller industries, the "inefficient" industries, so called, now sustained by high protection, to a fiercer struggle for existence.

On the side of such modifications other powerful interests could be arrayed. The agrarians, such as cotton and wheat farmers, who produce large quantities for export, could easily be brought into line. Bankers who make profits from floating foreign loans and handling exchange business would naturally gravitate in that direction. Transcontinental railways, eager for profitable long hauls, might look forward to increased business from a larger volume of international exchange. Shipping concerns, heavily subsidized already by the Government, fall under the same discrimination. Importing and exporting merchants could be easily marshaled under the new banner. Internationalists, alarmed by the growth of economic nationalism, would gravitate to that side for reasons of sentiment, and likewise a majority of American economists whose frame of reference is the ideology of classical economy borrowed from the English manufacturing classes of about 1850.

Here, then, is an array of interests tending in the direction of lower trade barriers. Noble ideas of international goodwill are at their command for a grand sentimental appeal. Speaking with reference to "practical" politics, it is possible, nay highly probable, that a new battle over the tariff will soon be staged. It would occupy the public mind and help to direct attention away from many domestic difficulties of the depression—

especially from collectivist tendencies deemed "dangerous" to historic practices and profits. Perhaps a respite from agitations over collectivist measures for attacking the crisis at home could be gained by a well-financed and well-staged battle over tariff reductions. But the respite would be brief, for the simple reason that there is no way of securing ever-expanding outlets abroad for the ever-expanding potentials of great technology by any system of foreign exchange and trade promotion (see below, pp. 74 ff.).

§

1. The statement of the industrialist thesis that American industry and agriculture produce more than the American nation can use or consume is not an incontestable description of an independent and unconditional sequence of facts, beyond the reach of human will and effort, except, perhaps, with reference to certain commodities. It rests upon the assumption that domestic demand and use are irrevocably fixed by the prevailing distribution of wealth or buying power, and are beyond the control of the American people. The implications of the statement are false and the assumption is challenged by contemporary thought and practice.

2. The prophecy of the thesis to the effect that the process of conquest, annexation, penetration, pressure, and force applied in a quest for markets *will* provide outlets for the surpluses of industry and agriculture has been belied by events.

3. A large part of "the stake abroad," acquired by the process of trade drumming, pressure, and *Machtpolitik,* is an illusion, as defaults, depreciation, and the passing of dividends demonstrate; another part of the stake operates to curtail the very foreign markets which it was presumed to open, by supplying capital and technique to competing foreign industries; a third part of the stake operates to pour into American markets materials which compete with already distressed domestic agriculture and industry; and there is no method of accounting by which to ascertain whether the final balance-sheet results of the stake have been advantageous or detrimental to the economy of the American nation.

4. The possessions, concessions, and privileges obtained by the processes of conquest, annexation, and pressure have not provided additional outlets for American goods large enough to absorb a proportion of the output commensurate with the public expenditures and risks involved, and besides have introduced into the United States raw-material imports which increase the surplus of agricultural produce for which outlets were to be, presumably, obtained.

5. A renewal of the industrialist process inaugurated under President McKinley is physically impossible, if deemed both desirable and likely to provide outlets for the "surpluses" of American industry and agriculture. Given the posture of other world powers, the United States cannot attain the position occupied by Great Britain in 1715 or in 1815. An attempt on the part of the United States to renew the process on its own motion or to gain undisputed supremacy on the sea would lead to an encirclement as merciless as that which throttled Germany in 1918, if there is anything at all in the experience of history. If physical courage, pride, or cupidity dictated such an effort, it would be a betrayal of the national interest to make it.

6. By the naval-limitation treaties and the renunciation of war as an instrument of national policy, the United States has denied itself the right to renew the unlimited industrialist process, were it physically possible and desirable from the point of view of the national interest.

7. Owing to the present distribution of "backward places" among the great powers of the world, no substantial increase could be made in the colonial possessions of the United States without a war with a major power or combination of major powers, except in the Caribbean area where the posture of social and economic affairs and the available resources are not such as to guarantee adequate outlets for the "surpluses" of American industry and agriculture. Nor is there anything in the commercial experience of Great Britain, especially since 1920, to justify the belief that an enlargement of colonial possessions would afford a steady and expanding outlet for the "surpluses" of American industry and agriculture.

8. The rapid industrialization of the leading nations of the

world, and even many minor nations, enables them to supply
themselves with the standardized products of the machine,
diminishes the purely raw-material areas of world trade, and
tends to curtail international commerce in standardized machine products.

9. The policy of applying pressure and coercion in making
outlets for the surpluses of American industry and agriculture
and of restraining imports by high tariffs is a contradiction in
terms. In the long run the end which the policy was designed
to attain is a physical impossibility, because exports must be
paid for by imports and not enough non-competitive imports
can be secured to balance a constantly expanding export of
American manufactures and farm produce.

10. The policy of seeking outlets for the surpluses of industry and agriculture by the application of diplomatic, consular,
trade-agency, and naval pressures, with corresponding commitments to an "adequate defense for the American stake abroad,"
has involved enormous increases in military and naval outlays
—running now in the direction of a billion dollars a year, has
created an immense naval and military bureaucracy with
powerful attachments of supply interests, and has produced
friction zones in many parts of the world beyond the competence of the American Navy, as now constituted or as it may
possibly be constituted, to defend effectively—zones in which
insignificant incidents may flame into war at a moment's notice.

In short, practice under the industrialist thesis has not provided the outlets for the "surpluses" of American industry and
agriculture as promised and it is beset from start to finish by
internal contradictions in thought and outcome. If unanswer-
able confirmation were needed, it could be found in the collapse
of American industrial and agricultural export in the economic
disaster of 1929-1934 which followed the pursuit of the policy
of drumming and pressure supported by all the agencies of
diplomacy and naval power. If anything is known by its
fruits, then the merits of the industrialist thesis are known
by its fruits.

Assuming, however, that the policy of the thesis is necessary
to realize the goal of ever-expanding exports, and that it is
possible to attain that goal, given the posture of world affairs,

a still more fundamental question remains: Is it *desirable* from the point of view of domestic economy and American civilization? It means, if experience is a guide, the increasing predominance of manufacturing over agriculture and the urban way of life over the rural way of life. It means an ever-larger proportion of talents concentrated on the manipulations of business as distinguished from agriculture and an ever-increasing proportion of the working people transformed into urban proletarians—"asphalt flowers," as they are known in Europe—toolless, homeless, and propertyless, dependent upon the sale of bare labor power—proletarians trained, if trained at all, in narrow mechanical specialties likely to be destroyed at any time by new inventions. It means also the increasing accumulation of wealth in the hands of the directing classes, with the manners, standards, and artificialities which undermine the very qualities of courage and leadership requisite to the successful operations of those classes. If possible in practice, the policy is to be condemned as undesirable in terms of consequences.

CHAPTER IV

AGRARIAN STATECRAFT

THE second way of escape from the dilemma in economy offered by American statecraft, called for convenience agrarian, can also be subjected to the test of historical experience. Stripped of contradictions in practice and considered, like the industrialist thesis, in its fundamentals, it consists of the following features. Its center of interest and affection is agriculture, with attachments of exporting and importing merchants dealing in goods and capital, as contrasted with reliance on industry, finance, and commerce primarily. It is intra-nationalist, and anti-imperialist: it favors the annexation of contiguous unoccupied territory which can be defended without a large naval establishment and can be exploited by self-governing American farmers and planters. It opposes a large naval establishment as a danger to democracy, a menacing burden on finances, and a fomenter of international rivalries and war. In economics, it advocates free trade, tariff for revenue, or moderate tariffs, in order that surpluses of agricultural produce may be exchanged in the best market for manufactures through the medium of the lowest-cost carriers on the seas. It assails bonuses, ship subsidies, discriminations, and other bounties to manufacturers and carriers as levies on planters and farmers, imposed by government at the behest of special interests. In its view, government is primarily an agency—not too energetic—to defend the territorial heritage and keep order at home; not an agency of powerful outward thrusts to force outlets abroad for domestic surpluses. In upshot, therefore, the agrarian conception calls for the simple exchange of commodities in the most favorable markets, for peace among nations, and for international goodwill arising from a reciprocity of trading interests as contrasted with rivalry, bitterness, and war springing from the use of the engines of state to force capital, goods, and services upon other races, nations, and peoples.[1]

At no time, however, in the history of the country have the items in the agrarian program been so fully applied in practice as were the principles of the industrialist conception between 1897 and 1933. About the middle of the nineteenth century, when the dominance of planters in the Democratic party was practically unchallenged, practice came rather closely into conformity with agrarian theory; but this state of affairs did not long endure. Later, many of the fundamental elements of the agrarian conception were either abandoned by the Democratic party, or radically altered. Only its opposition to the conquest and annexation of distant places occupied by races alien to American nationality has been maintained with fair, although not complete, party consistency. By 1928 the Democratic program of national interest was, in all substantial propositions, including the tariff, for practical purposes so nearly identical with the industrialist program that opposition between them almost disappeared. Yet it cannot be said that the agrarian conception has entirely vanished from American thought respecting foreign policy and commercial relations. Elements of it are so persistent, in spite of the confusion, and are so vigorously espoused by members of both parties, that it must be considered as offering an escape from the economic jam—the surplus of goods and capital—which besets the life of the nation.

THE NATURE OF THE AGRARIAN THESIS EXAMINED

Shorn of irrelevancies and reduced to system, the agrarian tradition embraces the following elements bearing on the subject of escape from the crisis in economy and thought:

1. There are surpluses of manufactures, agricultural produce, and capital which cannot be used at home.

2. These surpluses can be disposed of abroad if tariff barriers made by special interests are "lowered," other impedi-

---

[1] During the dominance of the planters in the Democratic party the acquisition of land at the expense of neighbors was, of course, a feature of agrarian strategy.

ments to the free flow of trade are removed, either directly or
through reciprocity arrangements, and international coöperation is substituted for the policy of government pressure and
Machtpolitik.

3. Other nations are moving in the direction of free trade [2]
or at least can be induced to lower their tariffs and to modify
their systems of licensing, quotas, bounties, and subsidies,
which operate against the free or easy flow of goods.

Q. E. D. The problem of the surpluses is solved, prosperity
is "recovered" or "restored," the crisis is dissipated, and the
national interest is secured.

Although there is now emerging under the leadership of
President Franklin D. Roosevelt a new and different conception
of national interest, the pattern of thought just described is
so widely cherished as a solution of the problem of "the surpluses" that it deserves analysis and criticism with respect to
its intrinsic offerings and merits. Like the industrialist thesis,
it purports to be a statement of fact, an assertion of possibility, a fixed order of action guaranteed to produce results
desired, a prophecy, and an interpretation of world economy
and history. Under these heads it will be appraised.

With respect to the statement of alleged fact pertaining to
surpluses of goods and capital, the agrarian thesis does not
differ from the industrialist scheme of thought. It rests upon
assumptions concerning the fixity of the economic arrangements and the distribution of wealth now existing in the United
States. It accepts the hypothesis that the surpluses, and the
economic jam produced by them, cannot be disposed of, in the
main or in large part, by alterations in the distribution of
wealth in the United States—that is, by changes in the using
and consuming power of the people of the United States, to
be effected by public and collective action. It is not necessary, therefore, to add anything here to the criticism of these
assumptions, as economic and historical verities, advanced
above (p. 47) in the consideration of the same item in the in-

---

[2] It is one of the ironies of history that this is the principal part of the
agrarian thesis which Jefferson himself abandoned in his later life in favor of
protection to American industry for the purpose of developing a domestic
market for agricultural produce. *The Idea of National Interest*, p. 317.

dustrialist thesis. They are founded on a conscious or unconscious acceptance of current economy as a deterministic and permanent order of nature, largely beyond the reach of human will, effort, and policy.

As a preliminary, then, we may first consider the parenthetical statement in Item 2, namely, tariff barriers are made by special interests. This is more than an incident in the agrarian thesis. It is used to support the fundamental proposition that the foreign commerce which would or could provide outlets for American "surpluses" is choked or throttled by import restrictions imposed under the pressure of special interests antagonistic by nature to the general or national interest, and that the exclusion of these special interests from domestic politics would permit the removal or reduction of the said barriers. These assumptions have a wide popularity among American politicians and publicists, and almost the universal endorsement of the economists. They dominate the wishful thinking of many books written since 1929. But is the statement true, and does the implication assigned to it follow as a matter of course?

The answer is what is known in law as a demurrer. The fact is admitted as alleged. Tariff barriers are raised largely as a result of the pressure brought by special interests on the Government of the United States, in a quest for higher returns on capital. But these special interests include such widely diversified branches of industry and agriculture that they represent the bulk of the capital invested and labor employed in industry and agriculture. So extensive are the interests reflected in these tariff barriers that only 10.7 per cent of the imports admitted into the United States under them, as they stood in 1927, entered into direct competition with domestic production.[8] In other words, an immense area of domestic production is protected by them, meaning an aggregation of special interests so diversified and so nation-wide in character as to constitute an approximation to a generality of interest.

Now we come to the implication of the statement, namely, that those who advocate a reduction of tariff rates represent

[8] Alfred Rühl, *Zur Frage der internationalen Arbeitsteilung*, Vierteljahrshefte zur Konjunkturforschung, Sonderheft 25, Berlin, 1932.

a general national interest, as distinguished from the special interests so vigorously condemned by agrarians. It may be granted, in passing, that academic economists reveal in their thought the pure disembodied spirit of national interest untainted by earthly considerations; and that they come to the subject uninfluenced by class or group affiliations or by their sources of economic support. But with respect to the practical leaders also found engaged in propaganda and lobbying for tariff reductions, history must record that they also fall under the denomination of special interests: importers of foreign goods, bankers who export capital, heavy investors in foreign securities, manufacturers who export a large proportion of their output and need no defense against foreign competition, exporters seeking to favor their foreign customers, and the growers of certain farm produce, such as wheat and cotton, who have large surpluses on hand—all special interests fully aware that they cannot export freely unless the intake of foreign imports is enlarged, against the wishes of other special interests protected by tariff barriers. As between these two groups of special interests, the one seeking high tariff barriers and the other demanding a reduction, history can make no discrimination with respect to their virtues. If, however, resort is had to the elaborate statistical tables compiled by Dr. Alfred Rühl, published in the work just cited, then a higher degree of generality in national interest must be assigned to the first of the two groups (including labor) in this contest of wits and power, namely, the proponents of high tariff barriers.

With this preliminary out of the way, the essential part of Item 2 may be drawn under scrutiny: the surpluses of industry, agriculture, and capital *can* be disposed of abroad if tariff barriers are "lowered," other impediments to the "free" flow of trade removed, and international coöperation substituted for the policy of government pressure and *Machtpolitik*. This is an allegation of possibility and a prediction. Here the same process of thought is involved as in the consideration of the industrialist thesis and at the risk of wearisome repetition must be reviewed in this connection. When an engineer declares that a certain result *will* flow from a certain order of actions and material arrangements, he makes a declaration that can be verified by experience or by an actual test of the hypothesis. When it is said that outlets *can* be found abroad for American surpluses of industry, agriculture, and capital by reducing tariff barriers and eliminating other government impediments to the "free" flow of trade, is the statement a description of a predictable order of occurrences, which can be subjected to verification and authentication?

The answer is and must be negative. Although the proposition is usually put forward by its proponents with the assurance that accompanies a verifiable axiom in physics, it is not even akin to such an axiom. The parts of the proposition that cover the order of actions which, it is alleged, will produce particular results possess none of the precision of the parts constituting a theorem in physics, to which positive mathematical values may be attached. The formula varies in construction from "lowering trade barriers" to "free" trade, although few in the Democratic party would now go to the latter extreme. There is nothing definite in the formula, "lowering trade barriers." Is there to be a universal and horizontal reduction by international agreement, let us say ten per cent, twenty per cent, or any other figure? If so, what is the figure? Why is it chosen? Why should it be universally applied to the varying cultures of the respective countries? How is it known that the precise figure will produce the precise result, namely, dispose of the surpluses of American industry, agriculture, and capital? If an apparent absolute is taken, namely, "free" trade, are governments, with their navies and armies, their diplomatic apparatus, their educational and other cultural institutions, their wealth, prestige, and influence thereby automatically eliminated from the operations of commercial exchange? These questions can only be answered, if answered at all, from historical experience; and unfortunately for the hypothesis there has never been a world-wide test of the principle of uniformly low trade barriers or free trade—international exchange unhampered by tariffs and discriminations of any kind.

Only one modern industrial country, Great Britain, has ever operated for a long time under a tariff designed primarily for revenue; and Great Britain, during the period of so-called free trade, levied duties on certain articles for revenue, had at first the advantage of little or no competition in industry on the part of other countries, and used her navy and army extensively in many regions of the earth conquering, annexing, and otherwise bringing within her sphere of influence new backward places with which she carried on trade. Moreover, during her period of tariff for revenue, Great Britain never had free access to the markets of other great powers, such as Germany, France, Russia, Japan, and the United States. But some conclusions of fact may be drawn from her experience.

With cyclical fluctuations, the foreign commerce of Great Britain, given the peculiar position of industrial supremacy in which she found herself and given the low stage of industrial development in other countries, rose in volume, if not in proportion, until near the close of the nineteenth century. Perhaps it might have continued to rise indefinitely had France, Germany, and the United States been content to remain producers of foodstuffs and consumers of manufactures. But after competition grew acute, Great Britain could not find expanding outlets for her growing production of standardized machine commodities. The export of her great staples —cotton and woolen goods, iron, steel, coal, and machinery— contracted after 1920, despite the power of her navy and empire; and Great Britain abandoned her so-called free trade in favor of selective protection and discrimination. This, in summary, is the historical upshot of the one great national experiment in "free" trade. Neither under that system nor under protection has British industry been able to find adequate outlets for the surpluses of its plant capacity, real or potential, and to provide anything like full employment for British labor, save during the World War.

The United States furnishes another partial test of "free" trade. This country is larger than Great Britain, France, Germany, and half a dozen other European countries combined. It has a greater diversity of climate, soil, and resources than several European nations taken together. Within this immense area there are no tariff barriers, high or low, and commodities may move freely in commerce from one end of the country to another.

In the great federated American Republic—a commonwealth

of nations within itself—are to be found all the conditions required for an ideal system of free trade internationalism— a strong central government to keep order within the entire area, a common language, complete domestic peace, the same monetary system for all parts of the trade area, a mobility of labor facilitating the gravitations of capital to "natural" opportunities. Here is a league of states, and here is a Supreme Court with compulsive jurisdiction over conflicts among them. Here in the United States, in short, can be found an almost perfect microcosm of the idealized economy of international free trade—the conditions favorable to the free flow of goods, unimpeded exchange, mutuality of benefits, compensating costs, and beautiful "equilibrium."

Yet periodically the economy of the United States is convulsed by panics, and in the best of business years there is a large body of unemployed laborers. There are huge surpluses of manufactures in manufacturing regions, and huge surpluses of farm produce in adjoining regions. No tariff barriers, high or low, prevent their "free" exchange.

If it is the tariff that hampers and blocks the exchange of surpluses among the nations of the earth, why is it that surpluses are not exchanged among the regions within the United States, differentiated, as various nations are, by climate, soil, industries, and skills, where no tariff barriers intervene? A possible answer is that there are many commodities not produced in the United States for which American surpluses could be exchanged abroad; but the reply to this allegation is that nearly all such commodities are now on the free list under the American tariff system.

The experience of the United States with freedom of trade over an immense area, differentiated as various nations are by climate, soil, industries, and skills, utterly explodes the contention of the so-called internationalists, dominated by low trade-barrier predilections, that international efficiencies, comparative costs, mutual exchange through price, and supply and demand will make for equilibrium and higher standards throughout the world. American agriculture was not rising in the scale of living standards even during the years of rapid industrial expansion, 1920-1929; on the contrary, owing to a lack of its own organization, concentration, price control, and ruthless leadership, it was utterly subjected to the organization, concentration, price control, and ruthless leadership of great industries in the United States and was sinking into mortgages, debts, tenantry, and poverty while the profits of industry piled higher and higher. When at length the process of draining agriculture had proceeded far enough, even industrial capitalism was almost paralyzed, partly from lack of buying power among the American farmers supposed to enjoy at home the free-trade benefits of comparative costs, mutual exchange through price, and supply and demand. All over the United States, under the free trade régime, there have been and now are blighted regions and industries, immense stretches of squalor and ignorance, wretched educational facilities, inadequate medical services, and an almost total dearth of the amenities of civilization.

How then could it be expected that under a system of world free trade the general level of civilization would rise, the more advanced enjoying increasing prosperity as the more backward automatically received the benefits of mutuality in exchange? If knowledge of experience means anything and is employed in place of formulas taken from the rationalization of British manufacturing interests as they stood in 1850, there is absolutely no reason for expecting such an outcome from lowering international trade barriers. On the contrary, there is good ground for believing that the well-organized and ruthless machine civilizations would use their power of exploiting the weaker and unorganized agricultural and raw material regions to the limit, until the latter were drained and impoverished, and the débâcle of both parties hastened.[4]

In this development, moreover, it is likely that industries would gravitate as rapidly as possible to the regions where lowest cost of production is available—accessibility of raw materials, cheapness of labor, long hours, and low or negligible standards of social legislation and insurance. This is what has happened on a large scale in the free trade realm of the United States where regions once industrial and prosperous have been blighted by the wholesale migration of capital to sections of

[4] Zimmermann, *World Resources and Industries;* and below, Chapter VI.

cheapest production—the lowest standards of life, unorganized labor easily regimented by employers, absence of labor legislation, exploitation of children, long hours, and social squalor in general. And the transported industries immediately introduced, into regions occupied, the social and economic degradation that accompanied the rise of the factory system a hundred years ago—the degradation that had been mitigated only by heroic efforts of reformers.

Furthermore, in the free trade realm of the United States there has been a concentration of economic ownership and power in a few great regions of capital control. One financial center, New York, has drained the country of capital and energy, has employed financial power in speculative manipulations that have stripped millions of their savings and investments, and has subjected outlying and distant zones of enterprise to a merciless economic dictatorship. What reason is there for believing that under a régime of world free trade the same kind of unrelenting mobilization of financial power would not take place at a few centers of economic dominance, like London? If experience means anything, there is no reason whatever. Under such a system would not corporations, those giants that dominate industrial operations, move to the places where restrictions on exploitation, speculation, and peculation are weak or negligible, as they have moved to New Jersey and Delaware in the American empire of free migration? If experience is any guide, they would, thus bringing local enterprise and ingenuity under tribute to centers of power.

Then what about that equilibrium, that balance, that stabilization which is promised in the formula of free trade or low trade barriers? The answer of the American free-trade empire is incontrovertible. Within this empire we see economic chaos, confusion, imbalance, contradictions, and unrest. Banks, insurance companies, railroads, and industries, prostrate and unwilling to take the consequences of their own operations, beg the Government of the United States for loans, subsidies, and subventions to save them from ruin. Agriculture is poverty-stricken throughout large regions and the engines of government are employed to pump back to the farmers enough revenues to keep them dragging along, or at least to enable them to make payments on debts and mortgages. Here in the United States we see whole sections of urban life blighted, the feverish concentration of mobile industries in certain areas, drawing labor from the farms and from foreign countries, and then collapsing—casting millions of laborers adrift for the Government of the United States to support.

All this is the outcome of freedom of movement, trade, and exploitation within an economic empire bigger than Europe, outside of Russia. Surely a thinker must be blind to experience when he imagines that world-wide free trade, or any kind of tariff manipulation downward can automatically bring equilibrium, stability, order, and mutuality of interest and benefit to the wide world, with its diversity of cultures and varying levels of economy and civilization. If the elaborate features of the Roosevelt Recovery Program were necessary to bring some semblance of order out of the chaos of banking, industry, and agriculture prevailing in March, 1933, throughout the American free-trade empire, a system of world planning and control on a scale more vast and complicated would be required to reduce the chaos of world disequilibrium to some semblance of order—a system of planning utterly beyond the competence perhaps the honest intentions, of any international conference or agency representing nations as they are now constituted.[5]

Since there is no world experience by which to verify absolutely the hypothesis of lower trade barriers, and no test can be made in authentication, it is appropriate to examine the origins and nature of the underlying scheme of thought, or frame of reference, on which reliance is placed by those who seek an escape from the periodical, almost continuous, jam of "overproduction" within the respective countries of the world. This program stems mainly from the economic and social philosophy of Adam Smith, especially from his *Wealth of Nations*, published in 1776. It rests essentially upon certain dogmas which he took for granted and put forward as axioms

[5] If it be urged that an influx of foreign commodities at low prices under international free trade would set commodities in the United States in circulation, the answer is that there is no way of *knowing* that it would. Moreover, there is every reason for believing that highly concentrated industries would probably enter into foreign cartels for protecting themselves by extra-legal control at the expense of agriculture, as long as agriculture could stagger along.

of political economy—with exceptions that vitiated them (below, pp. 162 ff.). The first of these assertions is that "in every country it has always been and must be the interest of the great body of people [the national interest] to buy what they want of those who sell it cheapest. . . . The proposition is so very manifest that it seems ridiculous to take any pains to prove it; nor could it have been called in question had not the interested solidarity of merchants and manufacturers confounded the commonsense of mankind." The second is a kind of corollary: "It is the maxim of every prudent master of a family never to attempt to make at home what will cost him more to make than to buy. . . . What is prudence in the conduct of every private family can scarce be folly in that of a great kingdom." With the same certitude that marked the original tone of Smith's work, these maxims have been repeated since his day; they appeared frequently in the literature of controversy after the decline in American foreign trade that followed the crash of 1929.

On examination these statements are seen to be maxims, not axioms. An axiom is a self-evident proposition which carries with it no disruptive presuppositions. But Smith's assertion that it is to the interest of the great body of the people to buy in the cheapest market rests on assumptions and carries implications. It cuts into the economic process at the purchasing point, deals only with the consumer, covers an immediate and one-sided transaction, and leaves out of account the sources of buying power essential for continuous exchange. To prove that it is to the economic advantage of the people of a given nation to buy in the cheapest market of the world, it must be shown that the operation will have no countervailing adverse effect on the long-run continuance of their capacity to buy. That is a complicated problem which economic arithmetic has not yet solved.

If Smith's proposition was true in an age of primitive economy when trade was in the hands of small dealers and concerns operating on a competitive basis, with no concerted control over prices, it does not follow that it is true in an age of great corporations and mass production when prices can be privately manipulated and commodities are regularly dumped to get rid of surpluses, to break competition, and to gain monopolistic advantage. If it was true for Europe of his day, where fairly equal standards of life prevailed, it does not follow that it is valid when the low-standard masses of the Orient are equipped with the best Western machinery and management. If it was valid in an age when there was little or no international indebtedness, public and private, it is not necessarily valid in an age when capital is exported and imported in huge quantities and exchange is burdened with charges to meet political, as well as economic, debts. A maxim that seemed obvious to Adam Smith in 1776 is far from obvious in the present state of affairs.

Nor can Smith's analogy between a family and a nation be accepted as applicable to the case in hand. Nations are more than mathematical units mysteriously possessed of buying power. Nations are historic accumulations of culture. They have governments moved by ambitious statesmen. They have problems of maintaining order, of national defense, of taxation, and of satisfying great impulses which do not arise out of the mere exchange of commodities. It may be unfortunate that this is so, but the fact remains. Even the business of preserving the order in which the consumer buys in the cheapest market is not a matter of mere policing; it involves, in modern times at least, the adoption of social policies which affect the distribution of wealth—of buying power. The posture of modern nations and the nature of their intercourse with one another do not admit of any assumptions predicated on the proposition that exchanges are or can be mere transactions between private persons exercising the right to buy "freely" in the cheapest market wherever it may be. The nation is something more than a mere family of individuals. Governments themselves are heavy buyers and borrowers.

In fact, the whole hypothesis of free trade assumed a certain "natural" differentiation among nations in respect of soil, climate, and inherited skills, and the existence of similar standards of life such as prevailed in Europe in the age of Adam Smith. It was fundamentally pre-machine in origin. It did not foresee the radical transformations which natural science has wrought in productive processes or the parallel developments of great industrial countries, such as modern France, Germany, Japan, and the United States. It envisaged static societies, not highly dynamic societies competing with one another for territories, spheres, and markets. It contemplated the continuance of the relatively limited productive capacity of labor as in 1776 and did not reckon with any such unlimited productive capacity as modern technology has brought into the world. Nor did it draw into the reckoning an enormous export of capital and machinery to cheaper labor markets, destroying productive opportunities in the home market. The theory also takes for granted many dubious propositions: that trading rather than production in certain ways of life is the supreme concern of policy; that either a balance of agriculture and industry will result from this system of exchange or is of no importance; that the State can ignore shifts in the social basis on which it rests without peril to itself and to society; that there are no considerations of civilization more significant than commerce; and that the complexities of international relations can be reduced to purely pecuniary factors susceptible of successful manipulation by individuals under the guidance of the acquisitive instinct. But were Smith's maxims really axioms, it does not follow that, given freedom of import, there could be an expansion of exports comparable to the evident potentialities of plant extension under modern technology.

Were all import restrictions removed, there would probably be temporary spurts in transactions involving certain commodities and widespread dislocations in industry. But nothing in the nature and course of trade indicates that there would be a continuous expansion all along the line. If the experience of industry in the United States under its system of internal free trade affords any evidence (above, p. 76), and it certainly is germane to the question in hand, then under world free trade there would be a movement of manufacturing industries from the regions in which wages are high, social legislation is strict, and trade unions are powerful to the backward regions where wages are low, social legislation negligible if not absent, and labor unorganized. Reasoning from this economic experience, we may assume that industries under a system of world free trade would tend to move to the low-standard areas until a certain level was reached; and the general level would doubtless be lower than that prevailing in any of the present high-standard countries. Without accepting the gospel of pessimism,[6] there is at least no reason for believing that the general level would be higher than it is at present. This state of affairs certainly would not mean a continuous expansion of exports for all countries, but ultimately a substantial deadlock in the standardized staples at perhaps a reduced scale of production. At all events, it would represent no solution of the prime issue at stake in national interest, namely, the continuous expansion of production made possible by modern technology.

The validity of Item 2 in the agrarian thesis as a scheme of mechanistic economics, guaranteed to move surpluses of goods and capital among nations, may be also challenged by showing its relativity to the time, place, and circumstances of its origin and formulation. The body of doctrines on which the Item rests is appealed to by the proponents of lower-trade barriers or free trade as if it were a timeless, placeless body of natural laws, arrived at by descriptive and deductive processes and guaranteed to work, always and everywhere, in all circumstances, like the laws of hydraulics or electrical engineering. If it were such a body of natural laws, it would be a final closed system of world history, embracing all economic occurrences, past, present, and future—a scheme of human mechanics as inexorable as the system of celestial mechanics. In truth, the system is, and can be, no such thing.

It is one of the commonplaces of history that every system of political economy—that of Aristotle, Machiavelli, Adam Smith, Ricardo, and Karl Marx, for example—bears the stamp of the age, place, culture, and class environment in which it was written. The degree of truth in the system, as measured by its enduring qualities, depends upon its correspondence with evolving human experience and upon the extent to which it anticipates the course of history in process of development—an anticipation valid for the immediate future, or the long future. No mere historical accident or extraordinary intellectual feat placed the *Wealth of Nations* in Great Britain instead of Russia or Prussia during the last quarter of the eighteenth century. Nor was it the logic of Adam Smith's great work which was alone responsible for its enormous influence on the minds of

[6] Spengler, *Man and Technics.*

British statesmen during the century which followed. On the contrary, *The Wealth of Nations* was written at a time when Great Britain had struck down powerful commercial rivals in a series of wars extending over more than a hundred years, when British manufacturing was just about to leap forward under the impact of mechanical production, when the expansion of British trade was conceived to be the prime national interest. Macaulay is right in saying: "The fine inscription on the monument of Lord Chatham in Guildhall records the general opinion of the citizens of London, that under his administration commerce had been 'united with and made to flourish by war'."

When at length Great Britain led the rest of the world in the size of her navy and merchant marine, in the accumulation of capital for trade and investment, in the ingenuity and productive power of her machinery, in the skill of her craftsmen, and in her mastery of the industrial arts, in other words, when Great Britain was without a rival in machine production, it was in keeping with her manufacturing interests to have the largest and freest commerce with all parts of the world. Note must be taken of the qualifying phrase "in keeping with her manufacturing interests." Whether, in the long run, it was consonant with national interest utterly to submerge agriculture in a machine economy, to draw nine-tenths of the population into great industrial centers, and to make the very life of the nation dependent upon the vicissitudes of trade with the four corners of the earth is another matter, to be debated on both economic and cultural grounds. It was in keeping with British manufacturing interests to have untaxed food stuffs and raw materials to cut the cost of production for manufactured goods. Those interests, of course, desired no tariff on manufactures imported into the country. They needed none; for nearly half a century they had no competitors whose rivalry was to be feared or even taken seriously. But other times, other manners. In the twentieth century, Great Britain, surrounded by competitors in nearly all staple lines, goes back to protection for manufactures.

Accompanying the mighty upswing of British industry after the mechanical revolution was an imposing literature—written by Ricardo, Senior, John Stuart Mill, and other economists.

First-rate minds were devoted to providing logic and rationality
for the dominant economic activity, and they operated with
such force and acumen that they arrested the attention of the
whole Western world, or at least that part of it which read any
political economy. To be sure, the system of "economic liberty"
which the classical economists formulated was vigorously assailed by Carlyle, Ruskin, Kingsley, and a score of lesser
critics, but the critics were dismissed by most of the economists as "sentimentalists." To the Continent and throughout
the academic circles of the United States classical economy
spread rapidly, and was widely accepted, not as a passing
policy reflecting a given economic situation in Great Britain
at a particular conjuncture in the evolution of world economy,
but as a kind of science, good always and everywhere.

It became so strongly entrenched in economic thinking that
its propositions took on the color of axioms to be realized as
rapidly as possible—axioms from which deviations were regarded as aberrations disturbing to a fixed economic course
calculated to bring a high level of prosperity. Hence through
all the economic discussions of our time there runs a strain to
the effect that a lowering of tariffs would really contribute to
the stability of international economic relations, to raising the
general level of production and distribution, to expanding outlets for goods, to effectuating some kind of balanced economic
order. The constant use of such phrases as "recovery" and
"restoration of prosperity" indicates the tenacity with which
classical conceptions rule in thought, despite the fact that
practice runs contrary to them and that the empirical judgments of statesmen are founded on other considerations.

Yet it must be evident, even to the superficial observer, that
the internal economies and exchange relations of all regions
of the earth have been fundamentally altered since Adam
Smith first formulated his axioms and maxims applicable to
handicraft and agrarian economies and to the distribution of
political power obtaining in the latter part of the eighteenth
century. To dwell upon these changes is to belabor well-established facts. The great principle laid down by Smith respecting reciprocal benefits arising from the exchange of commodities among regions differentiated by climate, soil, and skills

still remains valid. But under technology, which has altered the face of the earth, the structure of industry, and costs of transportation since his day, it requires something more than the acquisitive instincts of exporting and importing merchants to discover whether any particular country can produce a particular commodity advantageously within its own borders. Only engineering rationality coupled with human genius can determine that fact. Moreover, owing to the concentration of industrial control in the hands of great cartels and corporations, the accompanying price system of exchange works against loosely organized agricultural countries and regions and leads to their exploitation for the benefit of highly organized industrial countries and regions. In other words, contemporary manufacturing and exchanging processes make inapplicable the simple ideas of natural differentiation and compensatory costs which were sound enough in the eighteenth century.[7]

Now we come to Item 3 in the agrarian thesis, which was once prophecy and is now an assertion of possibility: nations are moving in the direction of free trade or can be induced to lower trade barriers. In the middle of the nineteenth century, when the prophecy was formally made by the Democratic party, the trend of international exchange seemed to be in that direction, under British leadership; but suddenly the trend was reversed and it has been running strongly in the opposite direction to the latest hour. Indeed, more drastic devices than mere tariff duties have been added to the armory of protection: absolute prohibitions, the licensing of importers, and the establishment of import quotas for specified commodities. The old prophecy has thus been falsified by events; and that part of the thesis may be laid aside in the museum of historical antiquities.

Whether nations *can* in the future be induced to reverse the trend, to lower trade barriers, to abolish discriminations on behalf of domestic economy, and to leave trade freely in the hands of exporting and importing merchants unrestrained by State action is a guess or calculation as to possibility. The

[7] Erich Zimmermann, *World Resources and Industries;* and below, Chapter VI.

issue raises perplexing questions. How can nations be induced to do this? Who—what persons, groups, classes, or interests within nations—can effect this alteration in policy? Proponents of the low-tariff thesis can make no invincible answers.

Judging by their pleas and arguments, they seem to regard statesmen responsible for the policies of exclusion as irrational and purblind creatures, temporarily misled, who will in time discover their folly—their violations of "natural laws," or will be displaced by uprisings among the "intelligent" citizens of their respective nations. It may be that the tendency to the utmost self-sufficiency on the part of the United States, France, Germany, Italy, Japan, the British Empire, and other great nations will lead to a revulsion, although the tendency is in a large measure justified by one of Adam Smith's maxims, namely, that State intervention with the natural course of trade is appropriate to the extent that national security is involved.[8] At best, however, this hope for revulsion is a mere hope—an interpretation of history to come, which may or may not be falsified by events.

Since it is an interpretation or forecast of history in the making, the hypothesis may be tested to some extent by the canons of historiography. One thing is certain in history and that is: History does not exactly repeat itself. The precise conditions existing in 1898, 1856, 1815, or 1776 cannot be restored by human effort, and will not be restored, owing to the persistent movement and alteration in ideas and interests in time. From this it follows that the future conditions of international exchange will be different from those of the past. Things are what they are and will be what they will be; and it adds nothing to knowledge or policy to call the proponents of high tariffs, quotas, embargoes, and licenses irrational men driven by folly or corruption. This is sheer utopianism which refuses to take the world as it is.

The systems of trade restrictions erected by the various nations have accompanied the drastic changes brought about by technology and by the development of agricultural regions into industrial regions. They represent movements of ideas and interests more or less synchronous with movements in

[8] Below, p. 162.

technology and productive economy. It may be, then, that they indicate an irresistible trend toward a different form of international exchange—an effort to give effect, in the new technological conditions, to a fundamental principle: there is mutuality of advantage in the exchange of useful commodities in accordance with national needs as ascertained by engineering rationality in relation to domestic standards of life, resources, and the state of technical arts. This, too, is hypothesis, but it seems to be more in harmony with the actual trends in policy and practice than the conception of *laissez faire*.

§

1. The first Item in the agrarian thesis, alleging the existence of "surpluses," like the corresponding Item in the industrialist thesis, is not a description of a deterministic order of economic occurrences, but rests on the *assumption* that the "surpluses" of industry, agriculture, and capital in the United States are inexorable quantities beyond the reach of domestic policy affecting the distribution of wealth and buying power among the American people. Its validity is now being challenged and attacked by thought and practice.

2. Like the industrialist thesis, the agrarian thesis appeals to special interests—to other interests: cotton and wheat producers, exporting industries, carriers, exporting and importing merchants and bankers, and capitalists with large investments abroad.

3. The assumption in the agrarian thesis that outlets can and will be found for "surpluses," if trade barriers are lowered or free trade is introduced, cannot be verified by reference to historical experience. On the contrary experiments with free trade on a considerable scale indicate, though they do not prove, that the assumption is little more than hopeful or wishful thinking, in a search for an easy escape from the economic jam represented by the "surpluses."

4. The former prophecy of the thesis, namely, that the world trend is in the direction of lower trade barriers, if not free trade, has been falsified by events; for more than fifty years the trend has been in the direction of controlled inter-

national trade—higher tariffs, bounties, quotas, embargoes, licenses, and State monopolies.

5. The proposition that ever-expanding outlets for the "surpluses" of American industry and agriculture could be found under a régime of low tariffs or free trade rests upon nothing more than maxims devised for a pre-technological or handicraft era when the differentiation of national economies in respect of fundamental commodities was sharply marked and presumed to be permanent. It may be conceded that, given the practical monopoly of machine industry enjoyed by Great Britain in the early part of the nineteenth century, it was to the advantage of her manufacturing interests to abolish protective tariffs on imports; for those interests then had no effective foreign competition in manufactures and derived benefits from the import of cheap foodstuffs for labor. These maxims, therefore, had a direct applicability to the manufacturing interests of Great Britain at one stage in her economic development. But they are not timeless and placeless natural laws guaranteed to find outlets for surpluses of goods always and everywhere, and they have been abandoned by Great Britain as rules of commerce. The perdurance of these maxims, this system of ideology, in American thought about international trade is to be ascribed to the tenacity of an intellectual heritage—a hang-over from classical conceptions and theories of political economy—a lag of ideas behind the movement of interests.

In short, the agrarian thesis is not a system of natural laws, good always and everywhere, which will guarantee, in application, ever-expanding foreign outlets for the real and potential "surpluses" of American industry and agriculture under the almost unlimited productive capacity of contemporary technology. As a scheme of thought tested by historical experience and the current practices of nations it can be properly characterized as utopian. The fact that men will fight and die for a utopia bears no relation to the possibility of attaining it or to the judgment which history yet to come will pass upon it.

CHAPTER V

FATALISM AND THE DRILL SERGEANT

To the programs of industrialist and agrarian statecraft offered as solutions of the contradictions in economy must be added other schemes of thought and practice tendered in the same connection. Such projects are without number. They range from simple proposals for manipulating currency and credit to gloomy philosophies of doom. But those that receive the most consideration in contemporary thought may be brought, with more or less completeness, within the scope of six conceptions: acceptance of the crisis as a decree of fate or nature; a renewal of lending abroad, perhaps in the form of government credits; war as a means of absorbing or destroying surpluses; communism; fascism; and defeatism.

The first of these programs for dealing with the dilemma in economy proposes to ease the strain by inner adjustment—patient and uncomplaining endurance of the emergency as fate. It is, superficially considered, the easiest; and it is fortified by certain religious traditions and by the common spirit of lethargy. According to this philosophy, mankind is to continue to stagger from crisis to crisis, from war to war, salvaging something from each wreck on the route to an unknown and unpredictable future—perhaps the past repeating itself endlessly in forms generally similar though differing in details. Within this conception may be enclosed the moral grandeur of stoicism or the maudlin hope of imbecility. In this view of things the history of mankind is over-arched by tragedy—for weal or woe; great spirits may accept it in the exaltation of unrational faith, as an unavoidable doom; small minds may remain cheerful in the deeps of adversity.

Realistically considered, this way of facing the present dilemma is supposed to mean "do nothing about it"; but in fact it usually means repeating the same things, under the

same kind of government policy and practice, that has
eventuated in the crash in which nations now find themselves.
It accepts a renewed concentration of human energies on the
pursuit of private gain, reliance upon the acquisitive routine,
and unquestioning government support for private interests in
the old style. Its proponents are undismayed by the fruits of
historical experience—feverish efforts at commercial expansion, reckless loans to reckless governments and corporations,
hasty plant extensions, enormous increases in fixed obligations,
collapses, defaults, contractions, dislocations, accompanied by
social calamity and private distress. Thus the spiritual idea of
resignation becomes involved in the practical interests that
expect to profit from the patience and endurance of stoicism.

However widespread the stoical view of the emergency may
be, it is not likely to prevail sufficiently to snap the tension between the ideal and the real. It is not likely that all the millions who have lost their employment, property, and standards
of life in recent storms will quickly sink their suffering in the
Lethe of gratified acceptance of tragedy. Nor will all movement of thought cease at the command of those who place their
inner peace, or their personal interests, above a consideration
of the historical crisis and programs for resolving it. Even in
high places it is believed that any dissipation of the present
economic depression will be followed by another dislocation
and by renewed dismay in the presence of wretchedness and
desolation. In any event, the stoical conception receives no
sanction from contemporary knowledge of history as the involution of ideas and interests in time movement (above, p. 21).

Likewise involving no substantial alteration in present practices and conceptions of economy is the second escape offered
to policy, namely, foreign loans on a large scale, made perhaps
in the form of government credits. Signs of the practice have
already appeared, in the credits extended to Russia by Germany and England, and in the cotton loan made to China by
the United States in 1933—for purposes not entirely clear.
The proposal has the appearance of simplicity and ease. It
wears no aspect of novelty, for it was presented to the public
in various guises with great insistence by business leaders and
by the Government of the United States, previous to the crash

of 1929; and it has since been advocated by economists of distinction, including Sir Arthur Salter, in his book entitled *Recovery*. Although the policy of lavish lending is included in other programs, it deserves examination in itself, especially in its new form of government control.

What is the nature of this single specific for the illness of industrial societies suffering from "overproduction"? By advocates of the lending therapeutic, it is insisted that the capital to be exported is "surplus" capital. It is called a surplus because it is exportable, and it is exportable because it is a surplus. The reasoning is circular and nothing can be gained by going around and around in that track. Can it be seriously maintained that, during the great outflow of capital from the United States following the World War, American agriculture enjoyed the returns to which it was entitled, that American wages in all departments were on a high level, and that there were no domestic capital needs to be satisfied? No houses to build, in view of the slum tenements in the cities and miserable shanties in all parts of the country, North, South, East and West? No hydro-electric plants demanded to furnish current for vast areas unserved? No rural regions to be supplied with roads, schools, hospitals, and the other amenities of civilization? No railroads to be lifted out of somnolence and equipped with the best of contemporary contrivances? No institutions of beneficence and esthetics requiring patronage? Even the most hardened apostle of realism will not deny that the United States needed at least a large portion of the capital which went abroad during the boom period of capital export.

But, it will be said, capital merely took its "natural" course —the quest for the highest possible immediate returns to its individual possessors. That much may be conceded, given the circumstances. Yet, whether the wealth of the United States was actually increased by the process remains a question unanswered by defenders of the lending procedure. At all events, it is certain that, had public intelligence permitted, high domestic taxes could have been laid upon the capital accumulations which became exportable under the policy pursued, and the proceeds of such taxes could have been expended on public enterprises in the United States—works and services of economic advantage, beneficence, and esthetic value. Surely the American nation would now be richer if millions diverted to armaments and wasteful building by foreign politicians from the capital accumulations of the United States had been taken by domestic politicians for expenditures on highways, housing, schools, museums, and libraries. Surely, also, the holders of billions of defaulted foreign bonds would be happy to exchange their depreciated paper for two per cent domestic bonds representing water works, electric plants, housing projects, and school buildings at home. It seems that nothing but interested sophistication could hold otherwise. At all events, the case is not one of an absolute surplus of capital for export, as in the matter of wheat and cotton, but of a conditional surplus—a surplus conditioned by the prevailing system of economy and by the policy of the Government, under whose approving auspices the export occurred.

Not only is exported capital withdrawn from American buying power and from domestic institutions of utility and beneficence; a part of it goes to foreign rivals in the form of loans that intensify competition against the United States in the world's markets; another part is used for purposes that are uneconomical, if not purely destructive. Some of it goes to the corrupt politicians abroad. Huge sums have been laid out in the erection of elaborate public buildings in foreign capitals, in the construction of boulevards, highways and public works, often badly planned, which serve no local productive purposes and weaken, rather than strengthen, the power of the borrowers to repay. Much of the exported capital has been definitely lost to American investors before whose cupidity bankers dangled bonds yielding eight and ten per cent interest. Under no circumstances can the wastes and losses be justified; even the bankers mainly responsible for them do not venture to defend either the loose policy followed or the results which flowed from it. Enough evidence was brought out in the Senate hearings on foreign loans to demonstrate that immense damage was done to American economy by the unrestricted pursuit of private gain in lending operations, and to indicate the necessity for some policy of restraint beyond the loose control of the State Department.

The very attempt to isolate the therapeutic of foreign lending from the whole body of economic operations, and to insist that it will make foreign trade possible, thus indirectly benefiting domestic economy, represents a deliberate and purblind exclusion of accompanying relevancies. It neglects the pertinence of the growth of industrial and agricultural maturity throughout the world ever since about the year 1870; shifts in the contents of trade, such as the decrease in the volume of exchange of food products; the new emphasis on raw materials; the approach of rationalization to completion, through the new technique; increasing tariff barriers and similar local efforts to avoid economic ruin; and other changes in world economy introducing new conditions for capital export. Why make capital exports if their purpose is to provide income that can exist only on paper and cannot be realized in gold or material goods? If lending is made for the purpose of receiving, and receiving leads to imbalance and crisis, what beneficial results can be expected to flow from the operation in the long run? The complexity of the conditions in which lending must function, and the disturbing events which accompany it appear to indicate that it must be treated merely as a phase of a larger process of trade and tariff control, if it is to increase the opulence of the United States (below, Chapter XII).

It seems, therefore, that the export-of-capital remedy for "overproduction" is no remedy at all, but a stimulant certain to be followed by relapse and discouragement. It may promote the export of commodities for a season. But at the same time it fosters the establishment of competing industries abroad, furnishes substance for the corruption of governments, and, what is worse, it encourages the development of spendthrift political habits. In due course a reckoning must come. If not utterly lost, the capital must be repaid with interest, and repaid in commodities and services, adding to the glut from which capital export is supposed to provide relief—unless lending to pay debts is to go on forever. No more than imperialism, protective tariffs, and free trade policies, does it offer a way to the continuous expansion of the productive capacities of industrial nations equipped with engines of technology possessing indefinite potentialities for enlargement.

Yet it is thought that wisdom may be gleaned from experience and that future lending to stimulate markets abroad for American "surpluses" will be controlled with a view to providing outlets. The Johnson Bill prohibiting loans abroad to governments and subdivisions that have defaulted on their obligations to American creditors was enacted into law in 1934; and Export Banks to facilitate the extension of credits have been established. If the sweep of the vague bans contained in the Johnson Act should be widened to cover new loans to private defaulters it would include nearly every important country in the world. American lending abroad, on such a basis, would virtually disappear, were the terms of such a measure strictly applied.

Russia repudiated the domestic and foreign debt of the Tsarist and Kerensky governments; Germany scaled hers to ruinous levels; France reduced the value of hers by three-fourths; Italy made a reduction almost as great; foreign holders of the internal bonds of England and Japan suffered similar losses from the devaluation of the pound and yen. The condition of most South American countries, as well as China, is so notorious as to call for no comment under this head. If renewed lending is limited to countries and their nationals who have paid all their past obligations, grain of gold for grain of gold, fully and punctually, then the prospect for loans and enlarged market outlets is painfully restricted. Perhaps only Finland is open to new loans.

If, however, old wrongs are to be sponged and new loans are to take the form of government credits controlled by policy, what policy and outcome will be possible and likely? Of necessity there will be a discrimination in offerings extended. There will also be limits on amounts. When the profit instincts and knowledge of private underwriting bankers are eliminated as sources of guidance, what criteria will be established in this respect? No answer is forthcoming in the statements furnished by the proponents of this therapeutic. Will loans be confined to those countries which provide markets for consumers' goods produced in the United States? If so, opportunities for adequate and expanding outlets of this character are nowhere evident on the horizon of the world.

If loans were limited to credits for the export of American machinery, or producers' goods, they would increase abroad the output of standardized machine products, with which the world market is glutted, or they would add to the stream of raw materials, already too large, or they would enable nations like Germany to re-arm with the help of American goods. In the first case it would be difficult to discover the possibilities of permanent relief from the "surpluses" of American industry, so eagerly sought. If, in the second case, foreign loans add to the output of those raw materials of which the United States even now has a "surplus," such as petroleum, this avenue of escape is not promising either. As to the third, nothing is to be said.

According to accepted formulas of contemporary practitioners, increases of production abroad which are advantageous to the United States are increases in raw materials not available in this country, and in special commodities, such as fine wines, woolens, and optical and surgical instruments, not now efficiently produced in the United States, if at all. The countries which furnish these special articles need little or no American capital; and surely the amount of American capital which could be taken by countries engaged in producing non-competitive raw materials would not be enough to supply adequate outlets for the "surpluses" of American agriculture and industry. Hence a renewal of large scale lending, whether by private bankers or in the form of government credits, if experience and the distribution of the world's industries and resources are any guide, offers no liberation from the economic dilemma in which the industrial nations of the world are now tossing.

Although not offered as a scheme of economy guaranteed to create continuous markets for "surpluses" of goods, war has long been regarded as a stimulus to commerce; and it is often put forward, however surreptitiously, as a release from grave domestic difficulties of any kind. Treitschke looked upon war as a medicine for humanity diseased; others have treated it as a way of reducing excess population—that is, the number of unemployed. Theodore Roosevelt's phrase, "we need a war," is frequently heard among practical men; and it is a commonplace in statecraft that a distracted and divided nation may be united and made to forget its domestic troubles temporarily by directing its energies against some other country. Politicians bent on the instant need of things, on keeping their party or class in power, on staving off growing opposition, have often resorted to it, with more or less immediate success in numerous cases. Hence war remains one of the potentials ever present, particularly in times of social crisis.

There is no doubt that war, temporarily at least, eliminates gluts of goods and men. By destroying accumulations of commodities and capital it creates a vacuum to be filled by renewed efforts. It engages feverish energies in production, without inducing a surplus, for the war commodities of industry are, in the main, immediately demolished in the process of eliminating the enemy. Railways and bridges are blown up, cities levelled to earth, building operations for civil purposes slowed down, and the production of luxuries curtailed. Business energies are concentrated on war industries and on the profits arising from that source, leaving other divisions fallow for later renewal and expansion. During war "everybody is busy" and after the war industry is speeded up to fill the spaces left by wholesale destruction.

The verification of experience leaves no room for doubt. It is well within historical truth to say that during the World War the working classes of Great Britain were fully employed and well fed for the first time in the history of British capitalism. The paralysis which was creeping over American industry in 1913-1914 was definitely broken in 1915 by the outburst of war in Europe; and American industry and agriculture then entered a state of high prosperity which continued until the close of the war. Although American agriculture, it is true, collapsed shortly afterwards, American industry, with billions of accumulated profits, quickly recovered from the post-war slump and was long kept busy filling the world vacuum created by the general holocaust. Perhaps the magnitude of the collapse after 1929 was proportioned to the magnitude of the efforts and apparatus required to offset the wholesale destruction of the war.

The remedy of war offers the chance of immediate relief.

And statesmen, as well as militarists who live by the trade, can easily unloose war; but they seldom find it possible to control the process and outcomes. War carries with it collateral consequences which outrun all purely statistical and economic calculations. The areas to which war may spread, the combinations of enemies which may be enlisted, the turn which alliances and "traditional friendships" will take, and the upshot in victory or defeat are unpredictable. War engages the deepest passions of the participants; it involves huge masses of people; it kindles the fire of national and class hatred; it glorifies violence and the destruction of property—those historic foes of ordinary industrial production. If waged on a large scale, as the World War demonstrates, it may be accompanied or followed by social earthquakes, revolutions, the overthrow of governments and constitutions, the assassination of statesmen, the disruption of economies, widespread repudiation of debts, enormous tax burdens for pensions and disabilities, currency disorders, and dictatorships military in character.

In short, those willing to evoke war, which is always imminent and possible, in an effort to break domestic jam, can never be sure whether the outcome will be an escape into the utopia of prosperity or into the ruin of their own class. "Glorious little wars" ending almost immediately in triumph are not always available for the great powers. So this remedy for the disease of "surpluses" is likely to be more dangerous than the disease itself, and will probably not be openly espoused, however secretly cherished, by responsible economists and statesmen, at all events unless the crisis spreads into perilous civil conflict.

Associated with war as a way out of the economic crisis is a collateral of war—huge expenditures for armaments, as affording more employment for capital and labor, profits and wages. It is one of the tendencies of history, apparently, for armament expenditures to increase as ordinary business activities decline. It is also evident that the spurt in business activities after the low level of the early months of 1933, in Europe, in Japan, and in the United States, was partly due to large increases in the military and naval outlays of the several governments. Like expenditures for housing, public improvements, school buildings, and similar civilian undertakings, armament outlays provide a stimulus for business. They have the sanction of patriotism, whether genuine or false; and powerful private munition and supply interests, as well as naval and military bureaucracies, apply heavy pressures on governments to augment such appropriations.

In its immediate economic effects the stimulation of business by increasing the demand for instruments of destruction is the same as the stimulation of business by expenditures for objects of civil beneficence. From the purely economic point of view, therefore, it makes no difference whether the new business set in motion is devoted to making poison gas, bayonets, and bacteria for military purposes, or to making food, shoes, clothes, and houses for the hungry and shivering. But like all such "shots in the arm," increased armament expenditures are only temporary. They must be paid for, and as a general rule there must be a resort to borrowings outside the regular budget. To this borrowing operation an end must come some time. Moreover, as armaments increase, the tension among nations increases; military and naval bureaucracies are tempted to make use of their magnificent possessions; and the possibilities of war are augmented. Hence it cannot be said that armament expenditures provide a sure cure for the disease of the "surpluses." [1]

Nevertheless, the diplomacy of the warlike gesture has been and may be employed in American politics to distract popular attention from economic crises and afford a covering for the suppression of discontents connected with crises. This fact is established and positively illustrated by the Venezuela "incident" in the second administration of Grover Cleveland. At that time the country was suffering from severe domestic distress. The disorders associated with the Pullman strike and the growth of Populism, with its frontal attack on capitalism and "accumulated wealth," alarmed the President and the politicians of his party, as well as the leaders in industrialist

---

[1] For a factual and sober (if necessarily somewhat ironical) treatment of increased armament expenditures as a partial cure for economic distress, see Paul Einzig, *The Economics of Rearmament* (1934).

statecraft. To all observers a sharp domestic tension, likely to break in violence, was painfully apparent.

At this juncture came the opportunity to arouse the multitude by a bold slash at Great Britain for an alleged effort to take territory in Venezuela that did not belong to her. Thereupon, President Cleveland espoused the cause of Venezuela and made a threat of war against Great Britain, more open than veiled. He surely knew at the time that the diplomatic fulmination was calculated to ease the domestic conflict. If he did not know this as a result of his own inquiring and thinking, Richard Olney, his Secretary of State, knew it. If Mr. Olney had not discovered it on his own motion, he acquired knowledge of it from Thomas Paschal, a Democratic member of Congress. In a letter addressed to Mr. Olney in 1895 Mr. Paschal summed up the whole case: "You are right, now go ahead. Turn this Venezuelan question up or down, North, South, East or West, and it is a 'winner'—pardon the slang— morally, legally, politically, or financially: your attitude at *this* juncture is the trump card. It is, however, when you come to diagnose the country's internal ills that the possibilities of 'blood and iron' loom up immediately. Why, Mr. Secretary, just think of how angry the Anarchistic, socialistic and populistic boil appears on our political surface, and who knows how deep its roots extend or ramify? One cannon shot across the bow of a British boat in defense of this principle will knock more *pus* out of it than would suffice to inoculate and corrupt our people for the next two centuries." [2]

Here, then, is the case. Armaments make war feasible. Increased armaments yield profits to capital and wages to labor. If war is not actually desired by a President he may use diplomatic situations to raise war scares which will tend to ease the domestic strain, stifle discontent. Although in Cleveland's administration war did not eventuate from his inflammatory proclamation to Great Britain, the escape was due rather to the conciliatory attitude of the British government than to the lack of direct provocation. Such situations

[2] Thomas M. Paschal to Richard Olney, 23:10:1895; "Olney Papers," Library of Congress; quoted in Alfred Vagts, *Deutschland und die Vereinigten Staaten in der Weltpolitik* (in process of publication).

are always at the hand of the politician in time of stress, and
if he is unwilling to bear the thought and labor required by
immense domestic effort, he may find an outlet in mere verbal
declarations, easy to issue, designed to turn the masses from
domestic irritations to the hatred of one or more foreign
powers. Accordingly, the peril is always imminent, but it can
scarcely be called action in the national interest, or a contribution to the solution of the problem presented by the domestic
crisis.

A fourth way out of the economic dilemma of "overproduction" offered to industrial nations is communism, associated
with the name of Karl Marx. Communism does not purport to
be a mere economic system to be substituted for the economic
mechanism of imperialism or of *laissez faire;* it is rather a
combination of historical interpretation with a solution of the
contradictions of modern society posited as a kind of triumphant upshot. As Marx once said, it is not a simple recipe
handed to cooks in the school of statecraft; it claims to be an
interpretation or explanation of the inevitable development of
capitalism under its own laws, crowned by a prediction of a
communist outcome. Such is the general outline of his scheme
of knowledge and thought.

It is difficult, no doubt, to reduce the voluminous writings
of Marx to a closed and logical system.[3] Some of his works
were closely knit and systematic; others were fragmentary
and directed to changing events contemporary to his life; and
still others—the least important—were dashed off for publishers in an effort to keep the wolf from his door. Moreover,
as a man of action, compelled to make choices and hazard
guesses, Marx often rendered judgments on current affairs
which were not verified by immediate historical events. Yet in
his writings there is a fairly consistent treatment of the nature
and tendencies of capitalistic evolution and a clear indication
of his matured conviction respecting the proximate and distant
issue.

[3] Those who imagine that Marx was always sure of his thought and his
formulas of expression will do well to correct their impression by reference to
his manuscripts, where it is evident that he constantly cut and carved his own
writings, revising his first and second impressions mercilessly. See, for example,
Landshut und Mayer, *Karl Marx,* Vol. II, facsimile facing p. viii.

The Marxian system of thought, so far as it bears on the dilemma now under consideration, is positive: the capitalistic system of production, accumulation, and expansion bears within itself contradictions which will result in its own destruction. The system will continue to expand, through crisis after crisis, until the backward places of the earth are transformed by industrialism and saturated with capital. Each periodical panic grows out of the nature of capitalism; and the wholesale destruction of capital through bankruptcy, defaults, and liquidation permits a renewal of the process of accumulation. But when the world is completely transformed by industrialism and saturated with capital the ultimate crisis of capitalism will arrive, because it will be unable, henceforward, to employ its profits; thus profits will disappear, and with profits, the system itself. Wars will accompany the process of rivalry so engendered, temporarily give new leases of life to capitalism by the widespread destruction of capital, and when the world saturation point is reached war will contribute to the destruction of governments founded on capitalism and capitalism itself. Then will come the spring into freedom (*der Sprung in die Freiheit*), the victory of the working class as the only class having the will and force and faith necessary to govern; and in the end will arise the world commonwealth of communist nations.

At bottom, the Marxian system of thought purports to be in part a description of fact, in part a prophecy or prediction, and in part a guarantee of a happy or fortunate ending, a millennium. That the capitalistic system rests on private ownership of the principal means of production and is motivated by the passion for profits is scarcely to be denied as fact. It is Ricardian as well as Marxian. In some respects the Marxian prediction made seventy-five years ago has been fulfilled. There has been a rapid spread of capitalistic industrialism to the uttermost parts of the earth, saturating backward places with capital and capitalistic enterprise. There has been crisis after crisis, renewal after renewal, in the course of expansion. There have been wars over commerce and empire, innumerable little wars culminating in the grand calamity of the World War which, notwithstanding its monumental and ruinous character, was succeeded by preparations for new wars on a scale still more vast and imposing, as the profits of the last conflict melted away. And at the close of the World War, so disruptive to economy and social order, one great government collapsed of its own weakness and bloodletting—the Imperial Russian Government—and power was seized by and in the name of the working class. All this is open to historical verification.

But whether the inexorable sequence with its long derivation, as projected in time by Marx, is correct, whether the prediction is generally true, remains a question on which empirical science and contemporary knowledge cannot render a verdict, that is, cannot verify or authenticate. Moreover, it is relevant to observe that Marx himself was not always sure that the result he desired would come in the end. In the Communist Manifesto he clung to historical experience and declared that, in the past, conflicts of classes had ended in the triumph of one or another, or in the downfall of both. He could hope for the victory of labor in the near or distant future and have faith in its cause, but his knowledge of past occurrences did not permit him to foreclose on the future with mathematical precision. It is possible to *believe* that his prediction is accurate, but it is impossible to *know* it, for knowledge is always subject to verification.

While forecasting a socialistic outcome, Marx nowhere gave any specifications for the operation of a socialist society to be employed by statesmen with assurance as to efficacy in producing desirable results. He was even less specific in matters of trade and exchange among societies founded on socialist principles. Moreover, neither he nor any of his followers has ever prescribed the exact rules for the treatment of backward places and primitive peoples by socialist societies, as distinguished from the treatment meted out under capitalist exploitation, supplemented by the labors of missionaries. How differences in climate, resources, soil, and advantageous skills among different peoples, and the commerce and price, or exchange-value, determinations founded on them will be handled under the projected affiliation of nations is nowhere minutely described in Marxian literature, or illustrated in the practice of Soviet Russia.

Will the fortunately endowed socialist societies or nations open the doors of immigration freely to less fortunate peoples and races? Will they give outright a portion of the fruits of their skills and resources to their poorer neighbors, or will they insist on exchange on the basis of *quid pro quo?* The first, though conceivable in theory, certainly would be out of line with historical practice, and an act of deliberate self-sacrifice on a colossal scale never before witnessed among nations. If the second alternative were chosen, foreign trade would be limited as in the long run under early capitalism, to a fair balance of reciprocally useful commodities and services. As a scheme of foreign policy, therefore, the Marxian map of the exit from the current dilemma is entirely lacking in working specifications.

Widely proclaimed as offering an egress from the conjuncture in which nations are imprisoned, and as a counterblast to Marxism, is another scheme of thought and practice loosely characterized as fascism. Strictly speaking, however, it is not a system of thought at all, but a celebration of irrational power and temporary makeshifts. It is not even offered by its proponents as a substitute for the industrialist and agrarian operations which have eventuated in the crisis. It is rather an attempt to freeze the crisis by employing the force of the drill sergeant. As illustrated in Italy and Germany, it means the seeming triumph of the lower middle classes and the actual domination of high capitalism over the working classes through the agency of a dictatorship, resting on military force and financed in a considerable measure by large industrial interests, especially those affiliated with armaments. It is in spirit, despite some contradictory professions mainly for foreign consumption, capitalist and imperialist, and its foreign policy is frankly the policy of *Machtpolitik.* It has, especially in Germany, waged a wordy war on great industry and technology, but it does not overthrow or abolish them. Nominally repudiating their logical outcomes, it allows them to proceed in certain hobbles and restraints. Neither in Italy nor Germany has there been any demonstration that fascism does or can or intends to keep great technology employed at full potential tempo, and to effect an expanding distribution of its products at home and abroad. During its ten years of tenure in Italy, fascism has tossed to and fro, making experiments in "corporate" politics, loudly celebrated as representing something "new," and as resolving the economic crisis; but the exigency of the demand for markets for "surpluses" is still pressing and the standard of life for the Italian masses is certainly as low, if not lower, than it was before the advent of fascism and still more sacrifice is demanded of them.[4]

What the proximate or distant outcome of fascism will be, it is impossible to know, that is, authenticate. That a society can be kept "frozen" by force for a long time is evident in pages of history, those of Tsarist Russia, for example; but previous experiments in the freezing process have been made in agricultural societies and under the sway of hereditary monarchs and aristocracies. No such long-time glacial operation has been maintained in any nation employing technology and science on a large scale, under a non-hereditary dictatorship. Dictatorial governments may hold power for many years, no doubt, especially since they command armies, poison gas, and other instruments of destruction and terror. So far as domestic affairs are concerned, their tenure might well be indefinite. But the logic of their dominion is force, and in due course they must satisfy the passion by which they are sustained or lose their grip; and a satisfaction of that passion leads to war, which may end in defeat and dissolution.

If fascism is a final and permanent system, then progress has come to an end, which is doubtful. In any case its future is veiled. It may be regarded as an effort to organize industry, agriculture, and labor, thus serving as a preliminary to socialism. From no point of view can it be considered as opening the way for a return to *laissez faire*. But how it will even seek to meet the issue presented by the productive potentials of technology is nowhere evident in its program or performances.

---

[4] For Mussolini's public confession that the Italian standard of life had been lowered and might have to sink still lower, see his speech quoted in the New York *Times*, May 27, 1934.

And yet, since its inner logic is war, it must make full use of them or incur the risk of meeting defeat at the hands of nations employing their technology at high tempo. It, therefore, has a fateful contradiction in the rationale of its own working policy.

The sixth interpretation of the dilemma confronting industrial nations predicts the doom of Western civilization—not a release into freedom and prosperity. It holds that mechanized civilization is rapidly exhausting the cultural powers from which it sprang, has divorced the middle and working classes from energizing contacts with the soil, and has deprived them of the physical strength and moral courage requisite to the functioning and perdurance of a great society. Hence, just as the governing classes of old Rome declined in virtue and in capacity for grand policy and action, so the industrial and working classes are now sinking in virtue and losing the power to subdue the Frankenstein monster they have created, despite feverish outbursts in Italy, Germany, Russia, and other countries. In this view of world history, the present crisis is merely a phase in the decline of all Western civilization—a long-drawn-out agony, devoid of hope.

The scheme and cast of thought represented in this thesis are very old, but they have been given spectacular form and wide circulation by Oswald Spengler, in *Preussentum und Sozialismus, Der Untergang des Abendlandes, Der Mensch und die Technik,* and *Jahre der Entscheidung.* From preceding theses it differs in two significant respects. First of all, it is the thought of historical conservatism, of the landed gentry, as distinguished from the thought of capitalistic economy, Ricardian or Marxian, and from the agrarian democracy of Thomas Jefferson. It is born of a distrust of, and hatred for, the small metropolitan man, celebrated by Ricardo and Marx, and, in harmony with the Aristotelian politics, regards "that highest type of agriculturalist, the country gentleman," as the best bulwark of society, and the hope for the triumph of blood over gold, of young culture over a sterile civilization.[5]

[5] See *Preussentum und Sozialismus,* which though later in date of publication, as Spengler says, contains the germ of the huge work, *The Decline of the West.*

In the second place, although Spengler, in the closing pages of the *Decline of the West*, mingles hope with fate and seems to rejoice in the prospective triumph of a new Cæsar and blood over the banker and money—all in vague language which is scarcely intelligible to a sober reader—his pessimism as to outcome is positive in the closing pages of *Man and Technics:* "The exploited world is beginning to take its revenge on its lords. The innumerable hands of the colored races—at least as clever and far less exigent—will shatter the economic organization of the whites at its foundations. The accustomed luxury of the white man, in comparison with the coolie, will be his doom. The labor of the white is itself coming to be unwanted. The huge masses of men centered in the Northern coal area, the great industrial works, the capital invested in them, whole cities and districts, are faced with the probability of going under in the competition. The center of gravity of production is steadily shifting away from them, especially since even the respect of the colored races for the white man has been ended by the World War. *This* is the real and final basis of the unemployment that prevails in the white countries. It is no mere crisis, but the *beginning of a catastrophe.* . . . Optimism is cowardice." [6]

Concerning the Spenglerian thesis expressed in the *Decline of the West* little can be said by way of authentication and verification. Pessimism and optimism are sentiments, not sciences, philosophies, or virtues. Millions of scattered fragments, called history as record, can be forced into the Spenglerian picture—the morphology of world history; but millions of other fragments can be forced into an equally contradictory hypothesis by a mind equally powerful. Yet there is a statement of possibility in that picture. The rise and decline of great societies is a known fact of history. The possibility of a similar dissolution in the West has long been a theme of philosophical consideration. It is an ever-present challenge to the makers of policy. But the "causes" of declines are not known, or at best are dimly discerned, and they are the subject of endless controversy and dispute by scholars most conversant with the facts material to the case. Nor is

[6] *Man and Technics,* pp. 102 ff.

there in the nature of things any reason why a calm and judicial survey of the facts in past declines, or speculation respecting the probabilities of future declines, should turn an investigator or thinker into an optimist or a pessimist. Incidents in the decline, if it comes, will undoubtedly give distress to individuals and lead them into pessimism, but whether the decline itself will lead to a finish or merely mark a descending dip in an upward curve of civilization cannot be determined by any instruments of knowledge available to human use.

In asserting as known the decline of the West—a thing that is not known—because verification can occur only in a distant future, Spengler is merely offering his opinion or hypothesis, which may or may not be authenticated five hundred or a thousand years from now. Besides founding his history on his opinion, Spengler is at war with himself in his own thought. At one moment he speaks of the future as fated, and at the next moment he rails in moral indignation at statesmen for their failure to understand or to adopt this or that policy. This is equivalent to saying that water must run downhill, and then insisting that acceptance of the fact, or indifference to it, is an evil to be deplored. If all is fated, then there are no right or wrong choices over which to grow heated. Again, Spengler pronounces doom on the West, calls optimism cowardice, declares that "our duty is to hold on to the lost position, without hope, without rescue"; and in the next breath he foretells the arrival of the Cæsar, who is to overcome decadence and set things right. At bottom, therefore, Spengler's system of thought is not a system at all, but an effort to rationalize and to clothe in history his tumult of troubled emotions, over which presides an evident longing for the return of Frederick the Great. To contemporary policy he makes no contribution, except to confound the bewildered.

§

In summary form, the stoicism of "doing nothing" and the pessimism of resignation to doom present no positive clues of policy to the statesman. In reality the former means repeating the things that have been done in the past—the very things

that have eventuated in present deadlock; while the latter
means flight to the desert, or standing by in naïve or mock
heroics. If mere thought can accept calamity as a fate, state
craft cannot, because it is, by nature, a form of action directed
to ends.

Among the exits just considered, four assume action—
foreign lending, war, communism, and fascism. Each is an
interpretation of history, past and coming; each presents a
certain scheme of policy and procedure. But none of them is
an inexorable demonstration, as compelling as a differential
equation.

A study of experience with foreign lending and of the conditions which limit its operations lends no countenance to the
theory that it can furnish a release from the distress in economy
and thought. By general confession, war offers only a temporary relaxation of the tension, a highly dangerous one at
that, and merely postpones the deluge. The essence of Marxism as practice is also violence—the overthrow of capitalism
by force; nowhere in the system of Marxian thought are there
unequivocal directions as to ways and means of resolving the
crisis—bringing great technology fully into human uses. It
is true that Marxism differs fundamentally from fascism in
that it proposes to accomplish this titanic design, but as theory
it offers no working blue prints; and in operation, as exemplified in Russia, its proponents, having destroyed the alleged
obstacles of capitalism by violence, still toss to and fro in
feverish efforts to attain an efficient application of the technical arts. Fascism is an attempt to freeze the crisis by force,
not to resolve it, and has no program for bringing great technology into full use; on the contrary, it looks backward rather
than forward for its inspiration and its guidance in the
crystallization of policy.

Although, judging by the history of wars and revolutions,
physical force may play a rôle in the making of future institutions and adjustments, violence has its own limitations. It
may lead, as Marx and Engels pointed out in the Communist
Manifesto, to a destruction of both parties participating in it.
Force has no assurance of successful outcome. Moreover, it is
certain that the wrath of men and women cannot provide them

bread, cover their nakedness, give them shelter, or maintain any culture save that of the barracks. This is particularly true of a nation that is compelled, if only by the necessity of defense and war, to make use of the delicate and rational mechanism of technology, physical and social. After violence has triumphed or exhausted itself, the rationality of technology must be restored and maintained, if anything like an industrial civilization is to be continued and developed. Furthermore, since masses of the people are involved in the processes of mass production inherent in the operations of great technology, they must be educated in the rationality of the system and convinced of its practical efficacy; and into that rationality must inevitably enter ideal conceptions of the uses, present and future, to which it may be put. When the wrath of violence has burnt itself out, the small voice of reason, moderation, patience, research, and experimentation, will still have to be heard. Otherwise even such civilization as we now have will disappear.

CHAPTER VI

HISTORIC INTERNATIONALISM

ASSOCIATED directly or by implication with industrialist and agrarian statecraft and yet holding a more or less distinct place in contemporary thought is the program of escape from the crisis in economy through some form of internationalism, accompanied by collaboration and coöperation among nations. This type of thinking places the "causes" of the crisis somewhere in the relations of nations and makes adjustment of their "external" relations the clue to the riddle of the economic and intellectual emergency. It is expressed in various maxims and precepts, but its emphasis is placed on procedures outside the life of the participating nations, such as the decisions of international conferences. In general it gives precedence to what is called "world prosperity," expects to derive domestic felicity from that source, and overlooks or minimizes the thrusts, drives, necessities, and configurations of internal economies. Sir George Paish has put the formula in the following words: "Wise nationalism builds the prosperity of each nation on the prosperity of the World." [1]

Although marked by no little confusion, this conception rests upon the assumption that there is in fact some kind of world system, world order, or world economy which now exists in more or less damaged condition and can be put in better working order by agreements and collaboration among the representatives of governments in international councils. And it is primarily to this international coöperation, rather than to domestic policies and measures, that statesmen must look for relief from the jam and disorder of internal economies. While the conception does not, of course, exclude domestic readjustments, its stress is clearly upon escape from the domestic emer-

[1] Address before the Academy of Political and Social Science in April, 1934.

gency through the formulas and measures of diplomacy and international conferences.

This idea has the sanction of high authority. Nearly all the writings on international law and international relations posit the conception of a world system—"family of nations"— usually without tracing its historical and ideological roots and conditionalities; and both criticism and constructive suggestions under the head of historic internationalism rest upon the assumption that the conception of world "order" or "concert" corresponds in some way to an objective reality.

In the "Draft Annotated Agenda for the London Monetary and Economic Conference" (1933), drawn up by the preparatory commission of experts acting under the auspices of the League of Nations, the implications of world order, system, or economy repeatedly appear. The paper speaks of "the whole system of international finance," "the necessary guarantees of political and economic international order," "the normal interchange of commodities," "an international economic system," "a comprehensive program of world reconstruction," "normal conditions," "return to a normal situation," "bringing world economy back to a more normal condition or, at any rate, to the situation which obtained a few years ago," "an improvement in the world economic situation," "recovery of an economic system threatened by bankruptcy."

It is true that the experts do not exactly describe the *system* or *order* to which they repeatedly refer; nor in speaking of "recovery" do they say whether it is the system of 1928, or 1914, or 1876 which they expect to restore. They admit, moreover, that the "system" is somewhat chaotic and that it is in peril of dissolution, unless the governments of the several nations take concerted action to save it. Yet they evidently have in mind a world system or economy—one that has existed or exists now in a disturbed state, and may be put in better working order by international coöperation. In this system to be "restored" or "recovered," "governments should set themselves to re-establish the normal exchange of commodities" (p. 9), and international trade should be allowed to "flow again in its natural channels." Evidently "normal" and "natural" are considered by the experts to represent an arrangement of things having structure and functions, subject to objective description, and forming a fixed point of reference by which to shape policy and determine the direction of action.

Writing after the preparation of the "Agenda," and with the freedom of a private citizen, Sir Walter Layton, who had been associated with the commission of experts, is even more emphatic in his emphasis on the conception of a world system of economy.[2] He declares that "the economic crisis cannot be solved, and can hardly even be palliated by the action of individual governments. . . . In short, there has rarely been a clearer case of a vicious circle, or one on a larger scale." The main task, he says, comes under two heads, "the restoration of order in monetary and financial matters, and the liberation of international trade from the restrictions which are throttling it." But even a sound financial system can do little to create a condition of economic expansion: "In attempting to restore the economic activity of the world we must not repeat the mistake made ten years ago of trying to reëstablish an international financial system without first making certain that the economic background is such that the world is free to develop as an economic unit. An international financial system and economic nationalism are mutually incompatible. . . . What is needed is nothing less than a reversal of the whole trend of tariff policy since the war." Evidently the ideal image in Sir Walter's mind is a clear-cut "system" of free private enterprise and free trade and it is not beset by the contradictions and compromises which mark the conclusions of the experts representing many national interests.

Sir Arthur Salter, to all appearances, also has in the background of his mind a picture of a world system. Although he sees coming upon mankind "a new world order" in which planned economy is to occupy a large area of industry and trade, he entitles his book "Recovery" and declares that the "tasks of the first post-war decade were to *rebuild the framework* within which man could pursue his normal life of making, selling, consuming, to clear the channels of trade that had been blocked by the operations of war and to open others, and, finally, to restore a single and stable medium of exchange."

[2] *Foreign Affairs,* April, 1933, pp. 406 ff.

The practical measures which Sir Arthur proposes and defends all look in the same direction—a stable medium of international exchange, and low and stable tariffs in all countries, resulting from "international discussion and agreement." Thus governments would be released from the perplexing and often corrupting influences arising from their efforts to intervene in the "natural course" of trade, and the most-favored-nation principle would be generally applied in tariff treaties. While he admits that industries are concentrating in the hands of great corporations, changing "the free competition" of the past, and that economic planning may be necessary in the public interest, his world system is in effect the system prevailing before the disruption of the World War.[3]

The world system not only exists or has existed, or exists in badly damaged condition and may be brought into better shape by international action of governments; its functioning is necessary to a high standard of life for each nation. This complement is a part of the conception of internationalism—a world system, world order, world economy, or natural course. The experts of the preparatory commission, after urging international collaboration to get the broken-down system into operation, conclude positively: "Failure in this critical undertaking threatens a world-wide adoption of ideals of national self-sufficiency which cut unmistakably athwart lines of economic development. Such a choice would shake the whole system of international finance to its foundations, standards of living would be lowered, and the social system as we know it would hardly survive" ("Agenda," p. 6).

Many such philosophers, speaking unofficially, take the same view. Sir Walter Layton is convinced "that independent action, unless wisely conceived and studied in its reaction upon other countries, is likely to deepen the general depression, and that any benefits which accrue to an individual nation are at best only relative."[4] Sir Arthur Salter is equally convinced that economic nationalism means a reduction in the scale of living for all countries. He says that if America arrested or almost abandoned foreign investing, sacrificed her export trade, and cultivated an isolated self-sufficiency, it would necessitate

---

[3] *Recovery*, pp. 5, 334 ff. (Italics mine.)   [4] *Op. cit.*, p. 406.

a "lower level of prosperity" for the United States. This line of development, if generally pursued, he is sure, would mean "loss to every country, impoverishment to countries like Switzerland which have no similar resources, and an organization of the world into separate units and groups which would soon be dangerous and ultimately fatal to world peace." [5]

Coupled with the conception of world order or system is another fundamental principle of historic internationalism; namely, that peace among nations is "normal" and desirable, and can be attained and maintained by the establishment of agreements among them, without making drastic alterations in their domestic policies, measures, economic configurations, and actions. This assumption posits the existence of some kind of international system and the ethical canon of desirability. In writings expounding the view, the language of legalism and diplomacy is extensively employed, more or less consciously. The nations of the world are taken for granted as actualities and as abstractions, much as natural persons are taken for granted in private law. These abstractions—nations—are supposed to be normal beings, just as the natural persons of private law are regarded as abstract normalities, at least if they are outside an insane asylum.

In the formulations of this conception, nations are presumed to have fixed geographical boundaries, to conduct themselves normally within their own borders, and to be equal in rights and duties, save for occasions of philanthropy. Little if any consideration is given to the fact that nations may suffer from internal spasms and revolutions and thrust powerful interests into all parts of the world thus profoundly disturbing their relations with other nations. [6] With internal revolutions, internal

---

[5] *Recovery*, p. 220. A somewhat similar strain runs through communist internationalism: no nation can have a high degree of prosperity through its own efforts; nationalism will lower the standard of life; and nothing short of world conflagration and reconstruction can give any nation a life of reasonable abundance. This is not strange, for Marxian economics is the obverse of Ricardian economics and makes other applications of Ricardian teachings.

[6] In strict justice it must be said that among the internationalists there are some who recognize the impossibility of effecting permanent peace by mere agreements and pledges. H. N. Brailsford, for example, states the case in the following terms: "While on paper the League [of Nations] is well equipped with all the powers necessary to prevent or stop the physical act of war, it

economic transformations, imperial expansion, and feverish quests for markets thus minimized in significance if not left out of account, the next step is taken in applying the thesis of prosperity through internationalism: by "collaboration," "co-operation," "conciliation," "conference," "negotiations," and "adjudication," the relations of these normal persons, that is nations, may be maintained on a pacific footing, with resultant mutuality of benefit.

Around this type of thought about international relations has appeared a vast literature, many formulas of diplomacy sanctioned by treaty, and numerous institutions of collaboration and adjudication. Like other literature it grows by additions, refinements, logical inferences, and commentaries, rising higher and higher into the realm of abstractions. When the formulas and practical institutions of peace fail to work as expected, for example in the case of Japan and Manchuria in 1931-1933, thinkers of this type do not reëxamine their presuppositions, but search for additional formulas and institutions to "implement" those already in existence, on the theory that they are on the right track and merely need to go further in the direction on which they have set out. Just what this collaboration and coöperation imply in terms of the internal adjustments of nations to one another, in economic and cultural institutions and practices, is seldom if ever mentioned; and it is openly or tacitly assumed that the use of words by diplomats or the incorporation of words in treaties can alter "the tough web of fact," making it fit the linguistic formulations.

This type of thought about international relations is, of

---

lacks the means to redress the grievances or meet the needs that may drive a wronged or ambitious nation into war—pressure of population, the need of markets, the lack of raw materials, the suppression of nationality. With none of these can the League deal directly, for all of them belong to the sphere of domestic jurisdiction, which it must not invade. It has the power to stop war, but lacks the ability to bring about by peaceful means the changes which desperate nations attempt by violence to hasten." *Encyclopaedia of the Social Sciences*, Vol. VIII, p. 217, article, "Internationalism." It would be interesting to know how many internationalists, so-called, are willing to face the realities of their aspirations frankly and to concede to an international authority or agency the power to control effectively (if possible) the nationalist thrusts which furnish propulsions to conflict and war.

course, not purely ideal and logical. Its sponsors constantly refer to facts and conditions in supporting the thesis that international peace is desirable and possible. They say, for instance, that means of rapid communication "tie" the United States to Europe and Asia, that the spread of democracy gives a common cultural base to modern nations, that trade and investments bind nations in an economic unity, that the United States, having become a "world power," is compelled to assume heavy responsibilities as a member of the family of nations.

To be sure, the facts cited do not prove the case, namely, that the peace of internationalism is possible and that collaboration can effect it. On the contrary, the same facts are employed on the other side to "prove" that greater preparation for war is necessary and that war is to be expected. While William Howard Taft was emphasizing the fact of rapid communication with Europe to show the necessity of .collaboration, William Randolph Hearst was using it to justify the construction of more airplanes and war vessels. While the "world power" principle was invoked in urging the policy of collaboration, on the one side, it was also invoked on the other in support of increased naval construction and war itself.

Nevertheless, the literature of peace and prosperity through collaboration grows rapidly and its formulas are part and parcel of American thought about international relations. The Atlantic and Pacific oceans are spanned by cables, the radio, and ships; commerce draws nations together; investments unite them; hence the United States as a world power has special international responsibilities; peace and collaboration are desirable and possible, given these conditions. "America's vital economic interests are at stake: they have bound her so closely to the other States of the world," says John B. Whitton, "that she cannot possibly ignore the political problems which thus far may have been discussed by European states alone." [7]

Therefore, the United States for the sake of its interests and the maintenance of peace—world order—should take part in the discussion and settlement of the international disputes in Europe and Asia—even disputes which have hitherto been

[7] *International Conciliation,* May, 1933.

regarded as outside the sphere of American diplomatic concern. Of course, Mr. Whitton does not really mean that the United States "cannot possibly ignore" these political problems, for it can and does ignore many of them; he means that the United States *should* not ignore them or will do so at some peril or disadvantage to its interests. In other words, the United States will find international peace possible and desirable; and active participation in the world system, family, or concert of nations, as they are now constituted, can contribute to, if not assure, the attainment of security and prosperity for the American nation.

Even many isolationists who scorn the internationalism of coöperation and collaboration do not reject the idea of world system, world economy, and concert of nations, while spending billions in preparation for war to the ultimate. Many of them seem to believe in the reality of the idea, if others only pay lip-service to it. They are willing to participate in international councils, as the increasing participation of the United States in the operations of the League of Nations between 1921 and 1933 indicated. But such collaboration has limits. It is confined to matters purely humanitarian, such as control of traffic in women and opium, and to matters pertaining to economic affairs when some distinct advantage in terms of industrial or agrarian statecraft may be obtained for the nationals of the United States. Thus for reasons not identical with those of historic internationalists, these isolationists, if only inadvertently, contribute to the spread and support of the idea that there is a world economy, order or system in which, or out of which, are and may be derived proceeds essential to the prosperity and welfare of the United States—proceeds considered in terms of the industrialist or agrarian conception of opulence.

Prominent among the dogmas of this historic internationalism—running from complete free trade and permanent peace at one extreme to the special-interest collaboration of isolationism at the other—are three contentions: the evil of the domestic crisis can be eliminated by finding foreign outlets for domestic "surpluses" through international adjustments of some kind; the quest for economic prosperity in the United States primarily through domestic measures (changes in economic structure and functioning) means lowering the national standard of life; and such a quest implies a denial of international collaboration. The central theme of dependence on world economy appears under various guises in the current formulations of certain editors, publicists, propagandists, politicians, and economists: "the prosperity of the United States depends upon foreign commerce"; the United States "cannot enjoy prosperity alone"; the American standard of life "rests on the export trade"; foreign commerce, "though a small percentage of the total commerce of the nation, supplies the margin indispensable to the maintenance of national welfare"; nothing but "coöperation with other nations" can measurably relieve the strain of economic depression. To condense them into the formula of Herbert Hoover, expressed while Secretary of Commerce: "In peace time our exports and imports are the margin upon which our well-being depends."

A note of necessity, beyond human will and policy, runs through them all: the very welfare, well-being, and living standard of the nation hang upon international trade and collaborating internationalism. Although most expounders of the hypothesis shrink from stark determinism, Raymond L. Buell asserts it without qualification: "The future of capitalism depends not upon the curtailment of production but upon the increase of purchasing power. This increase can be brought about only by the removal of the excessive burden imposed upon the consumer by unwise tariff restrictions and also by finding new markets for our most efficient export and import industries." [8] In other words, the *only* escape from the dilemma in which capitalism is floundering lies in seeking and finding new markets for our most efficient export and import industries and in relaxing "unwise" tariff restrictions; this modification of current policy and practice, plus this discovery of such new markets, *will* guarantee the requisite buying power to capitalism. Here is the absolute assurance of the mechanical engineer or the infallibility of omniscience.[9]

[8] The New York *Times*, May 1, 1934.   [9] See Chapter I, above.

CRITICISM OF HISTORIC INTERNATIONALISM

When the language purporting to describe the internationalism of world economy and collaboration is closely examined
and its underlying substance is disclosed, it becomes evident
that the fundamental frame of reference for this type of thinking is usually English classical economics—a scheme of thought
and rationalization worked out with rigorous logic in respect
of the peculiar economic position of the manufacturing classes
in Great Britain at the middle of the nineteenth century
(above, p. 85). The elements of that scheme may be re-stated
here briefly. Private property in the means of production is
assumed as "natural," "normal," or "fixed"; units of property
are possessed and controlled by individuals. Wealth consists
of tangible things—land, buildings, commodities. The several
activities constituting national economy are carried on by individual owners or partners; and individual initiative, stimulated
by the profit motive, keeps the engines of industry and trade
running, with competition to protect the public against exorbi-
tant prices and earnings. The individual owner or merchant
knows how to make the best possible use of his property and
energies, and, if the State does not interfere, individuals within
the country and in the markets of the several countries carry
on activities which redound to the general benefit—world prosperity and national prosperity. The world consists of countries
endowed by nature—climate, resources, etc.—in such a fashion
that a mutual exchange of "natural" commodities arises from
the division of labor and resources, adds to the enrichment of
all participants, and makes for international concord. Great
Britain, well endowed with coal and iron and mechanical contrivances, is the natural metropolis for manufacturing, while
other countries are by "nature" fitted to supply raw materials
and foodstuffs in exchange for British goods.

Fundamental for the classical theory of the international
system are certain corollaries, especially the doctrine of comparative costs, mutuality of benefit, a stable monetary standard, and free competition. Drawing upon the handicraft and
agricultural economics of Adam Smith, Ricardo, as Dr. Erich

Zimmermann points out, "could rightly treat of linen and copper, of wheat and cutlery, of wine and coal merely as objects of commerce, as commodities traded not necessarily by like, yet by decidedly similar and equivalent, methods." In other words, under calculations made before the rise of giant metallurgical industries, great capitalism, cartels, and super-national finance, the classical theory did not do much violence to reality when it proclaimed the rule of division of labor, comparative costs, and mutuality of benefit as governing desirable operations in international commodity exchange—the "System."

At that time practically all the relatively stable sections of the world, Western and Oriental, were, to use Dr. Zimmermann's apt phrase, "vegetable civilizations," that is agricultural and handicraft, not mineral, civilizations—in a large measure, self-sufficient autarchies. Few if any industries had a special economic power to compel, to dominate and exploit the markets of the several countries. The degree of equality and likeness among them was such that nations could be called economic units with a certain degree of accuracy, and their nationals could trade with one another on a substantially identical footing as to comparative costs and mutuality of benefits. There were exceptions, of course. For example shrewd Yankees could buy furs from ignorant Indians on the Pacific Coast, at a few cents each in trinkets, and sell them in China at a profit of a thousand per cent. But such exceptions did not destroy the general rule of mutuality.

Conceding the relevance of this system of thought to the circumstances in which it rose, is it good always and everywhere? In a large measure, admittedly, it does not now correspond to the capitalist system as operated. Private property, some of it precarious, is still assumed and present, but individual ownership, control, and use have been extensively supplanted by corporate ownership and directorial and managerial control. Trade between units of particular nations, especially in fundamental commodities of manufacture, is largely trade between corporations and often they are combined in international cartels for pro-rating and dominating the market. With respect to the prime staples of modern trade—textiles, chemicals, steel products, machines, etc.—the great industrial nations are competitors rather than producers of commodities differentiated by their climate, soil, and resources. Modern physics and chemistry, analytical and synthetic, provide innumerable substitutes for "nature's" products, thus overcoming a considerable part of the differentiation provided by nature. What a nation can now advantageously produce for itself is a complicated question in physics, chemistry, and technology, rather than a simple question of observation by the naked eye. So far as "natural differentiations" of system prevail today, they are to a considerable extent regional, not national.[10]

With respect to contemporary international trade, the theory of natural differentiation, comparative costs, mutuality of benefit, and equality of footing—which once offered the appearances of a certain "order" or "system"—has been completely invalidated by science and heavy industry. In the world's several national markets, the commodities of vegetable civilizations have been subordinated to the commodities of the mineral civilizations, especially coal and iron civilizations; and the latter are largely confined to the North Atlantic countries —Great Britain, France, Germany, and the United States. With their control over heavy industries and huge capital accumulations, they practically dominate the vegetable economies of the world and hold them at their mercy under a régime of free and equal commerce. By pushing their heavy industries against the weaker and less organized vegetable economies of the world, they thrust downward their own agriculture in common with other agricultural economies, destroy the balance of mutuality, and are already well advanced on the road to the point where the disproportion of benefit reacts against them, bringing them to an impasse in their own development.

Although economists who speak of the world order and the impossibility of prosperity through self-sufficient action are, consciously or unconsciously, thinking in terms of classical assumptions respecting international trade, most of them are well aware that giant industries, super-national finance, branch factories, and other features of modern economy have decid-

[10] Erich W. Zimmermann, "The Resource Hierarchy of Modern World Economy," *Weltwirtschaftliches Archiv*, April, 1931.

edly altered the picture of 1776 or 1850. When they speak of world economic unity they usually supplement the historic picture by reference to international investments, cartels, international investment trusts, the wide distribution of the stocks and bonds of the several governments and private corporations, and other features of modern economy which constitute an interlacing of interests. They proceed here on the assumption that the integrity of such international obligations can be sustained, that the process of interlacing is desirable, that it works for a mutuality of benefit (whatever uses may be made by governments and industries of international loans), that the process can be continued indefinitely, and that when it breaks down the supreme task is to restore it to its historical functioning.

In fact the world economic order, on examination, does not now take on the appearances assumed in classical economy, even as supplemented by the interlacing of finance and investment. That it is in sad disorder is almost universally admitted; but many economists, who concede this, hold that the distress is due to the dislocations of the World War and hope to "restore" or to "recover" the system of things prevailing at some previous date, not generally agreed upon. That the World War, reparations, and debts did radically upset the "system" of 1914 and disturb the exchange of manufactured and agricultural commodities cannot be denied. But were not the World War and its dislocations, in large part at least, an outcome of the international economic operations which characterized the "world order" of 1914 or 1898 to be recovered or restored? If so, why "restore" that which proved so disastrous for mankind? If on the other hand the World War is not to be ascribed in any degree to the operations of the world "order" previous to 1914 but sprang from other sources, entirely outside the economic realm, do those sources continue to exist? If they exist and may bring on another war, in spite of all efforts and successes in "restoration," why labor so hard at restoration in the economic field? It would be the better part of wisdom, in this case, for each nation to build its own bomb-proof economic shelter. No matter which horn of the dilemma is taken, the restorers and recoverers of world economic unity are at an impasse.

Thus the fundamental economic theory underlying historic internationalism of the classical brand—the theory of natural differentiation and mutuality of interests—does not fit the present state of affairs, and is in process of disintegration as a guide to policy. As a matter of fact, at the time it was advanced it was an oversimplification of the situation it purported to cover. It posited an economic man to the exclusion of the national cultures—ideas, loyalties, passions, political traditions, the development and clash of races and nations, and other actualities abundantly manifest in world history. It likewise gave too little consideration to the differences in the stages of civilization which existed in Europe and other parts of the world, and to swiftly changing processes of history. All this is now acknowledged by economists and is apparent in the utter confusion of their science (above, p. 10).

In the circumstances, the idea of world economy and natural course is dissolving in contemporary thought. That it does not correspond to existing actuality is generally admitted. That it is a kind of hopeful dream is conceded by the very application of the term "recovery" or "restoration," and by the admission that it is likely to be destroyed by economic nationalism. That it is clouded by disconcerting diversity of opinion as to its meaning among those who speak of it is revealed in the conflict of formulas presenting the creed. As Erich Zimmermann has clearly put the case: "The concept of world economy . . . is subject to diverse interpretations. It may mean, for instance, the aggregate of national economies— with their economical and other appendages—participating in world trade, or it may be viewed as the budding system of a new extra or supernational capitalism in which the world market is assuming greater importance at the expense of the national market, and in which international loans are playing an increasingly important part. Seen in either light, world economy is passing through an era of radical readjustment, structural and functional. Not only is the economic position of nations changing in their relation to one another and to the whole, some becoming more self-sufficient, drawing away from the world market, others boldly plunging into world economy; but wholly novel phenomena make their appearance, such as the economic exclave (*e.g.*, the Chuquicamata works of the Chili Copper Company), the penetration of even highly developed economies by foreign capitalism functioning not only as a lender, but also as manager, entrepreneur, and producer (*e.g.*, Ford in Germany), the international exchange of scientific experience through inter-corporate channels (*e.g.*, the I. G. and Standard Oil Arrangement), the Five Year Plan, fascistic economy, and what not!" (*op. cit.*, p. 431).

The so-called world "order" then presents a profusion of things, processes, and conflicts—highly industrialized countries with interlaced finance, enterprise, technology, and corporate relations, countries in process of industrialization, countries with different degrees and kinds of vegetable and mineral production, various stages of civilization and economic levels, different degrees of corporate concentration and management, movements and gravitations in industry to and from agricultural economies, various methods of securing raw materials (trade, colonies, protectorates, and concessions), varying degrees of resource-integration in single industries, different degrees of governmental and banking intervention in the finances of industries, tariffs, bounties, subsidies, quotas, and licenses for international exchange, combinations among buyers and sellers varying from country to country, interlacing and disintegration of ownership through stock market operations, varying amounts of capital accumulations, varying concessions and privileges in other countries through financial and political intervention, and so on through the huge complex of rights, titles, and occurrences which make national and international business a more or less going concern. To call this an "order" or an "economy" or a "unity," to treat it as something mechanical, on a plane surface, to be maintained *in statu quo* or restored if damaged, is to do violence to thought and to the covered reality.

What we have, then, in the total situation of international relations is system in part, subject to laws valid while the system operates, system in process of rapid change, a large area of occurrences which has the appearance of chaos, areas of apparent necessity (such as the distribution of natural resources), and areas of apparent choices where the course of things may be inclined one way or another by State intervention—the whole complication of things intertwined and moving forward in time, that is, in process of rapid change in details and interconnections. If this indicates a complexity of institutions and occurrences too vast for the human mind to encompass by formulas, nothing is to be gained by any false simplification. The borders of the discussion must be widened beyond the assumed rationality of falsely isolated economic occurrences, to include the totality of culture and world history, that is, beyond the competence of economists as such.

In these circumstances any effort to recover a hypothetical world system from the past and to restore its assumed rationality is based on a delusion. The system of 1914, let us say, or rather the complex of order and movement and conflict covered by the name "system," was itself a long product of world history. It was built up under certain conceptions of economy, statecraft, and policy; it was in a measure the fruit of national policies and choices made with reference to existing conditions. Those policies were curious mixtures of *laissez faire,* mercantilism, protectionism, state socialism, imperialism, and colonialism, related to the given opportunities. The World War did not come as a *Deus ex machina* to disrupt the system; it was one of the fruits of the system. It had been shortly preceded by the Spanish-American war, the Boer war, the Russo-Japanese war, the Italo-Turkish war, and the Balkan wars—all of which were entangled in commercial and territorial policies, rivalries, and ambitions. To assume that no such disturbances will arise again and that the system of 1914 (or of any other date chosen by the restorers and recoverers), if reëstablished at international conferences, could be confidently employed as the basis of American interest and policy is to make an assumption, at least—a dubious and dangerous assumption.

The confusion respecting "world order" or "world system" reigns widely in American thinking about "international commerce." Efforts to discover a correct line of foreign trade policy by objective studies of the movement of goods in this system in recent years have so far ended in defeat, and in the nature of things are destined to defeat. One of the best trained

and most experienced theorists and practitioners in this field—
a statesman who has studied profoundly the course of international trade and has served in important government positions
—confirms, by a memorandum to the writer of this volume,
opinions independently formed after a long study of contemporary works dealing with the economics of international trade.
It may be said, without fear of successful contradiction, that
objective studies of trade operations and movements have
yielded no correct system of trade policy, no program of action
commanding general assent, and that there is no prospect of
attaining this end by scientific research founded on the assumption that there is a "natural" order of international
exchange.

The memorandum to which reference has just been made
opens by stating that for years economic specialists employed
by the Government of the United States had been literally
groaning under the burden imposed by "our narrow national
commercial policy." Many of them had long dreamed of a
political régime which would permit them to work out a "rational" policy, to reëxamine our traditional tariff system in the
light of international developments, and "to place our economic relations with other countries on a sounder and more
reasonable basis." Yet, the memorandum continues, when the
inauguration of Franklin D. Roosevelt as President promised
a relaxation of the taut tariff lines, many of the Government's
experts, "in sight of the promised land," began "to doubt the
possibility of working out a rational trade policy on a basis
that would satisfy a trained economist." The reason was not
a lack of courage, but a realization "that we are working in
the midst of economic chaos, without the slightest chance of
any economic theory, however sound, being allowed to work
itself out without political or social interference. . . . Certain
economic principles do operate and their effect can be clearly
separated from the interfering factors, but that is not much
help to men who are called upon to work out a sound and
consistent commercial policy."

"If the world were not so deeply mired in economic nationalism," the memorandum explains, "we might be guided by the
rule of relative costs, with all its implications as regards inter-

national division of labor. Its possible shortcomings might be ignored in certain conditions, and infant industries left to shift for themselves. If a fundamental principle is necessary, there seems to be nothing better in sight."

So far the background of the argument is familiar: there is the hope of the *laissez faire* school clouded with doubts arising from the actuality of "political or social interference." These are serious, as the antithesis of the memorandum runs: "But what are we to do with the social and political commitments? Is it rational to think of international division of labor and ignore the disparity of national standards? Shall we allow Japan to supply the world with cheap tennis shoes and grass rugs, regardless of the reason for the cheapness, in the hope that the Japanese will buy the automobiles and radios that we can produce more efficiently? How many Japanese will buy them when underpaid labor is the country's biggest asset? And what political structure will survive the working out of 'economic laws'?"

This is not an encouraging outlook for *laissez faire;* apparently the system will not work as contemplated. So the author of the memorandum turns to an alternative. The only thing he sees to do now is to do something which should have been done at an earlier economic stage but was outside the practical realm, namely, "deliberately to plan or construct an economic State that will yield the utmost to its citizens, considering the limitations of the natural resources and international environments." Such a State would protect itself against the outside world and "place its foreign relations in the hands of a central authority." And this would be "the only consistent thing to do in view of the centralization of domestic economy." The United States is now being pushed in the direction of economic isolation. There is a bare chance of saving something from the "tradition of international solidarity, but when it becomes quite evident that we are in danger of ruining ourselves, we shall have to take a chance with as good a standard as is possible with our own resources, which may not be low after all." Such is the deliberate pronouncement of an economic expert of high competence—a student, a practitioner, and an authority of wide experience in commercial affairs. The sentiments and the reasoning seem to be conclusive.

It may be safely said, therefore, that historic internationalism, founded on the idea of world order, world economy, natural course, family, or concert of nations, and relying primarily on the policy of coöperation and collaboration, does not conform to the realities and tendencies of affairs (above, p. 24). Whether espoused by exponents of international peace as a pure value in itself, by exponents of *laissez faire* free trade (avowedly or obscurely), or by isolationists as sentiment or expedient, historic internationalism neglects, or at least underemphasizes, the following indubitable facts: the foreign policies of nations are aspects of domestic policies and configurations; if foreign policies are to be controlled, domestic policies must be controlled in relation to the ends of foreign policy; and control over domestic policy, difficult as it may be, is easier for the people of the United States than control over international events, through international conferences beyond the jurisdiction of the Government of the United States. Moreover, historic internationalism may be employed as a convenient escape from the necessity and perils of attacking at home the problem raised by great technology, mass production, and the distribution of wealth.

Speaking practically and with reference to the writings, speeches, and private memoirs of isolationists who make gestures in the direction of international collaboration, the substance of purpose and hope among the "realists" of this persuasion is clear. They believe that the United States Government should make no treaty commitments to peace which would interfere with American capitalists in the enjoyment of protective tariffs, in pushing foreign trade and investments, and in enforcing their interests abroad by engines of coercion, by war if necessary. They favor the anarchy of the acquisitive instinct at home and abroad, with the Government as an adjunct, not a control—an adjunct to employ force and violence whenever these private interests are seriously thwarted in obtaining concessions, pushing trade, and making collections or other realizations.

To be sure, this doctrine is not often so baldly stated, but such is the substance of isolationism as revealed by the writings, speeches, and private memoirs of outstanding isolationists. Lay and minor figures in the group, and orators speaking for public consumption, do not often employ language of realism, but the leading sponsors of isolation—Theodore Roosevelt, Philander C. Knox, Andrew W. Mellon, Henry Clay Frick, Calvin Coolidge, John Hay, and men of this type—have exemplified the hard realism in words and practice: a free hand for capitalism at home and abroad, with government support for it.

Leaders among isolationists given to verbal approval of peace through collaboration have always had in view a positive economic content for their policy; they have known more or less exactly what they wanted, and have had the money to pay for it; but the internationalist of the historic tradition has usually been legal, if not sentimental, and has seldom sought to visualize his scheme in economic terms, except perhaps in terms of *laissez faire* at home and free trade abroad. He has not appreciated the extent to which the thrusts of a given economic system into world affairs determine government action in international relations, whatever the formulas of diplomacy. He is inclined to give private economic forces a free hand while seeking to avoid the consequences by collaboration, conciliation, and adjustment in international conferences where collective will and power are notoriously weak and the possibility of control over troublesome economic thrusts is less evident than in the home councils of the respective nations. Nor does he often display awareness of the fact that the type of internationalism which he advocates in economy, if adopted, will redound more to the advantage of one nation than another, owing to differences in industrial advance and natural resources —that, in cruel truth, internationalism may be a covering ideology for the aggressive nationalism of one or more countries.[11]

Allegations respecting the efficacy of foreign trade, tariff modifications, and commercial manipulations, and the possibility of finding outlets for capitalism's surpluses through the

[11] For an analysis of historic internationalism, see Clark Foreman, *The New Internationalism* (1934).

internationalism of collaboration and coöperation are at bottom formulas, not axioms. Those who reiterate them do not show the percentage of goods nor the variety of goods that must be exported to maintain the well-being of the nation. They do not indicate the amount and variety of imports requisite to accomplish that end. They do not, and cannot, demonstrate that any amount of foreign trade alleged to be necessary to the maintenance of the present or any other standard of life *can* actually be secured by any process of coöperation and collaboration. These clichés are, in fact, simply fragments taken from the interested ideologies of the past, and their nature and reiteration are to be explained, for practical purposes, by reference to the parties who employ them.

Hence, when the formula appears: "The American standard of life depends upon foreign trade, and international collaboration can secure that trade for the United States," the first appropriate operation is to inquire: Who are engaged in reiterating this assertion? An examination of facts in the case results in certain positive disclosures. In the forefront of those who employ this formula are representatives of certain interests that are private and partial in character. Exporting and importing merchants, and their associates in the intellectual élite, reiterate it, individually and collectively, for reasons not difficult to fathom. Exporting bankers gravitate to that side. So do industrialists who manufacture extensively for the export market. One-crop farmers with a surplus to sell in foreign markets show a tendency in that direction. Old investors who advocate the cancellation of European debts owed to the Government of the United States are often found emphasizing the demand that a way be cleared for an increase of American exports and imports. Ideologists of the Adam Smith school, who accept the eighteenth-century handicraft conception of "natural" commerce, repeat the doctrines of the scholastics without subjecting them to analysis in the light of modern technology. Economists of capitalism who take the position that capitalism must expand through foreign trade and imperial operations generally agree with exporting merchants and bankers on the proposition that this is the only alternative to strangulation. They cite the examples of England, France,

Germany, and Italy to illustrate the case, not always happily for their argument. And, strange as it may seem at first glance, many Marxian socialists hold the same view and postpone their utopia until capitalism has saturated the world market, reached a dead end, and collapsed through sheer inability to find new outlets for accumulating goods and profits.

On the other side of the argument, it must be understood also, particular interests are arrayed in urging the utmost degree of reliance upon domestic productive forces, as contrasted with faith in international collaboration. Manufacturers who produce mainly or entirely for the home markets demand trade restrictions against foreign competition. They know that exports must bring imports and that the imports of raw materials and other goods on the free list cannot expand rapidly enough to balance an ever-expanding export of American manufactures and raw materials. They wish to monopolize the domestic market and to have the government protection which gives them the largest possible profit. They emphasize the amount and variety of commodities that can be produced in the United States, if ample protection is granted to producers. They speak of maintaining a high standard of life for American labor against the "pauper" labor of the Old World and the Far East, if tariff walls are high enough.

Yet it is evident from recent addresses and speeches of certain protectionist philosophers that they are now tossing in a fever of indecision between historic forms of isolation and historic forms of internationalism. Confronted by the breakdown of their system after 1929, and by the domestic implications of protectionist policy in economic planning, in wider distribution of wealth or buying power, in limited profits, and in higher taxation, they are beginning to consider a leap in another direction, that is, taking the dubious chance of "recovering" prosperity in a freer world-market of exchanges (above, p. 64). They realize that they are at an impasse and that their old methods have not worked; but they are trembling in uncertainty on the verge of the future.

Underneath the surface they seem to be searching frantically for a middle ground which will preserve their domestic market, as they would like to have it, without government interference in operations, profits, and incomes, and yet give them an opportunity to invade the world market under international agreements for joint exploitation or a pro-rata sharing of specific and regional markets. In their anguish to avoid domestic control over their historic profit system, they may rally their forces in a last desperate effort to smash domestic planning by consenting to and assisting in the modification of old trade barriers and the official manipulation of international agreements under traditional auspices. In the long run the hope is bound to be dashed, but it may give its exponents a brief lease of life and political power. In any case it is the hope of an aggregation of special interests whose past policies and measures have eventuated in the present calamity.

The upshot is clear: when historic internationalism is given an economic content and systematic form, it is fundamentally the internationalism of Cobden and Bright, appropriate to the situation of the British manufacturing classes near the middle of the nineteenth century, or it is the internationalism of industrialism or agrarianism, seeking market outlets in the old style through international and regional collaboration. Where this internationalism has no economic content it is pure sentiment and can furnish no realistic guidance for national policy. In all forms it has failed, and must fail, to provide measures for bringing great technology into full use, assuring a high and continuous standard of life, and guaranteeing national security. It has failed and must fail for the reason that it does not correspond to the realities and practices of nations, and does not attack the problem of the crisis openly and directly with clarified purpose, predetermined plan, and engineering rationality.[12]

[12] For additional criticism of the two forms of economic internationalism, see Chapters III and IV above; for a direct attack on the problem of domestic prosperity and security, see Chapter X below; and for possible forms of a new internationalism, see Chapter XII below.

CHAPTER VII

THE ETHICAL ROOTS OF POLICY

NONE of the systems of thought already offered as solutions of the problem presented by the crisis in economy, whatever pretensions to absolutism, determinism, and omniscience may be made in their name, can give to policy the unequivocal direction guaranteed to work. These systems of thought all rest on a study of past performances out of which the crisis has come, and past performances connot reveal the categorical rule for relaxing the tension, because they have brought us into the present dilemma, that is, have been found wanting in various and grave respects. Defeat does not, in the nature of things, of itself supply the clear mandate requisite to victory. For exigent reasons also science can furnish no equation of triumph; it is an instrument of purpose and, as science, has nothing to say about the uses to be made of its findings (Chapters I and II above).

The knot cannot be untied by historic systems of thought or by science. It must be cut. These systems of thought and reliance on the scientific method have led us up a blind alley, to a dead end, from which there is no escape. We must retrace our steps and consider again first principles. Our duty, our form of action, in the presence of the crisis is written in no known law of iron destiny, in no statistical curves showing past performances, in no axioms arising out of experience. Nothing that is known even tells us that we must do anything at all about the crisis. The very conception of action with reference to it is grounded deeply in the human spirit, in the desire or wish to do something about it—a propulsion beyond the reach of a statistical or rational probe. It is at this point that inquiry must start and thus a reversal of scientific procedure in the old style is required; the knot is cut by an act of will.

The essence of the crisis itself is dissatisfaction with the present disarray of things. Were there no dissatisfaction, there would be no crisis. Now dissatisfaction springs from the belief that the present state of things is not wholly good, does not meet the requirement of some ideal existing in the mind— some conception of greater economic security for the American nation, of well-being, deeper and wider than is now prevailing. Since this is so, the first task is to bring out in the mind as precisely as possible the ideal arrangement of things with which present defeats are contrasted in a manner to produce dissatisfaction—the crisis in thought. The ideal however dim is at the bottom of the difficulty. No ideal, no intellectual discontent. No intellectual discontent, no crisis in economy or thought.

The knot which cannot be untied by thought as meditation can be cut by act of will. The condition precedent to attacking the problem of the crisis is then to determine: What is the ideal arrangement of economic and social life which we desire to bring into being, and thus rid ourselves of the undesirable things which make the crisis for us? Simple as this formula is, it constitutes a revolution in the positive and scientific procedures to which contemporary minds have so widely enslaved themselves, to their own defeat. By no other procedure can confusion in thought and policy be avoided.

When we have formulated as clearly and realistically as knowledge will permit, the ideal—the kind of nation we desire to see brought into being, from which the causes of present discontents are eliminated as far as possible, then and only then can knowledge and science provide firm, and in some cases, unequivocal, direction to the realization of policy. For example, there is nothing in the statistics of industrial accidents and diseases which compels a state in the American Union to do anything about such accidents and diseases; but, if the state is dissatisfied with the condition they present and resolves to bring about a better (more ideal) condition, then knowledge and science can furnish guidance and fairly exact calculations for formulating and executing the resolution. Again, there is nothing in the facts of deaths and sickness that compels anybody to set up a scheme of insurance; but, if action in the premises seems desirable and action is resolved upon, then knowledge and science can furnish fairly deterministic rules of procedure. It is when desire exists, purpose is clarified, and action is resolved upon that the great and precious instrumentalities of knowledge and science have meaning and can set forth ways, methods, conditionalities, and determinants of realization. As the world appears in contemporary thought no other course is open to us, if we would avoid intellectual and spiritual defeat and resolve the crisis by bringing the real into some fair approximation to the ideal.

Since in its very essence the problem is national and public in character and involves the formulation of a new and better policy for the United States in its world relations, what is the type of mind requisite to grappling with it? Not that of the contemplative philosopher concerned with a logical consistency and an all-embracing generality convincing to his scholastic colleagues. Not that of the private person merely struggling for his own existence and bent primarily on the instant needs of immediate things—the pursuit of personal interests, pecuniary and cultural. Not that of the pure idealist who will accept nothing less than some perfect world order for all mankind—an order harmonizing with some system of world ethics. Not that of renunciation or resignation which offers only personal retreat by denying or minimizing the existence of the dilemma. Not that of the mere student or man of science committed by profession to neutrality respecting values. The question at bottom is a public question and any suggested solution must call for better choices and better actions on the part of the citizens and Government of the United States. Hence the only procedure in preliminary thought and subsequent decision at all likely to adjust the tension is that of the statesman—of the socially-minded, public personality engrossed in the public interest.

And what is the procedure open to the statesman, judging by historical examples, such as Hamilton, Jefferson, or Lincoln? He takes the world and his nation or political unit, as he finds them, using knowledge, experience, and insight or judgment in gauging the necessities which they present to his intelligence. He sees that within the border of these necessities there are appearances of choice, of policies that may be adopted, of actions that may be taken, of ends that may be attained. He clarifies his own purposes, and chooses among alternatives. This clarification and choice he effects with reference to some canon of the ideal or desirable, some picture of the world and his nation as he would have them be. Even a choice between two evils involves the consideration of desirability: this bad is better that that worse. In choosing and acting, the statesman estimates proximate and long distance outcomes with the aid of the empirical and statistical calculations available to him. Subject to hazards and aware of them, he clarifies his purpose, sets his goal, conceives a state of affairs more desirable than the one in which he finds himself, proceeds to action, and submits his program, ideal, decision, and action to the long judgment of his nation and the world. In the sphere of complicated human affairs this is the only procedure open to an intelligence that is not defeatist, passive, or utopian.

So-called scholarship, science, and independent research, if they are to grapple with the problem presented by the crisis in economy and thought, can take no other course than that followed by the statesman. They may, no doubt, cling to their neutrality, real or pretended, but in this case they cannot formulate new policy, which involves unneutral choices among possibilities of better things to be realized by action. In fact, with respect to national issues or any large area of human affairs in time and space, the scholar or man of science is not and cannot be neutral, for he must select facts and organize his reports on occurrences; and the very process of selection and organization is a process of valuation, of choice and emphasis. The offerings of private investigators—Adam Smith, Ricardo, Marx, Herbert Spencer, and William Graham Sumner, for example—like those of the statesman are and must be submitted to the same tribunal, to the judgment of history. And the only position in relation to the problem before us, which the scholar conscious of his rôle can take, is in effect, if not deliberately, that of the statesman, without portfolio, to be sure, but with a kindred sense of public responsibility.

This introduction of good, better, and best—ethics and esthetics—into economics and politics calls for more than the mere insertion of moral maxims into the interstices of private and class interests. It means nothing short of a revolution in

attitude, procedure, and emphasis, a frank recognition of the
fact that ethics and esthetics underlie and are essential to the
operation of any great society—a reversal of the approach to
policy made by the so-called empirical or practical sciences
(above, Chapter I). The conclusion or assertion, as the reader
prefers, is so fundamental to any attempted adjustment of the
contemporary crisis that it must be examined in relation to
conceptions of policy offered by inherited systems of thought,
considered on its merits, and applied to the issues in hand.

The three great schemes of thought which have been evolved
as solutions of the problem of the periodical crisis and have
gained ascendancy in foreign policies—*laissez faire,* imperialism, and communism—are alike in resting their structures on
material interests and in either rejecting or minimizing ethical
and esthetic considerations: of the Ruskinian type, for example. The beginning of this mode of thought on a large
scale is to be found in classical economy. The authors of that
system took man as they thought of him at the close of the
eighteenth century, and ignored for their purposes the fact that
the social order of Western nations was the product of a long
cultural development in which had been created the disciplines,
loyalties, integrities, and moral values indispensable to the
cohesion and operation of that order, such as it was. They then
made an abstract man motivated by material interests and
formulated a mechanistic system of economy based on that
assumption or premise. The severely logical among them
excluded ethical and esthetic considerations almost entirely.
Some, less rigorous in their logic, more sentimental, or perhaps
endowed with a more realistic sense, sought to insert such considerations into the frame of their system after it was com-
pleted, without disturbing its perfection of structure. But those
economists who thus took ethics and esthetics into account
generally contented themselves with the apparent afterthought
that the unrelenting pursuit of private interests would result
in "the general good" under "the invisible hand," or they added
homilies on thrift, industry, sobriety, and honesty—virtues
particularly useful in masses of working people who encountered no generous realization of material interests in their
sphere of operation. But none of these ethical and esthetic

side-lines in classical economy was allowed to disturb fundamentally the doctrine of material interest.

When the creed of *laissez faire*, especially as applied to free international trade, failed of adoption outside Great Britain, and the system of imperialism was substituted, the assumption that the pursuit of material interests is the prime mover was not rejected or modified in any way. On the contrary, it was taken for granted. To be sure, ethical phrases, such as the white man's burden and moral obligation, were freely and loosely used in the new literature of policy, but in practice they were treated as useful affiliates of material interests, not as independent and often opposing primordials.

It was in the intellectual climate created by the heavy emphasis laid on material interests that the communist body of doctrine came into being. In other words, Marxism stems immediately out of preceding conceptions. If the pursuit of interests is good for the immediate beneficiaries, then it is good for the working classes, whose secondary benefits have not been so evident and generous. Thus the very weapons forged for the promotion and protection of material interests in domestic and foreign policies were turned against those who had provided the armament. In this fashion socialism became hard, practical, and "scientific," as distinguished from "utopian." The statesmen of *laissez faire* and imperialism had made enormous practical gains in power and advantage by appealing to material interests and using violence in the conquest of domestic power and foreign markets; so the statesmen of socialism would take a leaf from the book of their mentors and pursue the same tactics under the guidance of doctrines similarly realistic in nature.

With special vigor and ostentation, many Marxists threw ethics and esthetics out of their system of thought. The ethics of thrift, industry, sobriety, honesty, and moral obligation to the benighted they regarded as mere covering ideology designed to delude working classes and backward peoples into humble acquiescence in the system of material interest imposed upon them in practice. The Marxian rejection of ethics was also supported by a firm belief that professors, philosophers, theologians, priests, and persons who specialized in ethics were

as a rule associated with, and servants of, the immediate beneficiaries of material interests—landed and capitalist, lay and
clerical. In these circumstances, Marxism in theory made a
rather clean sweep of public ethics. To be sure, Marx himself did not pursue material interests, for his life was one
long story of material sacrifice for himself and his family,
nearly always on the verge of starvation. Nor has Marxism,
in practice, rejected ethics; its promoters are full of moral
indignation; they hurl moral epithets at their opponents; they
speak of "justice" for the working classes; and they appeal
for "loyalty" to the "cause." But Marxism, especially in the
hands of systematists, assumes the predominance of material
interests, makes the communist outcome inexorable, and
treats the discussion of ethics and esthetics as largely irrelevant, if not foolish.

In fine, all these schemes of thought have been assumed by
their proponents to be somewhat in the nature of exact sciences,
from which choices and the use of ethical and esthetic interest
and imagination are largely, if not entirely, excluded. They
are made up of alleged axioms drawn from the structure and
flow of things, which are supposed to supply the "right" word
or "right" action for every occasion, contingency, possibility, as
a machine turns out the one article for which it is designed.
Yet when subjected to the test of practice, none of them does
provide automatically the words or actions which are accepted
as "right" by all true believers. Even Marxism, with its strong
emphasis on necessity in history, the inexorable course of
events, does not pretend to supply a complete bill of particulars so precise that a Marxian leader, confronting a set of
occurrences such as a crisis in capitalism or confusion in the
making and execution of a five year plan, can always find the
absolutely one thing to be said, done, and guaranteed to work.
The dictatorship of Soviet Russia is not untroubled by the
possibilities of choice or by deficiencies in honesty, reliability,
sobriety, and other ethical qualifications. Nor do the esthetic
designs of Russian architecture and commodities flow inexorably out of the material objective relations provided in the
proletarian order of things. Moreover the supreme purpose,
professed and avowed, is an ethical end—the welfare of Rus-

sian workers. Even when learned Marxists, such as Leon Trotzsky and Arthur Rosenberg, attack Soviet policy and practice as erroneous, they profess to aim at a greater good than socialism in one country, namely, international communism. Where there is difference of opinion, there is doubt, and choices, when made, are made with reference to good, better, or best means of reaching some goal, for the moment ideal, presented as a good—certainly not as an evil or as a matter of ethical indifference.

Admittedly, the statesman may conceivably have in mind only those choices and actions which will keep him in power or add to his power as a personal possession. But there have been few such simplified personalities in directing positions within historic times. Machiavelli, who is popularly supposed to have made brute power an end of statecraft, in fact took no such unequivocal view of the art. In his discourses he scorned the sheer brutal passion to rule and advised the utilitarian middle course. "Let no State believe," he said, "that it can ever formulate sure decisions, but let the State remember that all decisions are doubtful, because it so lies in the nature of things, and that one can never escape one evil without falling into another; wisdom consists, however, in discounting the quality of the evil and viewing the lesser evil as good." Deep in his consciousness lay the conviction that the commonwealth had precedence over private interests and that the conditions of State greatness were best assured in republics; while naturally he did not advance this doctrine in *The Prince,* he always had in the back of his mind a better ordered and nobler Italy.[1]

If this was true of European statecraft in the sixteenth century, it is still more true of the Western world in the twentieth century when statesmen, whether they are popularly elected or have imposed themselves by force, must make a certain appeal to the ethical and esthetic sentiments of the masses. They cannot win supremacy by announcing that their sole aim is the attainment of power for its own sake. They rise by pretending at least to offer something better to the nation over which they fain would preside, not by offering neutrality or something worse than the condition already existing. There

[1] Meinecke, *Die Idee der Staatsräson,* pp. 53 ff.

may be differences of opinion as to the value of the better offered, but there can be no doubt as to the supposed nature of the tender. It is the offering of something better, occasionally if not generally, of utopia—the restored virtue of Rome, the perfection of German *Kultur*, the welfare of the proletariat, the untaxed bacon of the British workingman, a chicken in every American pot, or the New Deal. The statesman must act; when he acts he makes choices; and when he makes choices he expresses a preference in accordance with some canon of ethical or esthetic desirability.

When the statesman begins to frame his policy, he encounters certain stubborn things which may be called necessities (above, p. 24)—the land, situs, and natural endowment of the nation, the people and their habits, the heritage of ideas, beliefs and customs, the state of the technical arts, the probabilities of war in the world, and provisions for war and defense. Some of these things are unquestionable necessities in the scene and can be described, weighed, or measured. Others are subjective, embedded in emotions, traditional ideas and sentiments; they are intangible, but the statesman must deal with them if he would remain in power. He may quarrel with some of these fixities of the nation, dislike them, and prefer others, but he knows that here preference will not avail. He may, for example, prefer the French language to the English tongue, but he cannot force the exclusive use of French in the schools, press, and law courts of the United States. Again he may think it desirable for every cotton mill worker to receive one hundred dollars a day in wages, but he cannot make his preference prevail. The borders between necessity and choice are difficult to discover with precision; many a statesman and inventor has accomplished the "impossible." But this does not prove that there are no conditionalities and determinants in the world.

Within the borders of these more or less impalpable necessities, the statesman, compelled by his office to act, confronts one of the oldest and newest questions in history: What is good? The more he clarifies his thought and prepares himself for his task, the higher, wider, and deeper is his inquiry into the nature of American society, into its place in history, into its potentialities to be unfolded by policy and action, and into the conception of purpose to be realized in its development. If to positive and empirical scientists, the idea may be repugnant, thought about national affairs cannot escape it. Policy, purpose, and action must reckon with it, must begin by formulating a frame of the desirable to be attained, an idealized conception of American society to which are to be referred choices of policy and action as they arise and are made. That the difficulties of this procedure are great is not to be denied, but no other course is open, save perhaps the blind following of acquisitive impulses expressed by private parties with pecuniary interests at stake—a procedure that has eventuated in the present crisis.

And where shall the statesman find guidance or a firm center of reference for the determination of policy conceived as the good life for the nation? In the more or less technical works on ethics he discovers, amid much confusion, the old contradiction between absolute and relative ethics. According to absolute ethics, good is eternal; it exists outside the human mind, in the idea of God or in the reason of things. Right and wrong are absolute; in every case of doubt certainty can be obtained by reference to a fixed, immovable center. Right is forever right and wrong is forever wrong, always and everywhere. It is wrong to steal, to lie, and to kill. There is a Supreme Good, an Ultimate End, a final authority. If the tribunal of last resort in matters of faith and morals is not the Pope, it is the conscience of the individual—at least among many fragments of mankind known as the Western nations. The statesman has only to look and he will see the one true path to the good; if he has difficulties he needs simply to consult his spiritual adviser. Thus ethics becomes a branch of mechanics, with some kind of chief engineer—theologian or pedagogue—at hand to indicate clearly and positively how the machine works and the place of the statesman as a cog in it. Absolute ethics is as unequivocal as physics and appears as the spiritual reverse of that deterministic science. In fact the two are so closely akin that they may be taken as one interpretation of the universe. Mediæval historiography, Calvinism, and nineteenth-century materialism are all made of the same intellectual cloth. They are characterized by certainty, absolute certainty, in theory if not in practice.

Yet there is no rule of right and wrong posited by absolute ethics which is not violated with sanction in practice. It is wrong to steal, but mercy tempers the judgment when a ten-year-old boy is caught stealing bread for his starving mother. It is wrong to lie, but not to deceive the enemy in time of war. It is wrong to kill, but not by the wholesale under the sanction of governments. Then there are large areas of conduct in modern society which are not covered at all by the code of absolute rights and wrongs inherited from distant ages and agricultural orders. For example, absolute ethics has no un-equivocal rules covering child labor, unemployment, safety in mines, sanitation in factories, hours of labor, wages, conditions of work, and a thousand other concrete realities of human con-duct that appear in contemporary society. The professors of absolute ethics, although agreed on the wickedness of adultery, are divided over the chief issues of conflict in modern legisla-tion, administration, adjudication, and foreign policy—the principal functions of statecraft. Catholics and Protestants, Jews and Gentiles, Buddhists and Brahmins, are here split into factions, torn by controversies, and as confused in policy as mortals who claim to possess no system of ethics at all.

At the opposite pole is the creed of "ethical naturalism," or relativity: all moral actions and ideas are relative; to use the language of a specialist, Sidney Hook, naturalistic ethics is to be conceived as "the equilibration of interests and their rational adjustment to environment. . . . The relativity of our ethical beliefs is prima facie evidence that good and bad depend upon our primary desires, and as these change the qualities of good and bad change. . . . Whatever I desire, says the naturalist, has the quality of good. This does not mean that the good is desired. It means that whenever we desire anything a certain irreducible quality arises which we call good." At bottom, according to this school, ethics is the frank or sublimated expression of individual, group, and class interests; in practice, largely acquisitive instincts which, as we have already seen, may defeat their own ends. Here is the ethical skepticism born of modern historical relativity: all things pass, all systems of thought are relative to transitory situations, there is no sifting and accumulation, nothing central remains, the shadow of death rests upon youth as well as old age. Stripped of all academic technicalities, this is the ethics of the main chance. Nothing is good in itself.

When the statesman transfers his attention from systems of ethical thought built up by specialists in the techniques of scholasticism to the simpler teachings of those upon whose writings most philosophical and theological schemes are erected —notably to Socrates, Plato, Christ, and Confucius, for example, he will find, not scholastic arrangements purporting to rest upon foundations of reality and self-consistent reasoning, but assertions of good submitted to the judgment of mankind. At the heart of all these teachings—whatever their theological implications—is a conception of the good life, of inner conditions of the human spirit and outward modes of human work and relations deemed desirable in themselves and conducive to a desirable order of things. These assertions are not *proved* by deduction, induction, and discrimination. They are put forth on their own merits out of experience and belief. Their practical validity depends upon the degree of their appeal to human beings in various conditions of life, not upon dialectic elucidations. When all is said and done, the great systems of ethics, as distinguished from mere scholastic glosses and compilations, are assertions of values; and a conception of the good life lies at their core, the good life on this earth, to be attained and realized, more or less perfectly, by practice. In the sifting that accompanies relativity, this conception gathers the support of historical accumulation.

The Christian ideal, so prominent in Western thought, separated from theological implications on the one side and from admittedly faulty practice on the other, contains certain fundamental conceptions of the good life here on earth—the good life considered as an inner state of spirit and outward relations of persons, conduct, and things. It was these conceptions which divided that ideal from the ideals of antiquity. First among them is the central belief that labor is in itself honorable as well as necessary, a source of virtue as well as wealth. "Industrial work," says Levasseur, "in the times of antiquity had always had, in spite of the institutions of certain Emperors, a degrading character, because it had its roots in slavery; after the invasion, the grossness of the barbarians and the levelling of the towns did not help to rehabilitate it. It was the Church which, in proclaiming that Christ was the son of a carpenter, and the Apostles were simple workmen, made known to the world that work is honorable as well as necessary." [2] In this form the ideal is presented by a modern writer on the positive history of labor.

If recourse is had to mediæval writers themselves, who combined a theological world picture with their picture of an idealized society, the case may be clearly presented in the language of Langenstein: "Heavy laborer's work is the inevitable yoke of punishment, which, according to God's righteous verdict, has been laid upon all the sons of Adam. But many of Adam's descendants seek in all sorts of cunning ways to escape from the yoke and to live in idleness without labor, and at the same time to have a superfluity of useful and necessary things; some by robbery and plunder, some by usurious dealings, others by lying, deceit, and all the countless forms of dishonest and fraudulent gain, by which men are forever seeking to get riches and abundance without toil. . . . Not so, however, do the reasonable sons of Adam proceed." They, on the contrary, accept labor as necessary to life. Those in the higher ranges of government and spiritual labor, "earn the right to be maintained by the sweat of others' brows" through services requisite to the maintenance of security and peace. While in this form of presentation labor is deemed a yoke of punishment, it is also considered as the only "righteous" way of life—one necessary and crowned with honor. [3]

Around this central conception of labor as honorable, though a yoke, was built the whole system of mediæval economic thought covering quality of work, wages, prices, and exchange. In that thought, "man did not exist for the sake of production but production for the sake of man." The use of wealth was not separated from the very definition of wealth. For example,

[2] Levasseur, *Histoire des Classes ouvrières en France*, Vol. I, p. 187; quoted in O'Brien, *Mediæval Economic Teaching*, p. 139.
[3] O'Brien, *Mediæval Economic Teaching*, p. 140.

a man was not considered rich merely because he had a store of armaments which he could sell at a high price to savages bent on destroying themselves and their neighbors. Capacity for the right use of wealth was deemed essential to the conception of wealth. Nor was price a simple question of the amount which could be got from another person whatever the state of his ignorance or necessity; there had to be an element of "justice" in price—an element inhering in the quality of the product and its cost in labor and materials, and bearing a relation to the needs and uses of the purchaser. The doctrine of *caveat emptor,* let the purchaser look out for himself, and blame himself if cheated in the processes of exchange, was repudiated. The seller was bound to deliver quality and quantity, and the buyer, or the community, was entitled to protection against all defaults in quality and quantity. Such methods and policies were deemed not only ethical, as the fulfillment of divine command, but also necessary to the stability, happiness, and perdurance of society—of objective social relations portrayed in positive terms.

Despite widespread violations of this ethical system by those who professed it, the break in history introduced by the Protestant Revolt, and the rise of the value-free system of mechanistic economics, elements of the mediæval conception of economy perdured and were re-formed and restated almost continuously. They lie at the basis of Carlyle's protest against Manchesterism. They form the substance of John Ruskin's economic writings, combining economy, art, and life, especially his *Unto This Last.* They are found in the speculations of the socialists, however violently their theological implications are repudiated. Many of them are central to the thinking of John Woolman, Thomas Jefferson, and Ralph Waldo Emerson. Many efforts to establish "fair practices," coöperative relations, and a stable order of economy under what is called "the New Deal" are predicated upon their functional authenticity. Their validity thus does not depend upon their Christian origins, mediæval development, or theological sanctions but upon their inescapable relevance to the efficient operation of any enduring social economy.

These ideal elements are not all mere theories in the air.

Fragments of the ideal are being realized in practice, illustrating the extensions and applications to be made in the conquest of misery, poverty, and ugliness—the crisis in thought and economy. In the construction of some houses, factories, parks, highways, bridges, and office buildings, in the design, substance, and marketing of many commodities, in the ways of many lives, are to be found exemplified the ideal elements of ethics and esthetics which it is the function of policy to effectuate on a national scale. For example, if all the best features of every American city were incorporated in the physical and social structure of a single city, a state of things more nearly approaching the ideal would be brought into being. If the best that is known and practiced in social and economic relations were brought to the center of American thinking, lifted up, dramatized, and employed in education, the dynamics of the ideal would be swiftly accelerated. The problem of ethics and esthetics in statecraft is not, therefore, one of levelling all things, but of selection, exclusion, and emphasis—of building upon and with the knowledge, experience, and achievements already authenticated and established. There will be creations now unconceived or only dimly foreshadowed, but at the moment they must be clothed in the forms of the known and partially realized. Such, in mere hints and fragments, is the ethical and esthetic heritage with which and in which the statecraft of new policy must begin and operate.

Yet in his efforts to bring into being more ideal elements of policy, the statesman cannot elude the impacts of systems of thought founded upon particular interests nor of those interests themselves. He is not operating in a social vacuum where ideals are realized without effort and conflict. Each of the organized systems of thought presented to him as offering an exit from the periodical, if not continuous, calamities of economy, is associated with practical interests of economy—capitalistic, agrarian, and proletarian. Each system of thought is intricately interwoven with a system of active interests. By birth, training, and associations the statesman is more or less affiliated with one or another of them. He may without thought or discrimination throw himself on the side of one or another. He may seek a compromise or an adjustment that will suffice for his day or he may take a longer view and make a more distant projection of policy. In any case he cannot evade the social forces dynamic in each scheme and must formulate a realistic conception of their nature and probable course.

On close analysis he will find that the industrialist thesis, including territorial and commercial expansion for market purposes, employs the term national interest to cover an aggregation of special interests possessed by private persons and corporations. These special interests are active in politics. They contribute money to party campaign chests. They seek the election or appointment of officials favorable to their designs, Through attorneys and representatives they enter into intimate connection with government officials. They press constantly upon the various departments and agencies of the Government in their efforts to effectuate their purposes abroad through diplomatic and consular intervention, protection, and benevolence. On some fundamental matters they may present a united front; on others they are divided and often at war with one another. Again and again the stronger of two special interests is able to bend action in its direction, and thus policy becomes a case of main strength—pecuniary, organized, or individual.

In the varied literature of these special interests there is no consideration of large national ends to be attained, of national interests as a whole set forth in the form of a balance sheet. Their operations are in a large measure fortuitous so far as the nation is concerned. They do not know and they cannot inform the Government or the nation whether any particular operation really does redound to the advantage of the country in the long run. Such concurrence of special actions is not based on general policy. Nor can it be squared with any consistent conception of policy. An official program based upon these interests and activities is not policy; it represents an affiliation of main chances.

The agrarian thesis has likewise been founded on a special interest—the agricultural interest, and it is divided into group interests—cotton, corn, wheat, dairy, and meat products, for example. In intent, with respect to immediate actions, these group interests within the agricultural range do not differ fundamentally from the interests of manufacturing and capital. Yet in reality they are, of necessity, more intimately national than the interests covered by the industrial thesis. For the most part they are individual not corporate in nature. The population embraced within this economic range is rooted in the soil as planters, farmers, tenants. Its concrete and immediate operations are in the United States, and are not extended to Europe, Asia, Africa, and the islands of the seven seas. American farmers form no cartels in cereals, sugar, fruit, and chemicals with the farmers of France, Germany, or Japan. They are Americans; their operations are almost entirely confined to the United States; their affections are in the main attached to a reality that is permanently in the United States —the land and ways of life on the land. Yet the agricultural groups also constitute a special interest and bring pressures to bear upon the Government of the United States. No more than manufacturing and banking interests do they present a reasoned policy of national interest, consistent and workable in maintaining a standard of life for the commonwealth.

Outside the realm of the propertied interests, though affiliated with them, are the labor interests, organized and unorganized. In the field of policy they count for little. On the whole, labor in the United States, has given slight attention to exigencies of large policy, domestic or foreign. It has been content to operate within the frame of capitalism and to exert pressure on capitalists for the purpose of obtaining shorter hours, higher wages, and more favorable conditions of work, with little or no regard for the effects of such demands upon foreign commerce and large domestic policy. In the main, organized labor has taken the position that capitalism can continue to operate on the level of the past half a century and that labor can, by pressure, share more abundantly in the good things obtainable by that process. While generally critical of "imperialism," it has shared in the fruits of the system and has at times more or less dimly recognized that the benefits it has enjoyed have come from an industrial economy based extensively on the commerce of imperialism. In general, labor has not thought its way very far into the realm of foreign policy. Socialists and communists, to be sure, have attempted to widen the horizon of labor's outlook but they have put forward nothing more than a vague internationalism, expressed in many phrases, which cannot be visualized as reality. If the actions of Soviet Russia are to be deemed an expression of communist foreign policy, then national interest and sovereignty are to be retained by communism as pivots of policy, at least for the indefinite future.

Around the American nation, as well as within it, are powerful interests. The ideal nation which the statesman outlines with more or less precision in his own mind, as the frame of reference for policy, is not an Atlantis surrounded by impenetrable seas; it is the American nation with a given geographical location in a world of nations, dependencies, and protectorates, with widespread commercial relations. It is not a question of an absolute ideal but a degree of approximation permitted by internal conditions and external constrictions, considering always the possibility of European and Asiatic wars. By profession other governments are motivated by conceptions of national interest. The aim of their policy, as they conceive it, is their welfare, not that of the United States.

§

Any hope for a successful escape from the dilemma in economy and thought makes necessary the formulation of *new* policy, and into that policy ideal elements of ethics and esthetics must enter.

Mechanistic economics cannot provide these ideal elements. Nor can any system of absolute, naturalistic, or relative ethics, of the scholastic or academic persuasion, furnish them. Reason and logic cannot establish their validity. They are at bottom assertions of values, not demonstrations of mathematics.

There is in the cultural heritage of the United States a body of professed values appropriate and indispensable to new policy —values abundant in literature and faith, and realized here and there in practice.

In the formulation and execution of new policy, the immediate task of the statesman is threefold. He must bring his practical sense to bear in creating his idealized conception of things to be achieved in the quest for security and stability. Having clarified his purpose and formulated it in a workable program, he must, after the fashion of the Fathers in 1783-1787, submit his proposal to the nation for discussion, deliberation, and adoption. With the requisite support and legislation obtained, he then proceeds to execution. This is in the American tradition and indeed in the only possible tradition which is compatible with the effective operation of a delicate technological society.

CHAPTER VIII

INTERESTS AND NATIONS AS PHASES OF NECESSITY

When the statesman, seeking the realization of some ideal —an escape from the dilemma in economy and thought— confronts the world as it is or appears to be, he discovers interests and nations as stubborn facts. His own nation or political society is for him a prime datum, and it lives and moves in a world of nations or political societies. It has interests, objects of attention and affection—objective things and relationships and subjective considerations of ethical and esthetic import.

Respecting the nature of State action to be taken in the realization of his ideal, four systems of thought, appreciation and interpretation are open to the statesman. Three of them— *laissez faire*, imperialism, and communism—are frankly founded on interests conceived in material terms. In the fourth system—pure *Machtpolitik*—the State is treated in theory as sheer power in itself, not governed by or devoted to the pursuit of interest conceived as material advantages; but in practice the State of sheer power is forced by the necessity of economic support and by the posture of international relations to have a care for its interest, to act with some reference to interest in the pecuniary sense.

Thus national interest appears inexorably in the field of operating statecraft. Neither policy nor action can avoid dealing with it. What then is the intrinsic nature of *interest* with which the State, as organ of society or nation, is closely affiliated and must reckon at every step? Is it to be regarded as a primordial particularity or force independent of the State, determining the forms and actions of States? Or is the State itself a primordial force, independent of interests and superior to them? Or, finally, if State and interest have evolved together, what is the nature of the affiliation? An exploration of the conception, interest, is in order.

THE NATURE OF INTEREST

As already indicated [1] the term interest, in its Latin derivation, means "to be between" (hence the use of the word as interest on money lent), and also "to be near," hence to concern, to attract attention, and to have value. In the broad sense, all people are moved by interest; no one does anything about a matter that is of no concern to him; that does not attract his attention, that does not affect in any way his sense of values. This is true of both "material" and "spiritual" interests—the profitable interest and the intellectual and esthetic interest. Hence to say that mankind is not moved by interest is false; the opposite is a truism. [2]

But modern usage is narrower in connotation. For a long time the term was employed indifferently in its wide psychological sweep; in fact, until the secular revolution which opened in the latter part of the fifteenth century spread out to the borders of thought. When political economy took the place of theology as a central concern of the intellectual élite, interest shrank to an economic conception in writings and negotiations involving policy, statecraft, and social affairs generally. The word was taken over into German in the later Middle Ages and meant in law "the share which arises from the property of any person through the activities of another, a utility lost or a damage suffered." Materially conceived, it now means a gain in wealth as measured by the prevailing economic standards—a gain in land, houses, material capital, money, credits, and exchangeable commodities.

But there is also the subjective side to be taken into account. Interest involves mental attention and strain of varying degrees. It is said of a man that he acts only on interest; this is a state of consciousness, a wish, a purpose, more or less deliberate

[1] *The Idea of National Interest*, Chapter I.
[2] Walter Sulzbach, *Nationales Gemeinschaftsgefühl und wirtschaftliches Interesse* (1929); W. Ostermann, *Das Interesse. Eine psychologische Untersuchung*, 3rd ed. 1912.

and rational, a determination to realize an increase in goods or wealth. The wish, however, may not be realized; the wrong means may be chosen, or unforeseen circumstances may defeat realization. Hence, although the person acts with a view to his interest, is governed by interest, he fails to attain his object. Again, it may be said: "This action redounds to my interest." Here is drawn into view an objective operation which does in fact yield a gain in goods or wealth. This is a fact which can be empirically disclosed: the specified operation either does or does not yield a gain in goods or wealth; or perhaps it would be more accurate to say, has yielded a gain in goods or wealth, for, owing to the vicissitudes of human affairs, prediction is hazardous. The subjective belief that a given action will redound to the interest of the believer may be realized, or it may be defeated by circumstances beyond his calculation or control, or both.

There is also another conception of interest connected with the use of the term in its plural form—interests. In this relation it is employed in two senses. It is used to describe outward realities such as material plant and equipment, or aggregations of plants and equipments. Thus a branch factory in Canada belonging to a corporation domiciled in the United States is called an American interest in Canada, and the totality of American tangibles in foreign countries is denominated a part of "the American stake abroad"—a collectivity of individual and corporate interests. The term is also applied to the *owners* of such tangibles, as for example, when we speak of utility interests, railroad interests, shipping interests, and aviation interests. There is a tendency in practice to regard the national interest as a mere aggregation of particular interests, or to interpret it in terms of the most active and dominant interests, even though they be in a minority—considered either as the proportion of persons or corporations involved or as the proportion of capital measured by pecuniary standards.

When policy is drawn into consideration, however, it is the animate owners of tangibles and those seeking to share in the benefits arising from the use of tangibles or to modify ownership in some direction that must be taken into the reckoning. As far as policy is concerned, interest inheres in human beings as motive or force of attention, affection, and action. As motive or force it cannot be defined absolutely, or isolated, or fully comprehended by the human mind. It is not a particularity such as a stick or a stone, nor even as a gas like hydrogen or oxygen. Yet in all formulations of policy, which necessarily implies action in relation to tangibles, interest—that is, attention, affection, and perhaps passion—is brought immediately into play. Those who merely discuss policy likewise bring their interests to bear, consciously or unconsciously, and their interests, both intellectual and economic (salary, wages, or income), are affiliated with some form of ownership or opposition to the present relations or operations of ownership.

The intellectual impossibility of isolating and defining interest in absolute terms is responsible for a large part of the confusion that reigns today in discussions of policy. There are many persons who treat interest as if it were an aggregation of outward realities, susceptible of isolation and definition, which determine the conduct of individuals and the policies of nations. Even critics who assail this view as inadequate often proceed on the same assumption, for they speak of "noneconomic forces" and "ideal forces" as if they too were particularities that can be isolated, defined, treated, and appraised in themselves. Thus material interest as objective realities of interest and subjective concentration of affection on them is regarded as actually existing in the world apart from "noneconomic forces" and "ideal forces." Such intellectual operations are, of course, simply scholastic and formalistic.

The worlds of matter and spirit, as William James said, have evolved together. History is not a record of "ideals" alone, or of "material interests" alone, but a record of the involution of ideas and interests moving forward in time, (above, p. 21). Interest, subjectively considered, may take the form of an idea, and every idea pertaining to earthly affairs is attached to some interest considered as material thing and is affiliated with social relationships. Neither can be separated from the other in operations called "understanding," "appraisal" or "measurement." In a strict sense there are no material interests outside the human spirit. A mountain full of iron standing in an empty world is not an interest. It becomes such only when human attention and affection are turned to the use of it and the apportionment of benefits. There are, to repeat again and again, no ideas without interests, and no interests without ideas. Hence, in connection with policy as action, those who treat "non-economic" forces as something like an insubstantial gas, wholly isolated from interested use of material things, "causing" or "producing" this or that movement of interests, are merely resorting to animism. The only operation that seems appropriate when "interest" is mentioned is to inquire: what ideas are associated with it? And when an "idea" is mentioned, to inquire: what interests are associated with it?

This will, to be sure, not satisfy those who imagine themselves to possess the omniscience ascribed by the theologians to God, and to be capable of isolating, defining, appraising, and manipulating, as separate entities or forces, the two intangibles —interest and idea. But it seems to be the only conclusion to which contemporary thought can come. The shrewd statesman who has clarified his purpose will appeal to economic interest in the material sense and to ideal interest in the non-material sense. He may emphasize the one in private councils and the other in public councils. He may mingle them cleverly in a balanced address to the masses or to classes. But as every student of politics from Aristotle through Machiavelli to Hamilton, Jefferson, Marx, and John Stuart Mill has known, interest and idea are inseparably united. If anything is known, this is known.

Export banking interests, for example, have their philosophy of policy and their apparatus of ideas. And when an idea, like the Monroe doctrine, the open door, or international coöperation, is employed in public or private discourse, economic or material interests, as ownership and benefits, are immediately involved in the thought of those who seek to explore their topic of consideration to its fullness. But men are not endowed with the power to isolate ideas from interests, to assign mathematically measured values to them, and to discover which is more potent than the other in the stream of occurrences called history. Even the very idea of "potency" is borrowed from physics, where it has measurable meaning, and is absurd when applied to human affairs in any other than an indeterminate sense. So we return again—ideas and interests are known to exist, if anything is known; they cannot be isolated in fact; they cannot be measured; they cannot be separately appraised, for appraisal is a form of mathematical valuation; but a realistic view of the world must include both. If preceding writers have emphasized one and minimized or excluded the other, then new writers will properly over-emphasize the minimized or excluded item, in an effort to preserve correctness of balance.

THE CLASSICAL THEORY OF NATIONAL INTEREST

In positing man as a rational animal moved by common-sense interest—acquisitive instincts—and endowed with knowledge sufficient to discover his own interests, the classical school of economists by general consent oversimplified the case. Many men are moved primarily by the acquisitive instinct, and are capable of realizing their interests. But others are highly irrational in fact, are sluggish, are not persistent, are governed by routine, and are indifferent to the acquisition of wealth after they have satisfied certain bodily wants. Besides, there are customary and moral restraints which interfere with the perfect working of human beings as acquisitive machines.

The classical theory also fails to take into sufficient account the ownership of property in different degrees and kinds, the class lines of contemporary society, the determining influences of class on government, the difference between the *mores* of landed aristocrats and capitalists, the possibilities of working-class revolts against ruling orders, the variety of cultural levels to be found throughout the world, and the gradations of economic power based upon the distribution of natural resources. Classical theory likewise neglects the warlike ambitions and propensities of feudal aristocracies, absolute monarchs, and masses of mankind, and the possible economic derangements brought about by politicians in their more or less demagogic efforts to get into power and keep themselves in power when safely installed—through economic legislation and foreign wars designed to quell domestic discontents.

Carried over into the domain of statecraft, interest, conceived in such positive and secular terms, covers material objects of desire—lands, houses, capital goods, gold, silver, and exchangeable commodities, belonging to the nation or its citizens. The pursuit of national interest by the State implies the protection, increase, and effective use of these interests. Maintaining and augmenting national interest is the supreme object of policy. The problem of achievement thus becomes one of the choice of instruments and measures calculated to attain the end posited. As in the sphere of private economy, however, a distinction must be noted between the pursuit of interest, the motive of interest, and interest as realization. A State, like a private person, may act on the motive of pure economic interest and yet be defeated by a choice of wrong methods, or by some opposing force not correctly estimated. Deliberate pursuit of a policy of interest, accordingly, is no guarantee of success in achievement.

In the first system of national interest, that of *laissez faire,* associated historically with the name of Adam Smith, the pecuniary interest of individuals is emphasized, so heavily in fact that many adherents overlook the rôle assigned to the State in the system. In some radical versions, the State appears as "a badge of original sin," as a necessary evil, to be confined to the apparently simple function of keeping order and affording protection to individuals. Extremists veer in the direction of utopian anarchy—a world of individuals and communities without government, pursuing their "natural" interests and attaining maximum opulence and satisfaction. This erroneous conception of Adam Smith's system of national interest is so widespread that the balance must be redressed by presenting both phases of his thought—nation and interest—phases clearly indicated by the short title of his work, *The Wealth of Nations.*

We may start with the datum so often distorted by Smith's less informed and less thoughtful followers—individual pursuit of interest. The theory runs as follows: Individuals are governed by the motive of interest, by the desire to make gains in objective goods. This motive sets them in action, employing talents, faculties, and property or capital. The individual is not only motivated by interest in gain, but he knows those actions and procedures which will realize that interest in objective gain—at least he knows them, to use Adam Smith's phrasing, "better than any statesman or lawgiver" (Book IV, Chap. ii.) In so acting "every individual necessarily labors to render the annual revenue of the society as great as he can." Thus individuals moved by interest and knowing their interest enhance the wealth of the nation. The individual so operating, Adam Smith says, "neither intends to promote the public interest nor knows how much he is promoting it. . . . He intends only his own gain, and he is in this, as in many other cases, led by an invisible hand to promote the end which was no part of his intention." To sum up the doctrine, the individual is moved by interest in objective gains; he knows his own interest, that is, how to realize gain, at least better than any statesman or lawgiver; and in pursuing his interest he enhances the annual revenue of the society, promotes the public good, the national interest. Interest, then, is the primordial urge, the *primum mobile* of life, and, if not interfered with by government, attains its ends with mechanical precision—the increase of individual and national gain.

As the free and interested activities of individuals within the society redound to the social good, so the free and interested activities of individuals in the markets of all nations redound to the benefit of all nations, if States motivated by other purposes will not intervene. Here lies the way to the highest degree of economic prosperity for all nations and to international concord. Richard Cobden believed that free trade was "the only human means of effecting universal and permanent peace." He argued, "The efforts of the Peace Societies, however laudable, can never be successful so long as the nations maintain their present system of isolation. The colonial system, with all its dazzling appeals to the passions of the people, can never be got rid of except by the indirect process of free trade. . . . The colonial policy of Europe has been the chief source of wars for the last hundred and fifty years. Again, free trade, by perfecting the intercourse, must inevitably snatch the power from *governments* to plunge their people into wars." [3]

In short, nations, as represented by their governments, do not know and follow their interests, but if let alone the indi-

[3] John Morley, *The Life of Richard Cobden,* Vol. I, p. 230.

viduals of the several nations, motivated by and knowing their interests, will enhance the wealth of all nations—promote the interests of each and all. Thus the mechanism of interest is made world-wide and ideal in upshot; economic dilemmas are eliminated, each nation is made prosperous, and the perfectionists' dream of universal peace is realized. But in this view interest is not an inexorable force. Its beneficent possibilities may be defeated by governments operating contrary to interest—presumably under the drive of other, independent forces.

Such, briefly, is the doctrine of individual interest in which the State almost disappears, a doctrine often supposed to have the sanction of Adam Smith. But a close examination of his work reveals other maxims or qualifications which completely vitiate the conception that individual pursuit of interest is the primordial datum, by introducing superior interest of the nation, society, or the State. First of all, Adam Smith excepted from the rule of freedom for the pursuit of private interests the particular industries "necessary for the defense of the country." The exception, which tears great gaps in the system of individual freedom, he then illustrated. "The defense of Great Britain, for example," he said, "depends very much upon the number of sailors and shipping. The act of navigation, therefore, very properly endeavors to give the sailors and shipping of Great Britain the monopoly of the trade of their own country, in some cases by absolute prohibitions, and in others by heavy burdens on the shipping of foreign countries. . . . It is not impossible, therefore, that some of the regulations of this famous act may have proceeded from national animosity. They are as wise, however, as if they had all been dictated by the most deliberate wisdom. National animosity at that particular time aimed at the very same object which the most deliberate wisdom would have recommended, the diminution of the naval power of Holland, the only naval power which could endanger the security of England."

If national animosities are independent entities in the world, and if goods necessary to national security are to be exempted from the free play of interest in industry and commerce, how much of commerce can be left to the control of free private interests in this age when entire nations and nearly all their resources are or may be involved in wars? The answer is that the exception of national defense and security from economic free play, for practical purposes, destroys the validity of the whole thesis of individual interest in the age of technological warfare. Moreover, the very navy which Adam Smith regarded as necessary to the security of Great Britain had sprung largely from commercial advantage; it controlled trade routes and bases in the British interest, and was, with its various shipbuilding and supply adjuncts and its bureaucratic appendages, an economic and political engine of immense potency, a special collective interest as distinguished from an aggregation of individual interests.

So highly did Smith regard defense and security that he made them a supreme national interest, a treasure to be prized above the wealth which individuals, motivated by interests, create and accumulate. "As defense is of much more importance than opulence," he said, "the act of navigation is, perhaps, the wisest of all commercial regulations of England." Thus after all, in classical theory, nations are not mere aggregations of individuals trading freely with one another, regardless of national boundaries. Nations as such exist and they seek to preserve their nationality, to defend it against aggression, and "wisely" make such exceptions to the law of freedom for individual interests as may be necessary to a supreme national interest—security and defense. Hence it would seem that nations must also place restraints on such commercial operations of their nationals as may lead to distant adventures likely to put all the powers of defense in jeopardy.

A second exception to the law of free play for individual interests included in the classical theory makes another deep slash in the perfection of the system. "The second case," said Adam Smith, "when it will be generally advantageous to lay some burden upon foreign for the encouragement of domestic industry, is when some tax is imposed at home upon the produce of the latter. In this case, it seems reasonable that an equal tax should be imposed upon the like produce of the former." This taxation on foreign imports, Smith continued, "would leave the competition between foreign and domestic industry, after the tax, as nearly as possible upon the same footing as before it."

The implications of this exception are evident. When a

country lays heavy taxes, direct property and income taxes, upon the produce of industry to maintain schools, colleges, universities, hospitals, asylums, institutions of beneficence, and schemes of social insurance, in short raises the standards of public welfare by taxation, then "it seems reasonable," according to Adam Smith's logic, to violate the law of freedom for individual interests in international exchange by imposing taxes on imports sufficient to put domestic and foreign producers on the same footing.

Hence the classical conception of national interest as an aggregation of individual interests guided by "an invisible hand" is vitiated, if not entirely destroyed, by reservations and exceptions. When national "security" or "defense" is introduced as a value or reality superior to and supreme over private interests and the opulence which those interests create and accumulate, it is made a primordial consideration in policy. The maxim of freedom for the international circulation of commodities under the impetus of individual interests is abrogated, or at least subordinated, to the exigencies of security and defense. Moreover, when taxes are imposed on domestic production for public purposes—in realization of social policy —the maxim of freedom is also restricted in application, and another primordial beyond the scope of private interest is brought into operation, namely social policy for which taxes are levied. Full reliance upon the *primum mobile* of individual interest which, under the "invisible hand," brings about the general interest is thus repudiated. Even the grand object of interest, opulence, is subordinated to another value, security, which is not measurable in the pecuniary terms of private interest. The State is thus restored to economy, the unity or integrity of the nation is posited as a datum, and a national interest superior to the pursuit of individual interests is made the supreme concern of domestic and foreign policy.

THE IMPERIALIST CONCEPTION OF INTEREST

Like the classical doctrine, the imperialist conception of State policy accepts material interest as a prime concern of individuals and society and differs from the former mainly in the degree and types of State intervention invoked in the name of interest. It allows for large areas of *laissez faire*—individual pursuit of gain. But it rejects the idea that each individual engaged in international trade, especially importing, knows the national interest and will realize it effectively in the ordinary course. For the classical view, it substitutes the idea that government, aided, advised, and to some extent controlled by private interests, is, in many relations, the best judge of the national interest and of the measures adapted to the realization of private interests, especially in matters of foreign trade. Indeed, governments operating on the hypothesis practically take the position that they are infallible guides to national interest and that to question their policies and decisions is akin to doubting omniscience and committing treason (above, p. 44).

In the imperialist system of thought, national interest does not automatically arise from the unhindered activities of individuals; it must be actively promoted by the State. The advancement of the national interest, generally considered as an aggregate of particular interests, becomes the end of State policy. Foreign policies result from practical conceptions of national interest and when long maintained these policies "control," or, in other words, act as determinants. The economic motive is taken as fundamental in individual activities and in the activities of the State. Such is the widely accepted view.

Yet it is relevant to point out that some writers of distinction and force, Joseph Schumpeter, for example, reject economic motivation as the prime force in that form of national interest promotion known as imperialism. Schumpeter denies the proposition that political imperialism is an expression of bourgeois interests seeking raw materials, markets, and investment opportunities and employing the engines of diplomacy, army, and navy for their purpose. He contends that imperialism is atavism, a hangover from the days of absolute monarchs and feudal aristocracies given to fighting as a trade and devoted to national honor as to the *code duello*.[4] He lays emphasis on the fact that English bourgeois went in for peace and free trade while Disraeli and spokesmen for the landed aristocracy, defeated in politics at home, sought power and an outlet for their

[4] *Zur Soziologie der Imperialismen* (1919).

energies in imperial adventures attractive to the masses whom they rallied to the slogans of "Empire" and "Greater Britain." He notes also devices for the pacific settlement of international disputes. In his view imperialism is sheer aggressiveness—a force in itself, without definitely calculated economic goals, expansion for the sake of expansion, war for the sake of war, dominion for the sake of dominion; it is, in sum, "the purposeless inclination of a State to forceful expansion without evident limitations." Though bourgeois in nature, a great capitalist country, the United States, has not taken advantage of opportunities to annex Mexico and Canada, is trying to grant independence to the Philippines, and has avoided war with Japan.

Over-emphasis may properly be ascribed to the Schumpeter theory of imperialism as a kind of hangover from the feudal age. It is true that the British landed aristocracy furnished a large part of the early leadership for imperialist expansion and activities, but this is not enough to make a complete case. That aristocracy itself had long been recruited from the bourgeoisie and had investments in capitalist enterprises; and many imperialist leaders, including Joseph Chamberlain and Benjamin Disraeli, can scarcely be called "aristocrats." After free trade failed to find the ever-expanding markets for capitalist enterprise, British bourgeois were active in all kinds of imperialist adventures, despite the pacific and "little Englander" wing on the left. In every one of the world crises, for two hundred years, British economic interests have been in the background, the foreground, or the center. Restless feudal lords do not make history in a vacuum. With respect to American imperialism it can be said truly that American bourgeois have not taken advantage of every opportunity to make war and annex property, but their acquisitive activities in Europe, in the Caribbean and Latin America generally, and in the Far East have been associated with every important diplomatic affair, every idea or formulation of policy, that has occupied the attention of the United States Government since its foundation. Sheer warlike propensity and a sense of moral obligation have entered into imperialist operations, but neither alone nor both combined account entirely for the imperialist phenomenon.

THE MARXIAN CONCEPTION OF INTEREST

Taking the materialistic and mechanical conception of the classical theory—for such it was despite the "invisible hand" and other ideal and mysterious factors occasionally mentioned in it—Karl Marx made another interpretation of interest. Governments, he said, are class governments; conceptions of policy are class conceptions or class interests disguised. The idea of individual pursuit of interests is, for Marx, a class idea —one that suits the ends of individual capitalists eager to be free of State intervention and permitted to carry on their operations in their own way with respect to their own ends; moreover, in his view, whatever the merits of the classical system as logic and whatever its utility to the class which propounded it, the misery of the working classes under even the partial practice prevailing at the middle of the nineteenth century belied the prophecy of general welfare to flow from it. And in the Marxian view, the commercial and imperialist activities covered by the term national interest are activities carried on by the capitalist class seeking to enlarge its markets for surplus goods taken away from the working classes in the form of profits—surplus values—and struggling to open new opportunities for investing capital accumulations derived from the same source. According to this interpretation, imperialism, as national interest, with all its accompaniments of martial spirit, national pride, armaments and wars, merely means the capture of the national government by the capitalist class and the use of its agencies—diplomacy, navies, armaments, and trade promotion—to enrich the class which directs political and economic enterprises under the cover of national interest and patriotism.[5]

In attacking imperialism and trade promotion as class operations carried on under the guise of patriotism and national interest, Marx did not deny the existence of the nation. The Communist Manifesto declared, it is true, that "workers have no fatherland," and this statement has often been torn from its context and made to imply that Marx was a foe of nationality as such. But this is a misrepresentation of the facts. Marx insisted that workers have no fatherland because

[5] For a summary of this view of interest see Sulzbach, *op. cit.*, pp. 70 ff.

the country is owned by landlords and bourgeois, because others have it; hence the workers must conquer it for themselves. This did not mean that nationality was, to Marx, something absurd—a thing to be fought, a dream or delusion. Class interest cloaking itself in patriotism and national interest must be opposed, the fatherland taken over by the working classes, upper-class interest destroyed, and the way prepared for a reconciliation of nations, leading ultimately to a federation of Europe.[6] In other words, Marx assumed that, given a triumphant working class in each country, the economic rivalries of nationalities would disappear and federation would be made possible. National interest by ceasing to be upper-class interest could be reconciled with international harmony—the classical outcome by another route.

Now it is appropriate to examine somewhat closely the conception that the idea of national interest is a mere covering for class interest, that the rivalry of modern nations spring from the rivalries of national capitalisms, and that the revolutionary triumph of the working classes in the several countries will destroy the State as a feudal-bourgeois apparatus of force, remove national antagonisms, and after a season of dictatorship usher in "the free union of free men."[7] The thesis as thus baldly stated purports to be partly a description of fact and

[6] Arthur Rosenberg, *Geschichte des Bolschewismus,* p. 19.
[7] Rosenberg, *Die Geschichte des Bolschewismus,* p. 20. The student interested solely in the truth of the matter finds it difficult to discover a closed Marxian theory of State, for Marx was an activist and revolutionist in politics as well as a theorist, and his ideas were constantly in process of development as his studies advanced and his experience deepened. And those who have tried to make a system out of Marxism, either for or against, have usually had some axe to grind. Marx himself was skeptical about efforts to forecast the distant future; although he sometimes indulged in such fancies, he was inclined to be scornful of them as "utopian." In his movement there were national parties, or rather socialistic parties, within national groupings. He evidently contemplated a highly centralized and dictatorial State (or governing organ, whatever the name). Bakunin violently opposed him on that ground. Otto Rühle, *Karl Marx; Life and Work,* p. 291, and Sidney Hook, *Towards the Understanding of Marx,* pp. 256 ff. Yet he also spoke vaguely about the coming free union of free men in which, apparently, national States or national organs of power (soviets, etc.) might be supplanted by free and voluntary unions. It must be admitted that there is little in Marxian writings about the future relations of national societies or groupings to follow the destruction of the class States and their class rivalries.

partly a prediction for the future—how distant, it is impossible to discover from the writings of Marx himself. As such, the conception leaves out of account many relevancies—the reality of common national feelings, racial, linguistic, and cultural unities, affection for fatherland and soil as a deep-rooted cohesive force, the zeal for power as a ruling passion with great numbers of men, however passive masses may be, and the immense amount of "social patriotism" that exists and may be generated in conflicts of States.

The love of the pomp and circumstance of war, the devotion of masses to military heroes, the proneness of democracies to elect military men to office, even if merely manipulated for political and class purposes, are at least latent forces in popular psychology and must be taken into account in any scheme of policy and action, either on the right or the left. It is also a fact that masses may be stirred to titanic and concerted effort in war, whatever its ends alleged or real, while the same masses cannot be stirred to a similar action for some purpose of domestic and civilian economy. A comparison of the concentrated energies of the American people in the war on Germany in 1917-1918 with the lethargy in the presence of 12,000,000 unemployed and distressed American citizens in 1933 may serve as an illustration. Nor can it be said in truth that capitalism always works automatically, that it seizes every opportunity for class advantage, as it should were acquisition a law of gravitation; for example, the United States did not wrest the trident from Great Britain in 1920, as it might have done; it has not annexed Mexico, despite capitalistic pressure; and it has not tried to annex Canada, despite the undefended border.

In short, notwithstanding the claims made, the Marxian conception of national interest is not "scientific," if that term is used with any respect for precision. On that score even its exponents differ among themselves. In the hands of some German theorists before the World War, Marxism was a science, an objective, material, value-free science "which proved that socialism as a state of society would come." [8] On the other hand, many Marxians have treated Marxism not as a closed

[8] Hook, *op. cit.*, pp. 27 ff.

science, but as partly established, partly predictional, and partly an instrument for revolutionary activity on behalf of the working classes.

In any case, Marxian theorists have given too little consideration to emotional and nationalistic propensities. Their practice may be regarded as exemplified in Soviet Russia. While abandoning tsarist Russification in dealing with nationalities within the federation, subject to economic fundamentals, Marxism in the Soviet government makes use of all the rights, titles, claims, and privileges of sovereign national States and frankly employs national interest and balance of interests abroad as a pivot of policy.[9] To be sure, Bolshevism as practiced is violently denounced in the name of true Marxism by the Trotzky party, as out of line, as a betrayal of internationalism; but where a comprehension of reality and action, rather than a will to believe, is involved, communism is so far operating on a conception of State and national interest, whatever may be the ideals to be realized in the future. Up to this point, as a conception of internationalism, as a thesis of policy, Marxism functions through the national State—or Soviet, if that term is more pleasing to communist thinkers.

THE CONCEPTION OF THE STATE AS EMOTIONAL POWER

The fourth system of thought concerning national interest rejects all systems—*laissez faire,* imperialist and Marxian—which are founded on the belief that the actualities of government and foreign policies spring from and are controlled by practical interests. This system makes the State sheer power, grounded in emotions. In support of the contention that community of economic interest is not the cement of national unity and does not form the motive of policy, Walter Sulzbach advances the following propositions: No nation is a perfect economic unity with balanced resources of climate, soil, and materials; minerals, forests, rivers, and the other resources of the world are distributed without reference to national boundaries; there are no natural economic boundaries between States; international trade is between individuals; normally

[9] *The Idea of National Interest,* pp. 2-3.

foreigners have the same right to trade in a country that its own nationals enjoy; buyers and sellers are ordinarily indifferent to the nationality of one another; the nearest and best market for the national of a given locality is often a foreign market just over the border, not a distant market within the same country; it is generally known that wars do not "pay," and yet nations learn nothing from this economic experience, are in fact indifferent to it. Then Sulzbach arrives at the grand conclusion that the problems of foreign policy and world politics which press for solution do not arise from conflicts of interest at all, but that the *a priori*, hostile attitude of States and nations causes certain economic developments to be burning points of political controversy.[10]

Having made these assertions, Sulzbach then describes several motive forces of imperialism as an expression of national feeling which, he says, are "empirically disclosed." First is the will to power, for its own sake or as a manifestation of national pride. "This must be accepted as a psychological datum." Second is the joy of battle. Here Bismarck is cited: "Peace-loving civilian work for popular welfare does not, as a rule, move and inspire the Christian nations of Europe as much as the willingness to divert the blood and wealth of subjects victoriously on the field of battle. Louis XIV and Napoleon, whose wars ruined the nation and closed with little result, have been the pride of the French, and the civilian services of other monarchs and governments drop into the background in comparison." Third is the high value placed on physical courage. Here Bryce is cited: "It is the greatest good fortune for America that it seldom has wars, for in no other country does military achievement carry a candidate further than there."

Finally, there is the honor of the nation. "The honor of the nation is the honor of the State and this is the warlike honor of absolute princes as soldiers." The conception comes from the feudal age; politicians, journalists, professors, and literary artists are its interpreters and exponents. If the leading statesmen will not see a matter of national honor at stake in a controversy, "public opinion" and the opposition will force them to take the "right" position or surrender their offices.

[10] *Op. cit.*, p. 99.

While classical economy and Marxism are open to criticism as laying too much emphasis on the rationality of the economic man, neglect of economic interest may be charged up against the emotional conception of nationality—common national feeling, patriotism, love of power, joy in battle, predilection for physical courage, and national honor—treated as primordial particularities, prime movers, original first causes of policy and international conflicts. It is impossible, in fact, to separate them from economic interest, for history, as Riezler says, is the involution and moving forward of ideas and interests in time.

There is no emotional outburst in international affairs on a large scale which is not accompanied and stimulated by economic interests of some kind. Von Tirpitz, as the minute and realistic researches of Ekert Kehr demonstrate, could not make the German navy out of sheer will to power, love of battle, and national honor; he could only do it by enlisting powerful economic interests—shipbuilders, steel industries, supply merchants, and overseas traders; the idea was suggested to him mainly by Alfred Mahan's portrayal of British sea power, which was a deliberately chosen instrument of commercial advancement—profit-making.[11] Patriotism, national honor, and flag-waving accompanied American operations in the Philippines after the outbreak of the Spanish war, but the enterprise was not pure joy and pure philanthropy; it was associated with a deliberate purpose to use the opportunity for commercial ends, as McKinley and his party leaders openly avowed. There is seldom, if ever, any war mongering without munitions mongering somewhere in the neighborhood. The potential passions of war and patriotism are constantly aroused and played upon by interested parties—parties with political motives and economic advantages in sight.

The sponsors of the emotional-complex theory of State policy cannot cite a single international affair that has arisen during the modern age—Morocco, Agadir, The Straits, the Boxer conflict, the Balkans, and the Russo-Japanese war, for example, which has not been preceded and accompanied by clashes of interested persons and concerns, with or without government

[11] *Schlachtflottenbau und Parteipolitik.*

assistance. Long before the Samoan affair, which brought
Germany, Great Britain, and the United States to the verge of
war, Hamburg merchants had begun operating in Samoa; they
were there before the German Empire was founded—before
the establishment of the North German Confederation, before
the very existence of the Reich whose honor was apparently
put in jeopardy. Jameson's raid in South Africa, which helped
to precipitate the Boer war, affords an illustration of the relations of private enterprise with imperialist adventures and
wars; and the actions of English and German bankers previous
to the intervention in Venezuela in 1902 show how economic
interests play upon political emotions. It is highly doubtful
whether the United States would have entered the World War
"in defense of democracy" if American nationals could have
sold munitions and supplies as freely to the Central Powers
as to the Allies, and if the Germans had not preyed upon American commerce. To rest international antagonisms and clashes
on emotions operating in a vacuum is to betray a lack of historical knowledge, the kind of knowledge that is empirically
established.

Still more impressive in this connection is the fact that
nations, whose will to power, love of battle, pride in physical
courage, and honor are engaged in international policies, are
themselves the products of history, including its economic
forces; they are not primordial entities existing from the dawn
of time. Not a single nation in Europe or in the two Americas
is a pure racial community; all are so mixed in population as
to defy analysis and classification by anthropologists. The
powerful monarchs who built national states in Europe paid
little attention to racial agglomerations; they conquered, combined, cut, and carved States with slight reference to racial
peculiarities and groupings. The very conception of the racial
or national State is modern, almost contemporary, in origin.
To say that race was the prime force in bringing about German
unity, or in creating the American nation out of thirteen sovereign states is to ignore other fundamental relevancies. That
race and language contributed to unity must be conceded, but
that they brought about the unification is only a part of the
story. There was a time when Germans fought one another on

the battlefield with as much zest as they fought Frenchmen or Slavs; when Bavarians were more friendly to France than to Prussia. The German *Zollverein* preceded the unification of Germany as a nation; and a popular writer of the time declared with considerable truth that "matches, fennel, lamphreys, cows, cheese, madder, paper, ham, boots and beer" had served to bind German hearts together more effectively than all the political ties formed at the Congress in Vienna. The influence of capitalists, commerce, railways, and finance in transforming the loose union of the United States into a nation is so generally recognized that it calls for no concrete documentation. Will to power and emotions are not enough to account for the formation of national States or for their foreign policies.

Nor is it true that classes in national States always put national interest, honor, and pride above their class interests. The history of revolutions demonstrates conclusively that when a class is ousted by an upheaval, leaders of the class and a considerable part of its membership flee from the country and enter into arrangements, if possible, with the governments of rival States for the purpose of making war on their own country. The action of English aristocrats after the execution of Charles I in 1649, the enterprises of French aristocrats and clergy in England and various parts of Europe after the first Revolution in France, and the counter-revolutionary adventures of the Russian émigrés after the accession of the Bolsheviki in 1917 serve to illustrate the point. Rather than stay with their nations and sacrifice their privileges, classes will emigrate on a large scale and seek to stir up wars against their own people. Thus national honor may become, upon occasion, extremely attenuated.

Scarcely less striking, in any full consideration of the emotional conception of national policy, is the fact that statesmen and agitators who use it for their own designs themselves make appeals to class interest, whatever their covering ideology. Georges Sorel exploited it in the name of the working class, making it the foundation and inspiration of the syndicalist movement. Mussolini employed it against communists and radicals in the labor movement, enlisting the support of the Italian middle classes who thus combined patriotism, the protection of property, and Roman grandeur in one "national resurgence." Likewise in Germany, Hitler and his party made a distinct appeal to the harried middle classes against organized labor and socialist forces, using vague socialist phrases to confuse the real lines of the social battle. Moreover, in both cases, the triumphant fascists took good care to distribute among their followers all the lucrative posts of government, central and local. Mussolini never denied Marx completely; Hitler was more Marxian than Marx in the use of class interest, while utterly repudiating him and his conception of interest. Prejudice may seek an escape through emotional confusion, but a cold survey of the occurrences that take place under the emotional hypothesis of policy reveals interests at work in such operations.

Finally, emotional complexes, uncontrolled by knowledge and calculation, give no certain guidance to policy. Admitting their existence, it is necessary to ask: "What of it?" If national feeling, will to power, joy in battle, love of courage, and national honor are the prime motive forces of policy, they are not separated in action from motives of acquisition and from the total situation of economic interests which condition their operations. Why not fight all the time for the joy of battle and love of courage? Opportunities are unlimited, at home and abroad. Do not discretion, calculations respecting chances of victory, consideration of the probable effects of any action on economic concerns—in other words a reckoning with the network of domestic and foreign interests—check, and to a large extent control, the expression of these emotional forces? Reliance upon pure emotion leads only to berserker rages and wars. To restrain emotional outbursts in any way by calculations of interest is to admit the reality and force of interests in the making of policies, as distinct from verbal theories. This is a commonplace of politics. Talking for "domestic consumption," that is, for chauvinistic purposes, is a favorite device of politicians, capitalist, fascist, and bolshevist—and it is discounted in all the chancelleries of the world. Emotions are a part of the historical process; so are interest and rationality. One or another may be emphasized for literary or par-

tisan ends. The existence of all is evident. Statecraft takes
note of them all, uses them all.

§

From this survey of systems of statecraft dealing with interests and nations, certain conclusions may be drawn. The
first is that each of the several systems contains fundamental
truths or fragments of truth, that is, describes realities and
practices which are indubitable, susceptible of historical verification. Each represents an effort of the mind to get at
primordial necessities and forces and to set them forth as
guides to policy. Within the composite picture they delineate
are all contemporary conceptions of such primordial necessities
and forces. The statesman must face, coldly and searchingly,
the realities and practices they claim to describe. He must also
face the various conceptions of them, for beliefs and convictions are realities and forces in the world of statecraft.
Although none of these systems can be accepted as an all-
inclusive system of knowledge and thought, closed, prescrip-
tive, and unequivocal, he must find his prescriptions, somewhere
within their overlapping circles of portrayal.

The second proposition is that nations, societies, States, as
such, appear inexorably in all these systems of knowledge and
thought. Even Adam Smith's immortal work is on the wealth
of *nations,* not of individuals in a world of individuals. Imperialism, while it conquers and absorbs races and nations,
pretends to redound to the interest of the particular nation
which pursues it. Marxism, despite its call upon the proletarians of the world to unite, is international in its outlook
and policy, operates on some theory of federation rather than
universality, and in practice concentrates on the seizure of particular governments as centers of power in given societies,
notwithstanding its antipathy to the State as a word or idea.
Only the apocalyptic and chiliastic members of the Marxian
school seem to expect a fusion of all humanity in a world conflagration. And the emotional-complex system of statecraft
makes the nation, not interest, the source of all State motion,
of all policy, petty or grand. In fine, nationals organized in

political States, represented by governments and motivated by interests and passions, stand as indubitable necessities in front of the statesman seeking possible choices of policy, domestic and foreign, with reference to some good or better order of things.

The third proposition is that interest—material security, gain, and cultural satisfaction—is a reality also and a center of concern for individuals, classes, and nations. But the conception of interest is inevitably vague; it covers other things besides measurables and ponderables open to mathematical enumeration and pecuniary accountancy. Near the core of this reality of interest, with its nebulous fringes involving nothing less than an interpretation of world history, are certain fundamentals: territory, for every nation occupies a geographical space; security; cohesiveness and coöperative capacity; economic resources and technical arts; a productive economy; and a cultural heritage growing out of the course, or, if you please, the differential accidents, of history. Despite their local rootage, interests show a tendency to expand beyond national boundaries through force, public and private, pacific or belligerent, making each projection of ideas, activities, and things a more or less world-wide radiation.

Yet none of these apparent necessities stands out in the scene with borders so sharply defined that it provides a positive bench mark for the triangulation of future policy. There is a core of substance in each, surrounded by an impalpable haze, changing and changeable as presented to thought. Great headlands and broad channels are indicated by knowledge, beyond question, but within the areas thus circumscribed many choices of direction and policy are possible to statecraft, to purpose, will, courage and virtue.

If this summation is lacking in precision, it is not because powerful minds have not been engaged in constructing the systems of knowledge and thought here explored. It is due, rather, to the fact that statecraft is an art of the humanities and, although employing exact knowledge, is not a branch of engineering dealing with invariables. Nations or organized political societies are realities, material interests affiliated with them are realities, emotional complexes called nationalism are realities, but they are changing realities in motion; in any case they are not realities which make unequivocal prescriptions to statecraft. Unless alternative policies forcibly presented to the human mind are illusions, unless statecraft itself is an illusion, then to some extent form and direction can be given to these realities, or choices can be made within the limits set by them. Otherwise mankind is imprisoned in the dogmatism of political doom and no adjustment of the crisis in contemporary economy and thought is possible to effort. In the nature of things, statesmanship as a form of action proceeds on the assumption that choices, directions, and achievement with reference to some good or better canons are open to it, whatever hazards of uncertainty as to means and outcome may arise.

The upshot takes the following form. Among the necessities confronting the statesman who seeks an escape from the dilemma in economy and thought are interests—private, class, and public—and nations, subject to motivations rational or interested, and irrational or passionate, without calculations as to ends. The boundaries of these necessities, which present so many indubitable manifestations, cannot be positively fixed, but policy must reckon with their reality. It is somewhere within the borders of these necessities that ideal elements of policy must operate, if they are not to be utopian in nature and defeated in outcome. While the philosopher not called upon to act may enjoy the luxury of utopianism—pacific or revolutionary—the statesman driven to action by his craft and profession must have some sense for the practical and must work with things that will be—in spite of his efforts—as well as with those that may yield to ideal purposes.

CHAPTER IX

AMERICAN NATIONALITY

Now we come to the application of previous findings and opinions to the problem of resolving the crisis in economy and thought—defining and realizing the national interest of the American people. We have considered the nature of that crisis, proposed exits from the dilemma, the setting of ideas and interests, and methods of procedure available to statecraft. From what has been said, it is evident that two elements appear in the problem—the American nation and its interest. The society with which American statesmen and citizens are concerned primarily is the American nation. The immediate manifestations of the crisis which they are attacking are within the jurisdiction of the United States. The focus of power on which they can bring pressure is the Government of the United States, unless it is assumed that they should and can operate effectively through the governments of other countries. The point of departure, therefore, is the American nation and its interest conceived as a state of security and well-being. In dealing with this nation, the American statesman confronts a social organization presenting phases of necessity—indubitable realities which must be accepted in the formulation of policy.

What, concretely as possible, is this American nation whose interest is to be conserved? Is it a mere fortuitous collection of individuals—human beings—struggling for existence within the geographical boundaries of the United States? Or is it a real community held together by ties of race, social cohesion, geographical setting, and cultural heritage—a community which is more than a juxtaposition of individuals and as such has an interest transcending the aggregated interests of individuals, classes, and corporations? Is there something in the cultural heritage, composition, organization, development, material resources, physical environment, and technical arts of the American nation which gives a certain irrefragable unity and distinction to American nationality, makes its interest, real and potential, different in nature and expression from the interests of other nations?

Even those Americans who fix their hopes upon some remote "parliament of man," a brotherhood of the human race, must reckon with nations and the American nation in particular as stubborn facts in the present scene. So we turn to a consideration of the American nation as a complex affiliation of human beings, interests, and ideas, with a historical background.

HISTORICAL CONCEPTION OF RACIAL NATIONS

For preliminary purposes, a nation may be defined as a people, politically organized, occupying a definite geographical area, and recognized as independent in accordance with the conceptions of international law. Peoples are older than nations so defined and were grouped by ties of blood or race long before great territorial States appeared in history. The political organization of States has not corresponded exactly or even closely to groupings of races. States have been more or less connected with races, both in origin and development, but nowhere, in modern times at least, have States and races coincided with a high degree of precision. The conception of a nation as a single race, politically organized and occupying a geographical unity of its own, is a comparatively recent conception.

In actual practice, at least outside contemporary Germany, the nationality of an individual has no necessary connection with race; it means membership in a nation. An English national is an English national, whether in racial origin he is English, Slav, Latin or Jew, assuming for the moment that there are in fact such distinct "races." Yet there is running through modern thought the idea that a race is in reality a positive particularity, that nations should be composed of distinct races, that such races should have an independent national existence, that purity of race is a requirement of cultural development, and that races are endowed with special mental and moral capacities.

The idea whether it corresponds to reality or can be realized in practice, is a powerful influence in shaping national politics and international relations, is both an instrumentality of propaganda, agitation, and conflict, and a more or less definite goal of many statesmen and schools of politics. Recently the idea was employed as one justification for a world war in the name of democracy—the self-determination of peoples, that is, in superficial conception, of "races." Thus in theory, a nation becomes a race or a branch of a race, and national interest becomes affiliated with racial interest, or rather with theories of racial interest.

This conception of the nation in modern Europe contains several definite notions. There is such a particularity as a race. The history of the race is distinct. It runs back into the distant past and is affiliated with the heroic figures of a mythos, sagas, traditions, and achievements. It has a mission, which is another way of saying that it assumes and manufactures its mission. It is superior to other races, at least in the most desirable and "noble" qualities. It has a duty to enlighten other races according to its own standards and often a moral obligation to conquer, subdue, and improve other races, or exploit them for the benefit of the superior. Frequently the idea of the racial nation is associated with a species of religious faith: God has created nations and imposed upon them the fulfillment of missions in world history. Sometimes it is purely materialistic: the race has special physical and mental endowments and of "natural" necessity makes the most of its opportunities at the expense of other races. In one form or another the idea lurks everywhere in the patriotism and policies of contemporary nations, with varying degrees of open avowal and emphasis.

It is a striking note in the literature of Italian fascism. "We, fascist Italy," declared Mario Carli, "feel that our loins have descended from Roman fierceness, nor are we displeased that a little barbarian influx has added to us that migratory impulse that may be considered as the patient period of waiting for the inevitable expansionist movement of peoples destined for Empire. . . . The Great War put us on our feet and fascism has revealed us. Italians, mindful of themselves, want to return and be the indomitable warriors that they were and outdo themselves. . . . A people of warm vitality and sound muscles like ours must energetically reject all doctrines that do not lead it immediately to a satisfaction of its thirst for power. This explains fascism. The rediscovery of the warlike spirit of a race that has always been at war with the universe. . . . Who can doubt any longer that Mussolini is the most complete man of our times, the magic guide of the nation's fortunes, whom God has generously conceded to Italy. . . . The Italian people . . . is a people of religious, rhapsodic warriors who will conquer the future with the mystic fire of their own faith, interwoven with songs and with flourishes and thrusts of the sword. . . . Italy will be regarded as a powerful nation, vigorous, willful, intent on its tomorrow, reawakened to a destiny of power and hence of dominion, by which all the old humanitarian doctrines . . . have been dispersed like unwholesome fogs in the fascist sun." [1]

France likewise has nationalistic race traditions of long standing. The French are French, a branch of the Latin or Roman race, heirs and perfectors of classical culture and civilization. It was once their mission to spread liberty, equality, and fraternity throughout Europe by fire and sword. They, as a race, are superior in military, literary, artistic and gustatory genius. They offer the refinement of *cuisine* and *politesse* to an inferior humanity. The English are a nation of shopkeepers, the Germans are barbarians, Italians are degenerate sons of the long decayed Romans, and the Americans are scarcely to be tolerated, save perhaps as collaborators in a war for the defense of French civilization. They speak of the "individualism of the Gaul and the intellectual realism of our Latin culture," of "the soul of France" which can be understood and loved only by rare spirits from the outside, and of "the refinements of her civilization." [2]

Across the Rhine is another racial and national tradition—the Teutonic, flowering in Pan-Germanism and Hitlerism. It, too, has a long history. Its more immediate sources can be traced to the Napoleonic wars, when the Latin conqueror,

[1] Schneider, *Making the Fascist State*, pp. 281 ff.
[2] Siegfried, *America Comes of Age*, pp. 20, 315.

Napoleon, overran, divided, carved up, combined, and dominated German states without mercy. Then a great school of German poets, philosophers, and literary artists arose to resist the conquerors and to put Germany in a position to expel invaders and impose her own will on neighbors. By them the German race was discovered and praised in song, poem, history, and philosophy. It was an ancient race, favored of God, the great race which was destined by God to overcome the decaying Roman empire, infuse new vigor into that declining civilization, introduce liberty and valor, break the power of the Roman church, outshine all others in literary, artistic, military, philosophic, and scientific achievements, serve as bearers of culture, take part in the spread of European civilization to backward places, challenge the British empire, and fight for a place in the sun. All these doctrines Hitler carried to their extreme consequence when he began in 1933 to drive Jews and various aliens out of their positions in German national life, to celebrate race purity, and to insist upon a distinctly "racial culture." Here is an unalloyed and simple conception of a nation as a race.

Curiously enough the underlying racial philosophy of English patriotism was largely borrowed from Germany during the early decades of the nineteenth century. The English, no doubt, early formed a conception of themselves as a nation, with various superior qualities, but they accepted their racialism as a matter of course, in a practical way, and did little to give it a philosophical, historical, literary, and artistic form. Safe on their island throne and free of invasion after 1066, never defeated in a great European war, never overrun by triumphant armies, they managed to keep their social cohesion without resorting to special stimulants of race pride, assurance, and enthusiasm.

But English scholars read the German works on history in which race pride was a dominant motive, hidden at times amid vast learning and multitudinous footnotes. From German scholars they learned that the Teutonic race was especially gifted in the arts of government and in the love of liberty, from the days of Tacitus onward. So Palgrave (*né* Cohen), Kemble, Freeman, Green, and Stubbs took over the German thesis respecting the Teutonic genius and mission, re-wrote English history in those terms, showed to their satisfaction that Anglo-Saxon invaders burst into Roman Britain, extirpated Britons, Celts, Romans, and other early residents, founded a pure Teutonic nation and civilization, and then taught the world lessons of democracy, liberty, and representative government.

The Teutonic thesis of the racial nation and racial State may be most effectively summarized in the formulas of an American writer, John W. Burgess, founder of the School of Political Science in Columbia University.[3] The Teutonic race is especially endowed with genius for organizing political societies; Teutons are the founders of national States; they have solved best the problems of self-government and liberty; it is their duty and mission, in the economy of Providence, to assume leadership in the creation and administration of States; they are under obligation to bring backward races under the dominion of their law and order, by conquest wherever necessary; and if backward peoples resist the operation, "the civilized State may clear the territory of their presence and make it the abode of civilized man." The branches of the Teutonic races are especially fitted to be conquering, imperial, colonizing, and organizing powers. This is their historic mission. It has divine sanction. "Certainly," says Burgess, "the Providence which created the human race and presides over its development knows best what are the true claims of humanity; and if the history of the world is to be taken as the revelation of Providence in regard to this matter, we are forced to conclude that national States are intended by it as the prime organs of human development; and, therefore, that it is the highest duty of the State to preserve, strengthen, and develop its own national character." Thus the cycle is closed; the racial State is a particularity of history; the Teutonic race has a peculiar endowment and mission; its path of duty is clear; the will of God decrees it.

Although noteworthy efforts have been made by advocates of racial doctrines to give to their formulations the sanction of science and learning, a study of the history of these theories

[3] *Political Science and Comparative Constitutional Law.*

in the process of making shows that such scholarship and science as have been employed in their construction have been intertwined with the hopes, passions, and aspirations of politicians, agitators, journalists, musicians, painters, sculptors, and literary artists. The scholars and scientists who have given solemn form and academic decoration to the racial theory of nations have themselves often been involved in the politics and conflicts that have accompanied the creation and evolution of the various doctrines. In other words, the theory of the racial nation did not spring full-blown from the hearts and minds of masses of people busy in shop, field, and factory. Nor did it arise from the study of objective facts. Its development and expression have been entangled with State and party antagonisms and wars, with defeats and victories, with efforts to recover from disasters and to justify policies adopted or agreed upon.

Yet this manifestation of the human spirit is not, as some critical writers are inclined to hold, pure myth. Behind it are certain common elements, susceptible of objective study. These elements are, in each case, a common language despite dialects, some general physical characteristics, such as color of the skin, the fact of long group association extending far back into history, many traditions generally accepted though not without protest by minorities, some literary and artistic peculiarities difficult to define, and well-established habits or responses to certain types of stimuli. And in several States the custom of baiting, oppressing and mistreating Jews is a common expression of the racial conception of the nation. A tendency to resort to measures of suppression in dealing with minorities in general is also a marked feature of racial nationalism.

When, however, the so-called physical characteristics of the so-called European race are examined in the light of contemporary knowledge of anthropology, painstakingly acquired by microscopic research, without thought of political uses, when monographic studies of such broad theories as the Teutonic conception of history are brought into consideration, the tenability of race as a particularity simply disappears, so far as the nations of Central and Western Europe are concerned. Taking color of eyes, skin, and hair, shape of skull, and other characteristics, which can be objectively determined, discovered, and enumerated, as the criteria of judgment, scientists have come to the conclusion that the population of England is decidedly hybrid and that, while many of its leaders have shared what is called Anglo-Saxon blood, many of them have shown little evidence of "pure Nordic traits." [4]

Summarizing numerous findings by scholars in anthropology, F. H. Hankins accurately states the position of disinterested science: [5] "As regards the popular tendency to identify race and nation, the facts for continental Europe are similar to those for Britain. France, no less than Germany and northern Italy, has been the common meeting ground of the three primary European stocks, plus various other Paleolithic stocks that have survived. Thus, the Mediterraneans constituted the indigenous element and now dominate in the South of France. The Alpines penetrated clear across the Alps to Brittany and today are dominant among the Savoyards, the Auvergnats, and the Bretons or Armoricans. The Nordics or Baltics, as Goths, Normans, Saxons, Teutons, Franks, and Burgundians, all of them highly hybridized, crossed France from north to south within recent times. One Teutonic tribe gave its name to the country. Down to the early Middle Ages France was predominantly Germanic in language and customs; and today the Germanic elements predominate over other ethnic stocks in considerable areas in the north, south, and west. In consequence, Dominian, after a careful and judicious study, is able to say that some parts of France are today more Teutonic than certain parts of Germany. If the population of Germany is less composite in certain areas than that of France, it is equally so in many others. A relative purity of Germanic elements along the Baltic and the North seas (but mixed even there with Slavic Poles and Wends) gradually gives way to the southward to an increasing complexity in which Alpine and Mediterranean elements increase. The entire area of France and Germany has been the battleground of tribes and races for the last 25,000 years. It has been repeatedly overrun by new conquerors and passing military adventurers who have temporarily

[4] Hankins, *The Racial Basis of Civilization*, p. 278.
[5] *Ibid.*, p. 285.

or permanently mingled their blood with that of the indigenous population."

It would seem then that the so called racial nations of Europe are cultural products as well as racial products, that race is not an original and pure particularity, a kind of first cause which operates under its own laws. Notwithstanding this fact, and despite the falsity of its racial assertions, racial nationalism is a potentiality of undoubted force which may be aroused and manipulated by groups, classes, and interests for their purposes and in pursuit of their policies, or sublimated as by Soviet Russia. Its verbal forms, its proclamations for domestic and foreign effect, its passionate manifestoes, make it a force to be employed by interest in international relations, however dubious race characteristics and races may be as matters of physiology and mentality. Of the personalities and classes which operate in this field of emotions and intellect, of the nations so motivated, of their collisions springing, in part, from such sources, the Government and people of the United States must take positive note in shaping both foreign and domestic policy. To speak of the international relations in the sphere of economy as free, rational operations in pure finance and commerce, or to speak of the European "system" as if it actually had a cultural unity, to ignore this racial nationalism, is to leave out of the reckoning realities of the first magnitude for politics.

RACIAL ELEMENTS IN AMERICAN NATIONALITY

Owing to its origins, its historical development, and its previous immigration policies, the United States cannot lay claim to racial nationalism in the European sense of the word, at least with a straight face. The very returns of the census on the distribution of races in the United States destroy the possibility of ever repeating here the psychological patterns and methods of French, Italian, German, and English nationalists. The past of this country is not buried in prehistoric depths which fancy can people with race gods and race heroes. It is an open book to common sense and obvious fact-finding. The number of Negroes, Teutons, Latins, Slavs, Jews, and

Orientals mixed with descendants of the colonial stock is so great and so evident that the most ardent nationalist does not dare to speak of "the American race." And should some American Hitler or Mussolini wax ecstatic about the glorious mission of "the race," his auditors would naturally inquire: "Which race?" Nor is it likely that any such attempt will be made, owing to the political perils of appeals to any single racial element and on account of the fact that the "British race" which is numerically strongest (below, p. 195) in the nation can only govern with the consent of the other races in the country. Nationalism of the European type is, therefore, impossible in the United States, but this must not be taken to mean that American nationality is an illusion. American nationality is a cultural polity possessing both objective and subjective characteristics.

The first and perhaps most significant fact revealed by an examination of data bearing on American nationality is the present abandonment of the long-standing conception of *laissez faire* in immigration and the substitution of drastic and selective control over additions to the existing stocks in the population. For many years the Government of the United States proceeded on the theory that this country was an asylum for the poor and oppressed of all lands and races. Certain social and economic conditions favored the adoption and continuance of this policy of free admission. Southern slave owners, aided by New England and foreign shippers, imported thousands of Negroes to be exploited on plantations and farms. If the competition of slave breeders in the Southern states and the criticism of anti-slavery opposition had not intervened, if slavery and slave importation had been continued on the *laissez faire* principle, then all sections of the United States where slavery was economically feasible might have been occupied by a toiling population of Negroes dominated by a white minority, with whatever consequences for American nationality such a policy might have entailed. But in the course of historical development the importation of slaves and slavery itself were abolished, although the free immigration of Negroes from certain geographical areas was allowed. In a large measure for reasons not wholly dissimilar, the doors of the country were thrown wide for free migration from all countries. Capitalists needed laborers to operate mills, mines, railways, and other enterprises, and speculators who held millions of acres of vacant land needed buyers and occupants to turn hopes into profitable realities.

But the conditions which led to the wholesale immigration of Negroes and free laborers of all races and conditions long ago disappeared. The rise of organized labor in the United States has brought into existence a powerful political force directed against "the influx of cheap labor." The pressures in favor of *laissez faire* with respect to American nationality have been relaxed with the disappearance of slavery and vacant lands, and with the saturation of the labor market; and a formidable opposition has been established. In these circumstances control over immigration has been substituted for freedom, and the doctrine of America as an asylum for the poor and oppressed of all lands has been abandoned in public policy. It is, no doubt, sometimes heard in public discussions. A few Americans try to keep alive the tradition as a value in universal ethics, and many immigrants who would like to bring relatives and co-racialists into the United States refer to it as if it were a fixed obligation; but the practice which it connotates has been abolished and a positive conception of American nationality now controls immigration. In other words, there is now in existence in American public law and policy a conception of American nationality. To use the picturesque language of Theodore Roosevelt, America is no longer a boarding house—for visiting immigrants.

Although the idea of race in the narrow European sense has not been incorporated in the conception of American nationality, the idea of race has not been entirely eliminated. On the contrary, the immigration legislation of the United States during the past twenty-five years has contained within its scope certain racial discriminations pertinent to American nationality. It is true that this legislation and the discussion that accompanied it have been variously interpreted, and that efforts have been made to minimize or discard the racial aspects, for various reasons, but a minute examination of the books, the congressional debates, and the periodical literature dealing with the subject discloses irrefutable evidence that racial convictions were mingled with the powerful motives which brought the legislation into existence. This is not the place, nor is there space here, to present even a summary of the findings, but certain selections may be given to illustrate the fundamental nature of the national ends which the legislation was designed to attain—racial, economic, political, class, cultural, and biological—and the diversity of opinions affiliated with it.

First of all may be presented the view which rejects the racial interpretation of the immigration bill of 1924, restricting immigration on the basis of national origins, according to calculations derived from a survey of American social composition as reflected in the census of 1920. Commenting on this measure while it was under consideration, the New York *Times* expressed editorially the theory that assimilability is the criterion of judgment: "The basis of restriction must be chosen with a view not to the interest of any group or groups in this country, whether racial or religious, but rather with a view to the country's best interests as a whole. The great test is assimilability. Will the newcomers fit into American life readily? Is their culture sufficiently akin to our own to make it possible for them easily to take their place among us? There is no question of 'superior' or 'inferior' races, or of 'Nordics,' or of prejudices, or of racial egotism. Certain groups not only do not fuse easily, but consistently endeavor to keep alive their racial distinctions. . . . A policy must be formed without discriminating unfairly against any given groups, but at the same time with regard to the interests only of the whole and not of any special part." [6]

As a matter of fact, however, during the preliminary inquiries and discussions, elaborate efforts were made to show "scientifically" that immigrants from certain European countries were inferior mentally and biologically and should be excluded on such grounds, as well as for general cultural reasons. With respect to mental characteristics it was claimed that the new psychological tests "have furnished us with the

[6] New York *Times*, March 1, 1924; quoted in Garis, *Immigration Restriction*, p. 285.

necessary yardstick to measure the desirability of the immigrant. The same tests will reveal to us, with relative precision, the hidden qualities which will demonstrate the fitness of the intending immigrant for citizenship, and will exclude those who are unfit."

By the use of the Army "intelligence measurements" the various countries of Europe were given an intelligence rating based on the relative performances of their immigrants in the United States. According to the schedule thus arrived at mathematically, on assumptions of intrinsic validity, Poland, Italy, Russia, Greece, Turkey, Ireland, and Austria were clearly marked for restriction, and the conclusion was reached "that Slavic and Latin countries show a marked contrast in intelligence with the western and northern European group." [7]

These operations and findings were vigorously attacked by other men of science. The assumption that the tests measured "intelligence" in itself, as distinguished from cultural opportunities and attainments, was challenged with undoubted incisiveness and effect, and the conclusions based on it were assailed as biased by prejudice and sentiment; but the allegations as to "intelligence" differences in races or nationality were widely accepted as affording specific ground for restriction and selection. [8]

Still more important, perhaps, in shaping the determinations of Congress was a report by the eugenics expert of the House Committee on Immigration, Dr. H. H. Laughlin, of the Eugenics Record Office of the Carnegie Institution. Indeed, Professor Garis states that this report "is often regarded as the principal basis of the Act of 1924." It was founded on a survey of asylums, hospitals, prisons, and other institutions for defectives, dependents, and delinquents, thus covering intellectual, biological, and cultural data. In some respects the findings appeared to show that the newer immigrants were equal to or sounder than the older stock; but in other respects, especially in feeble-mindedness, insanity, crime, epilepsy, tuberculosis, and deformity the newer immigrants fell below the older stock. In this way statistical reinforcement was pro-

[7] Garis, *op. cit.*, pp. 232 ff.
[8] *Ibid.*, pp. 236 ff., for a review of the critical literature, with citations.

vided for the growing conviction that the nations of northern and western Europe, popularly called "Nordic," supply immigrants superior in biological, mental, and cultural characteristics. Dr. Laughlin's report, like the declarations based on Army Intelligence Tests, was ably analyzed and criticized by other students of competence, and the implication that the "inadequacies of groups and races are innate" was badly shattered; but its influence on Congress was scarcely diminished by the adverse demonstrations and contentions.[9]

The European side of the cultural picture, sketched with reference to the nature of American nationality, was presented in a broad sweep by the lifelong student of labor and immigration, John R. Commons, in the following summation: "A line drawn across the Continent of Europe from northeast to south-west, separating the Scandinavian peninsula, the British Isles, Germany, and France from Russia, Austria-Hungary, Italy, and Turkey, separates countries not only of distinct races but also of distinct civilizations. It separates Protestant Europe from Catholic Europe; it separates countries of representative institutions and popular government from absolute monarchies; it separates lands where education is universal from lands where illiteracy predominates; it separates manufacturing countries, progressive agriculture, and skilled labor from primitive hand industries, backward agriculture, and unskilled labor; it separates an educated, thrifty peasantry from a peasantry scarcely one generation removed from serfdom; it separates Teutonic races from Latin, Slav, Semitic, and Mongolian races."[10]

The generalization was sweeping, but it represents a conception of Europe and of immigration which was all-pervading when the immigration measure of 1924 was up for consideration.

Out of these allegations, findings, facts, and sentiments, however "scientific," coupled with the steady pressure of organized labor, sprang the Immigration Act of 1924, which, with other laws, determines immigration in respect of American nationality. The broad outlines are clear, although the details

[9] Garis, *op. cit.*, pp. 239-251.
[10] *Races and Immigrants in America* (1908), p. 69.

are bewildering in complexity. First of all, the population of
the continental United States for the year 1920 was taken as
furnishing the racial criteria for selecting immigrants from
certain regions. This population (with some exceptions) was
divided into classes according to their respective "national
origins"—an impossible task, but it was done, in a way and
very roughly. On the basis of this classification an estimate
was made purporting to show the proportion which the number
in each national-origins class bore to the whole number of
inhabitants reported by the census in question. Then each of
the countries from which immigration was to be restricted
under the terms of the Act was assigned an annual quota.
This quota figure is the number bearing the same relation to
150,000—the total number of immigrants allotted to quota
countries—which the number of inhabitants of the particular
national origin in the United States bears to the total population of the United States as just indicated, with the exception
that no quota is to be less than one hundred. Thus the "balance" among the several white "races" composing American
nationality is to be preserved for the duration of the Act,
perhaps for all time.

    In the second place, the Act in operation accepts roughly the
line drawn by Professor Commons from northeastern to south-
western Europe, and provides for restricting the major portion
of European immigrants to the so-called "Nordic" nations.
For example, it favors the British Isles and Germany in particular, for these regions were given about two-thirds of the
total number of immigrants admissible from Europe under the
rule fixing the normal annual number at 153,714.

    In the third place, the Act of 1924 marked the culmination
of a long series of measures directed against immigration from
the Orient. It abrogated the Gentlemen's Agreement with
Japan and in effect added the Japanese to the Orientals already
excluded. Thus the gates of the country are now closed absolutely to persons from large specified regions of Asia and adja-
cent islands, including Chinese, Japanese, East Indians, Hin-
dus, and many other races and nationalities, with exceptions as
to officers, students, merchants, and certain other special
groups. In short, for the purposes of American nationality, an

invasion of Asiatics is now made impossible, and further restriction of immigration from the East is provided for in the measure offering conditional independence to the Philippine Islands, enacted in 1933, and revised in 1934.

Yet, in one respect, the Act of 1924 leaves open the doors for immigration not based upon the national origins composition of 1920. Entirely outside the quota system are immigrants born in Mexico, Cuba, Haiti, the Dominican Republic, the Canal Zone, or any independent country of Central or South America and their wives and unmarried children under eighteen years of age, as well as immigrants born in Canada and Newfoundland. In addition, immigrants from Hawaii and the Caribbean possessions of the United States are freely entitled to admission. When it is remembered that 759,269 Mexicans entered the United States between 1921 and 1931, the significance of these exceptions for the future of American nationality, if continued, becomes apparent.

On this point of unassimilable immigration there can be no uncertainty. Any class of employers in the United States that wishes to obtain or enlarge profits through the use of low-standard labor will press to keep the doors of immigration open to that kind of labor, even if it means flooding the communities concerned or the nation with races that cannot be readily assimilated. To this extent they are sacrificing the possibility of a coherent nation to their private interests. Moreover, where organized labor of the gentleman-craft type feels no competition from unorganized, casual labor, it will give little thought to the battle of the jungle that goes on at the bottom of the economic system. Whether the social composition of the American nation is such as to offer some prospect of long endurance is a matter of indifference to these seekers after individual and class gain.

No exact picture of the "racial" composition of American nationality as it is and may be in the near future can be drawn, especially as long as immigration from certain dependencies and the Caribbean remains undetermined. If, however, the findings of the Bureau of Census touching the national origins of the population in 1920 are to be accepted, then the white population as of 1920 includes about 40 per cent of British and

North Irish origin, 16 per cent of German origin, and 11 per cent of Irish Free State origin, with nationals of other sources in the following order of numerical importance: Canada, Poland, Italy, Sweden, Netherlands, France, Czechoslovakia, Russia, Norway, Mexico, and Switzerland (accounting for about 95 per cent of the total white population taken into the reckoning).[11] The meaning of these figures in precise racial terms, assuming that the word "racial" has definite connotations, must be left unsettled, in the very nature of things.

INSTITUTIONS AND CONCEPTIONS

When this American nationality as a social composition is brought under analysis, numerous elements appear. For convenience, though not philosophically, they may be classified as objective and subjective (1)—material conditions and social institutions on the one side and (2)—ideas, traditions, and conceptions on the other.[12]

In the first category there is the geographical setting associated with and involved in this nationality. The home of American nationality is a continental domain, with its material endowment stimulating and affording opportunity to the American people. This geographical setting forms an unbroken unity for the nation. The American nation has no powerful neighbors of another race or tongue on its immediate borders. It has no large enclaves occupied by other races, with kindred races just across the borders under other powerful governments, alien or of their own creation. Thus the geographical situs of American nationality is a unity, it supplies certain material stimuli and opportunities, and it is so placed as to foster few, if any, of the powerful passions of nationality which characterize European peoples. This is an objective situation concerning which there can be no doubt or difference of opinion.

Among the social institutions to be treated as objective

[11] *Recent Social Trends in the United States,* Vol. I, p. 20.

[12] For a remarkable consideration of objective institutions and relations and accompanying subjective conceptions and sensibilities, see the penetrating description of the old social order in Russia, as contrasted with that of other countries, in Trotsky, *History of the Russian Revolution,* Vol. I.

elements of nationality are many that differentiate America from European countries and give it a peculiar stamp. At the outset the negative side may be considered. There is in the United States no State Church, with common religious beliefs and sentiments and with a vested clerical interest bent on holding the population to a single cultural pattern. On the contrary, the church in the United States is a private affair; there are numerous sects; there is nothing approaching unanimity of faith. Less than fifty per cent of the people are recorded as members of churches and the variety of religious opinions prevents the establishment of a uniform religious pattern of thought and action. To intrude any religious question into a discussion of public policy is considered not only bad form, but also perilous to partisan policy. This tends to a universal secularization of politics and the elimination of disruptive religious conflicts.

That other distinctive European institution, a military caste founded on landed property, trained in the profession of arms and occupying an independent position, is also absent from American national life. As a republic the United States has no ruling family, such as the Bourbons, Hapsburgs, and Hohenzollerns, around which national traditions cling, which can be exploited for political purposes as forming a center of loyalties. American nationality is not, never has been, associated with a landed aristocracy in the European sense—a class devoted to the *politesse* of civilization, more or less interested in conceptions of *noblesse oblige* and public service, and paid for it.

For these and other reasons there is a high degree of intellectual homogeneity in American society. There are economic classes and sectional interests in the United States and numerous conflicts over class interests, but the lines between classes are not sharp, as often remarked by writers on American society. There is no permanent upper class as such definitely separated from the social body by legal rights, long traditions, and positive cultural distinctions. There is no consolidated proletariat of long standing, produced by generations of inbreeding in the congested quarters of the industrial cities. The United States has nothing that Amiel could call *le grand monde,*[13] or Marx could call a class-conscious proletariat, at all events on any considerable scale. From the traditional European point of view American society is classless, despite marked economic divisions and group conflicts. Such indeed has been the traditional American conception of American society. It is hardly going too far to say that, in theory, America has one class—the petty bourgeoisie—despite proletarian and plutocratic elements which cannot come under that classification, and that the American social ideal most widely expressed is the *embourgoisement* of the whole society—a universality of comfort, conveniences, security, leisure, standard possessions of food, clothing, and shelter.

The methods employed in the exploitation of the natural endowment of the United States have also given distinct characteristics to the institutions and sentiments of American nationality. On the industrial side, to be sure, the methods of capitalism have been dominant, but American capitalists— late arrivals on the scene of world history—have been more ruthless, changeful, adaptable, active, and imaginative than the European capitalists. If there has been more political corruption it may doubtless be attributed to the greater opportunities offered. The older generation of American capitalists sprang largely from the farming and working classes, and if, as the recent figures seem to show, the younger generation is more frequently recruited from the class itself, American capitalism is still capitalistic—untainted by the "refinements" of a landed aristocracy and without the ambition or the possibility of climbing into that level of culture. In other words, American capitalism has not been subdued in any respect to the long heritage of clerical and aristocratic pretensions and habits common to Europe. Few of the mercantile and family traditions which mark European society are to be found in its practice or spirit. If easily consolidated at any moment against labor or agriculture, its members are constantly engaged in internecine warfare, personal, corporate, and group.[14]

Even more distinct has been the agricultural phase of

[13] Matthew Arnold, *Essays in Criticism* (2nd Series), p. 326.
[14] C. W. Barron, *They Told Barron,* for abundant illustrations; Max Lowenthal, *The Investor Pays.*

American nationality. American agriculture has no feudal base; it has had slavery, tenantry, and farm hands, but no peasantry, with its good and evil aspects, no village solidarity such as is still to be found in France and Germany, for instance. It may be almost said with safety that American agriculture, during the past hundred years at least, has not been a settled way of life, but a life of land speculation and adventure, with the frontier ever beckoning—until about 1890. When machine industry destroyed the handicraft and artisan nucleus of village economy, and railways were thrust into every region, agriculture took on more capitalistic practices and spirit. In general, the American agriculturalist has not loved the soil as the European peasant loves it; he has been essentially a rationalist, buying and selling land or using it vigorously for productive purposes, with a view to personal gain in the capitalistic sense of the term. But while industrial capitalists combined in great corporations, farmers remained individualists despite their coöperative efforts and occasional uprisings in politics; their practices and thought were linked with those of the lower bourgeois rather than with the great industrialists of the upper ranges.

As everyone who is acquainted with the writings of Frederick Jackson Turner knows, the free land, the frontier, and the accompanying economy gave a certain bent to American nationality. In a large measure the spirit of American nationality arises from this source. As Turner says: "The Western wilds, from the Alleghenies to the Pacific, constituted the richest free gift that was ever spread out before civilized man. To the peasant and artisan of the Old World, bound by the chains of social class, as old as custom and as inevitable as fate, the West offered an exit into a free life and greater well-being among the bounties of nature, into the midst of resources that demanded manly exertion, and that gave in return the chance for indefinite ascent in the scale of social advance." Owing to the richness of the gains from agriculture and land speculation, millions of farmers rose above the subsistence level of the European peasantry and, while remaining on the land, took on or expressed the ideals of the urban bourgeois—universality of comfort, convenience, security, leisure, standard possessions of food, clothing, and shelter. Although religious as a rule, and devoted to various political ideals, American farmers have been rational and materialistic, with respect to the economic basis of social institutions and life.

American political institutions, objectively considered, likewise present certain characteristics of significance to national unity. Their framework includes in theory, and to a considerable extent in practice, the entire adult citizen population. Manhood suffrage, except for Negroes in certain states, has been so long established that memories of early restrictions have practically disappeared from the consciousness of the people. Indeed, although property limitations were once almost universal in the states, the wide distribution of property early gave the suffrage a broad base, and the successive extensions of the right to vote were never accompanied by the violent agitations and revolutionary actions which marked the advance of political emancipation in Europe and left deep scars in society. The struggle of women for the vote, though prolonged and more recent, was based on democratic traditions and the antagonisms engendered were quickly dissipated after victory.

With the exception noted, traces of exclusion and political subjection are seldom found in contemporary thought. On this basis American political institutions rest and are operated. From town, township, village, and county self-government through the state machinery to the federal system runs the principle of popular election, initiative, and participation, with a large degree of local autonomy in the lower ranges. In this way have been effected many fairly workable adjustments in the age-long conflict of centralism *versus* federalism, bureaucracy *versus* individual liberty and responsibility.

On the subjective side, American nationality finds expression in a number of traditions and emotional attitudes. They are correlated, of course, with the objective institutions briefly described above, have evolved with them, and have contributed to their development; yet they are ideas and forces to be reckoned with in formulating and applying any doctrine of national interest. Outstanding among them are traditions of human equality, of the worth and moral dignity of the individual, of equal right to participate in the benefits of civilization, of equality before the law, of toleration in religious and political matters, of freedom of person, press, and speech, and of the State as an agency of the people to be determined, changed, and used by them in the promotion of their interests. If there is much mythology in these conceptions, and glaring violations in practice, still there is rational and emotional content in them—a reality to which appeals are constantly made with evident effect in awakening and rallying popular support for proposed and adopted public policies. To these traditions Woodrow Wilson addressed himself in enlisting the nation in "the moral crusade" against the Central Powers in the World War. They condition the possibilities of future policies and furnish a dynamic for the development of policies. If the propagandist plays upon them, the statesman may make use of them. Indeed, to a certain extent, he is driven by the ideas and emotions that cluster around them.

Among the subjective factors of American nationality is one which is often characterized as especially distinctive, that is, belief in the desirability of change, in the idea of progress. The base of American civilization is not old; it is new. The whole structure has been erected in the course of three hundred years and its very erection has been a process of rapid change and development. There are living today American citizens who once talked with their fathers about their grandfathers who saw George Washington and other founders of the Republic, who knew the Republic as a group of states on the Atlantic seaboard. Within living memory have come the sweep to the Pacific, the construction of continental railways, the abolition of slavery, the closure of the frontier, and the uprush of great cities. Nowhere in the economic or intellectual life of America is there any foundation for the type of historic conservatism exemplified in the landed aristocracy of England and Prussia during the eighteenth century and celebrated in the writings of Edmund Burke, especially his *Reflections on the French Revolution*.[15] In the United States both economy and thought about economy have been fluid, and the idea of

[15] Karl Mannheim, *Ideologie und Utopie*, pp. 79 ff.

continuous change in the ways and means of life gives an extraordinary elasticity to American politics.

American mentality is also to a high degree mechanical in interest. Handicrafts and traditional agriculture were early uprooted by industrialism, and ingenuity was turned to the invention of machines and, what is more significant for nationality, to their extensive operation in factory, field, shop, and kitchen. American men and women by the millions drive automobiles, airplanes and tractors, wash, cook and sweep with electricity—make machines perform an infinite variety of work. This love of and preoccupation with machines has been the characteristic most often noted, perhaps, by European visitors and most severely criticized, especially by literary artists concerned with preserving "the refinements of culture" as by-products of stratified society, that is, the traditions of feudalism, bureaucracy, handicrafts, and domestic servitude, for example. However reprehensible in the eyes of critics, the mechanical aspect of American mentality is a stubborn fact, an inescapable phase of American nationality, significant for the organization and development of economy and for the formulation of public policies. At all events, it would seem to be an insuperable obstacle to a return to primitive economy and ways of life, to any possible restoration of the nation to a provincial status as a purveyor of raw materials for the industrial nations of Europe.

Upshot and Policy

In drawing conclusions from the facts presented above, certain cautions must be kept in mind. We cannot know "all the facts" that have been or are included under the head of nationality. Still less can we be sure of what is becoming, since that lies buried in the thought and emotions of this generation, the rising generation, and generations yet unborn. It was probably for this reason that Henry Adams said somewhere that nothing is more dubious than an opinion founded on facts—a profound truth within a paradox. In seeking to determine what has been and is, we can only select facts which seem relevant to the problem in hand, that is, significant for the formulation of conclusions. When we come to drafting conclusions we inevitably mingle thought with the operation. We posit criteria and ends which we deem desirable, make an assertion of will to believe and act. The force of that determination, its effectiveness in making history, depends upon the degree of accurate prediction contained within it and its influence on the course of affairs. Its moral validity in relation to an assumed absolute is a separate problem in itself—an issue not germane to the method of treatment here adopted. With this definite understanding we may proceed to a consideration of nationality as a subject of interest and the policy required by the conclusions drawn by the process admitted above.

Given American society, without the cement of a long-established monarchy, State Church, or fixed landed aristocracy, with fluid classes, with mechanical propensities, with traditions and practices of political equality and self-government, and assuming from the trend of things (above, p. 24) that the business of government and economy will become more complicated, it follows that there must be great cohesion among the population and an enlarging capacity for coöperation. Common conceptions of rights and wrongs must be further developed, if American society is to endure and make the most of its opportunities within its natural setting. This involves safeguards against increasing sharp color distinctions in racial composition; the country has enough distinctions of this character now, and is unable to resolve them without great friction and moral injury to all parties concerned. If it be said that these racial struggles within the United States are to be ascribed entirely to the willfulness and passions of the white population, or of a white class, still the fact stands that these antagonisms do exist, and certainly no national or humane interest can be served by intensifying and augmenting them. Lynching, persecution, and hatred cannot resolve such conflicts, and wisdom will avoid increasing their frictions and distractions.

In terms of policy this implies no more conquest of territory occupied by races which are not in fact readily assimilable to the population of the United States, for the idea of governing subject races and excluding them from the continental domain is contrary to the traditions and practices of the American heritage. So far as past errors are concerned, they may be undone by granting independence to the Philippines and Porto Rico, with immigration restrictions against them. In addition, the principle laid down involves the application of the quota or percentage rule to immigrants from the entire Caribbean region and from Latin America, as well as Europe. Nothing stands in the way of this extension of rule except the demand of planters, farmers, railways, and industrial enterprise for cheap labor to be exploited in town and country. The ruthless manner in which thousands of Mexican laborers and their families were deported to Mexico after the crash of 1929 indicates the spirit which has animated those who insist on keeping this flood gate open, to the long-run injury of the immigrants themselves.

So far as international law and comity are concerned, there can be no question about the right of the United States to regulate and restrict immigration. All other countries are governed in this relation by their conceptions of national interest, not by principles of universal philanthropy. They do not proclaim themselves asylums for the poor and oppressed of all lands. Within historic times they have not had enormous natural and agricultural resources to open up and exploit, or land speculators and capitalists eager for large bodies of free laborers and peasants to serve their purposes. Other nations control immigration by laws and administrative measures adapted to their own needs, desires, and economic requirements. Most Western countries, except in South America, exclude Oriental laborers in theory or practice, although none of them has, for reasons to be accounted for historically, adopted the American principle of selection according to national origins. All apply restrictive principles of one kind or another—physiological, political, and economic—and a few go so far as to permit immigration officials to suspend all immigration for economic reasons. Even within the British Empire, the dominions, after a long struggle, have secured the right to control immigration from other parts of the imperial aggregation.

While the right of each nation to regulate and restrict immigration is well recognized in international law and comity, the exercise of the right should be governed by discretion, a respect for other nationalities, a determination to avoid unnecessary complications, and considerations of national defense. Interests should be balanced and the greater never sacrificed for the lesser. The easy generalizations of the "Nordic" fanatics about the innate "inferiority" of other races will be utterly discarded by statesmen who have any sense for realities or the reports of scientific inquiries. While these fanatics cannot and should not be denied the right of free speech, statecraft should reject and repudiate their assertions and dogmas as unverified and as adding complications to international relations already vexed with too many complications. Equally to be rejected are the alleged disclosures of intelligence testers and specialists in eugenics which purport to show that certain deficiencies and inadequacies—appearing in defectives, dependents, and delinquents—arise from the innate characteristics of certain races. Such alleged disclosures ignore the infinite complications of economic, social, and cultural relations and make pretensions to validity which are utterly untenable. Psychologists and eugenicists, as such, are not competent to deal with these cultural situations and movements. Any race that is superior in fact may be content with the fact and refrain from announcing it; a race which is inferior does not become superior by making claims, however vociferous.

The issues, therefore, may be stated in the following form: By universal consent the United States has the legal right to regulate or abolish immigration with respect to national interest. No foreign government can or does claim that, under international law and comity, the United States is bound to open its gates to an unlimited influx of people from any or all countries. As a matter of physical limitations it is impossible for the United States to take care of the pullulating surplus populations of the earth and, according to the more recent conclusions of specialists in population movements, an absolutely unrestricted admission of immigrants by the United States would not give permanent relief to any overcrowded country. Finally, the United States has determined upon a policy of drastic restriction and there is no prospect of any relaxing of the bans already imposed.

Yet it is evident that the form now given to these bans is not designed with reference to a socially efficient nation. To say that an Englishman, a German, or a Swede as such will contribute more to effective coöperation in American society than a Macedonian, a Slovenian, a Turk, or a Japanese is to utter an obvious falsehood. Moreover, the ways in which Mussolini, Hitler, and other governing persons in Europe interfere with their co-nationals in the United States and use the latter for *their purposes* are well known and call for no comment here. It may be, indeed, that the addition of more "Nordics" under the present immigration law will actually contribute to the overthrow of the Government of the United States. In some coming time of international crisis the sway of foreign governments over their nationals in the United States may incline public decisions in directions absolutely contrary to national interest. Considered in the large, therefore, the so-called "racial bans" bear no sure relation to the great issue of national coherence and national security.

Given this situation, the problem of policy is one of effecting a reduction of immigration without wounding unnecessarily the susceptibilities of any nation or stirring up enmities perilous to national security. How can this be done? Various methods present themselves, and it may be assumed that ingenuity in social invention has not been exhausted. All immigration from all countries might be abolished or suspended for a term of years, with certain exceptions for political and religious exiles. Immigration might be limited to the parents, minor children, husbands, and wives of persons, citizens and aliens, now domiciled in the United States. The base line for determining national origins and applying a quota or percentage principle to new immigration might be fixed at 1890, or the percentage fixed at a point so low as to reduce all immigration to a vanishing point. Such a rule would permit the abrogation of the measures of exclusion directed against particular nationalities and make the American immigration law apply without discrimination to all independent countries, thus relaxing all tensions involving grave considerations of national defense.

That drastic restrictions of this character would awaken great opposition among foreigners and foreign-born in the United States and their co-nationals abroad cannot be denied, but if their will, founded on consideration for their nationalities as against American nationality, is to prevail, then the latter has no independent existence and is subject to the interests and passions of others. In that case the very conception of national interest disappears or is left to the determination of alien nationalities in the vital matter of population, with all its biological and cultural implications. In short, some national interest is to prevail—that of the United States or that of foreign countries—for the issue is not one of virtue or absolute rights. If it is a question of American national interest against the interests of other nations, there can scarcely be any doubt as to the outcome in the long run. The former will prevail, and should prevail, unless we are to assume that nations capable of organizing government and economy have no function to perform in the world.

This leads to the crux of the matter. The proposed restrictive policy can be attacked effectively only on grounds of universal ethics, such as a Christian doctrine or an international communism which envisages the destruction of national states or organizations. The policy does run counter to the assumption that all peoples of all races, colors, and conditions are brothers, to be treated as brothers, and to be admitted to every fellowship even at a cost of unlimited sacrifice. That the nations which profess universal ethics do not practice it, individually or collectively, does not destroy the conception or do away with belief in it on the part of large groups of people. But the exponents of universal ethics cannot show that freedom of migration is calculated to increase the area of the good life and well-being; on the contrary, they confront the possibility, rather the probability, that the practice of their faith would defeat its own end by enlarging the areas of low-standard life and human misery. Indeed, the degree of probability is so high as to amount to a practical certainty that, were the doors of the United States flung wide open, the immigration of all races, with the aid of rapid transportation and steamship-company pressure, would rise to a figure ranging from one to two millions a year, with the surplus populations of China, India, the East Indies, and Japan in the lead. In view of the fecundity of Orientals and the growth of their numbers during the past century, it is not fantastic to assume that in fifty years the population of the United States might amount to three or four hundred millions.

No doubt such estimates are hazardous, for, despite years of investigation, little is known of the conditions which make for increases or decreases in populations. But the enormous growth of populations in the West and the Orient during the past century, for which extensive, if far from satisfactory, records exist, cannot be denied; and there is ground for believing in the existence of potentials for an enormous growth in the future. Where the probabilities are so evident it certainly would not be in the national interest to disregard them and to take the perilous risk that something might happen to counteract known tendencies. Could an American nation, with three or four hundred millions of all races and colors, govern itself, be sure of efficient coöperation among its members, maintain an organized economy capable of sustaining such members, or, if regarded as a mere unit of a world economy without national implications, coöperate effectively with other units in a world economy of units? If anything is known, if reason is not a complete delusion, if the facts amassed by science and empiricism are not delusions also, then the answer is a negative, an emphatic negative.

Accordingly, American interest repudiates the philosophy and implications of universal ethics as applied to immigration and to the development of American nationality. The assumption for policy is, therefore, that the population composition as fixed upon the basis of national origins for 1920 at least, restricted in other directions, is to form the substance of American nationality now and in development. Existing race mixtures, language, traditions, and consensus of community feeling are not to be seriously altered by any enormous influx of other races, bringing different languages, traditions, and community feelings. This is to be the American nationality around which issues of interest in international relations will revolve. With immigration reduced and the rate of increase in population declining, it is probable that the population of the United States will become fairly stable within two or three generations, that assimilation will advance far more rapidly as new immigration is cut to the minimum, and that the racial combination so formed will be the cultural or social substance with which American statecraft must deal when formulating domestic and foreign policies.

§

1. The American nation is republican, secular, and essentially economic in character.

2. It is not feudal, clerical, monarchical, or "spiritual" in the European sense of that term; that is, it does not sustain an aristocratic and clerical élite engaged in the enjoyment of its own social and intellectual virtues and standards.

3. The American nation is not and cannot be racial, as race is conceived in Nordic fantasies, although composed largely of Northern European stocks.

4. American nationality has no mythological traditions, rooted in a distant past, but is hard, factual, and mechanical and has been built up in the full light of recorded history.

5. It has distinct political and economic ways of life due to its natural endowment and the process of settlement and expansion; and these ways of life give it peculiar characteristics, objective and subjective.

6. Social cohesiveness and capacity to coöperate on a large scale are indispensable to political and economic management on a large scale.

7. Current immigration policy is based on a fixation of racial composition as disclosed by the "national origins" principle.

8. An extension of that principle in some form to all areas not yet covered by it is desirable.

9. National policy, having regard for defense and the susceptibilities of other nations, will modify immigration legislation so as to eliminate avowed discriminations against other

nationalities, while retaining full power to preserve a cohesive balance of social composition.

10. To assume that other countries have a "right" to dictate immigration legislation to the United States is to assume that their respective national interests are supreme over the national interest of the United States, and is to ignore their practices in controlling their own immigration.

11. Policy will lend no countenance to racial fanatics who speak with pontifical assurance about the "superiority" of this race and the "inferiority" of that race. It will reject the alleged findings of intelligence testers and eugenicists respecting the "innate capacities" of races, as ignoring fundamental economic and cultural considerations, as not proved, and as not susceptible of scientific verification.

12. The principle for the guidance of policy in matters of immigration is the necessity for maintaining social cohesiveness and coöperative capacity, which are indispensable to political and economic management on a national scale.

CHAPTER X

NATIONAL ECONOMY AS INTEREST

FROM American *nationality* as a reality in the field of statecraft, as a cohesive organization of a portion of humanity for the operation of a regional economy, as a society to be protected against predatory and undermining forces, as potentiality that may more closely approximate the ideal, we turn to the best *interest* of this nation, considered as a conception controlling policy in connection with the quest for a resolution of the dilemma in economy and thought. What is the supreme interest of American society, as distinguished from a mere aggregation of special interests often conflicting in nature and inimical to national security?

THE MAXIM OF SECURITY AND ITS IMPLICATIONS

The answer offered here to this question is an assertion of a value: The supreme interest of the United States is the creation and maintenance of a high standard of life for all its people and ways of industry conducive to the promotion of individual and social virtues *within the frame of national security.* The continuance of American society, the establishment of ways of industry and life calculated to assure that continuance, and the orderly production and distribution of material goods, subject to the paramountcy of national security—such are the assumptions on which all that follows is based. Thus the problem is treated as one in ethics, esthetics, domestic arts, and engineering rationality; and the solution can be more or less accurately visualized as objective things, conduct, and relationships.

1. In this statement, national security, considered in terms of stable economy maintained at a high operating tempo and of appropriate defense, becomes the supreme and controlling consideration in national interest, and provides the positive

guidance to policy hitherto lacking in historic formulations. No assumption is made respecting the possibilities of creating some ideal world order (above, p 112) in which nations will cease to menace their neighbors by making drastic alterations in their domestic institutions and practices. But the assumption is made that there is little use in attempting to create and maintain a high standard of life and ways of industry conducive to virtue in the United States, if security is ignored and military defense against predatory nations is neglected. National security, therefore, comes first.

Strange as it may seem to superficial students of Adam Smith, security occupies the supreme position in the system of that great thinker (above, p. 162). Despite his emphasis on the utmost freedom in international commerce, involving dependence on its vicissitudes, he placed security above opulence, and favored any interference with the "natural course" of trade required by security. He also realized that this fundamental consideration is not to be treated in terms of mere physical defense—armies, navies, and war machines—for economy and defense are parts of the same thing. Economy itself depends upon defense to prevent disruptions of its current operations; and defense relies upon economy for the production of the instrumentalities of defense.

2. In terms of economy, national interest involves stability and standard of life deliberately adjusted to each other in a long time perspective. Conceivably a higher than fixed normal standard of life might be obtained for a given period by sacrificing security and stability, by incurring great risks beyond the power of military defense, with the almost certain knowledge of coming disruptions, dislocations, and impoverishment —the gambler's conception of the world and ways of operating in it. But here the assumption is made that *stability* in economy is a good in itself and conducive to those individual and social virtues necessary to the continuance of society. And emphasis on this element of stability carries with it certain implications with respect to foreign trade as a part of the process by which security and the standard of life are maintained. Inevitably it involves the utmost emancipation from dependence upon the economies, rivalries, revolutions, and wars of

other nations. It involves as a corollary the utmost emancipation from dependence upon the course of international exchange, which is, in brutal fact, subject to constant vicissitudes and disruptions, spreading havoc over great regions of the earth. No prudent family deliberately places any large part of its property and economic concerns in the hands of distant and quarrelsome strangers who periodically set their houses on fire; and, as Adam Smith would say, this maxim of prudence for the individual is applicable to the nation.

3. Since standard of life occupies a central position in the conception of national interest, along with security and stability, another proposition emerges: The supreme purpose of such foreign trade as may be carried on is the acquisition of imports deemed requisite to the posited standard of life.

This proposition means a reversal of the conception which lays emphasis on the export of goods immediately profitable to the private interests concerned, with little or no reference to the depletion of American resources and to the import of goods and services necessary to pay for exports in the long run. To illustrate the case concretely: since opulence consists of the possession of valuable goods, the United States is not necessarily enriched by allowing private interests to pump petroleum out of the ground, sell it abroad at low competitive levels, and exhaust this resource; the export of petroleum from the United States can only be conceived as enriching the United States when it is the one best means of securing imports which add to the opulence of the United States. And trade considered as the best means of securing imports requisite to the national standard of life is at the opposite pole from trade conceived as export profitable to private interests—trade forced upon other nations by high pressure salesmanship, lavish capital export, and the use of State engines, ranging from diplomacy to war.

4. In connection with security and stability, the following maxim also appears self-evident: No prudent man deliberately pursues operations likely to raise quarrels with his neighbors in which he is certain to be defeated and ruined by an overwhelming weight of men and metal. It is true that under the feudal code, an individual may feel bound to keep in a given

course although it will lead to a duel in which he is likely to be killed by his opponent; but a statesman, being an agent for the nation, not a principal himself, will not deliberately choose and persist in a line of action that even incurs the risk of bringing disaster upon his country.

The applications of this maxim of prudence are clear. The promotion of foreign trade by the engines of State, as a good in itself or as a profit-making enterprise, inevitably thrusts American private interests into the heart of other nations, spreads them to all parts of the world, and provokes rivalries and conflicts in widely scattered places which cannot be defended by the American Navy as now constituted or by any American navy that opposing governments or combinations of governments will permit the United States to build before striking—as Great Britain, France, Japan, and the United States struck at Germany. The solution of this problem is not to be found, therefore, as many naval bureaucrats insist, in more and more naval construction, but in the withdrawal of public support from private interests engaged in making outward thrusts perilous to security, and in the public control of foreign trading operations, in the interest of security.

Hence the imperative: If a nation has, and depends upon for its standard of life, vital interests outside its jurisdiction, which it cannot dominate and defend, then it does not and cannot possess economic security and stability. To that degree it suffers from economic weakness and is constantly in economic peril amid the endless diplomatic and military conflicts involving those interests. Prudence, therefore, calls for policies and practices which restrain and minimize indefensible commitments in distant places, for the United States cannot possibly expect to gain the unquestioned naval supremacy requisite to the effective defense of all outward thrusts of private economic interests.

5. The effort to realize security, accompanied by the transformation of foreign trade into its true function of increasing national opulence, involves a fifth proposition: The security and opulence of the United States can best be attained by the most efficient use of the material endowment of the nation and its technical arts; and, as a corollary, the least possible depend-

ence on foreign imports. This conception does not mean, as
hasty critics may declare, an absolute elimination of foreign trade. It means the maximum employment of the national
resources and skills and a minimum reliance upon international
trade, constantly in oscillation. Stress must be laid upon another point: we are not here discussing a universal policy for
all nations, but a policy for the United States which, owing to
the diversification of its resources and talents, could maintain
a high standard of life with all imports cut off—a thing not
contemplated in this chapter. And it must be added: it is
probable that under a régime of economic security and efficient industry, the foreign trade of the United States would
materially increase, for the full use of the American endowment would create a national buying power of enormous pro-
portions and a corresponding demand for foreign commodities
of peculiar distinction; but the imports thus stimulated and
permitted would be, in the main, luxuries and objects of appreciation and enjoyment not indispensable to the security and
basic standard of life of the American people.

When the problem of national interest in terms of economy
and security has been stated and a solution offered by ethics,
esthetics, domestic arts, and engineering rationality, two issues
still remain unsettled. Are American intelligence and virtue
equal to the task of realization? Will the maxim of prudence
be observed? If the answer to the first question is in the negative, the upshot will be an acknowledgment of defeat—not a
demonstration that the verbal delusions which have dominated
thought and policy in the past are valid. The point of possible
realization is debatable, of course, but it must be conceded that
contemporary knowledge of the domestic arts and of the physical requirements of human life is immense; that engineering
is the one science pertaining to human affairs which may be
fairly called exact; and that our ethical and esthetic heritage
carries with it evidence of great achievements potential within
the nation. Having been precipitated into a crisis by pursuing
one course, the nation may try another—a new course not
dictated by the false assumptions of the past out of which the
dilemma has arisen.

Will the maxim of prudence required by respect for security, stability, and standard of life prevail? There is no way of knowing. It is possible, indeed highly probable, that it will not immediately prevail. Given the power of private interests which make use of government promotion, the strength of army and navy bureaucracies and their associated private interests throughout the world, the ease with which newspapers and masses are mobilized for any kind of quarrel or war, and the great effort of intelligence and will required for the realization of security and stability, it is possible that Western nations, including the United States, will repeat old methods and routines until they destroy the very basis of civilization; but American statecraft, American intelligence, cannot approve this course, cannot refuse to make efforts to avoid it, without betraying national interest considered as commonweal, without moral and intellectual stultification.

CLEARING THE CLIMATE OF INHERITED OPINION

Owing to its intrinsic nature, the problem of national interest, expressed in terms of security,[1] stability, standard of life, and ways of industry conducive to individual and social virtues, cannot be stated or solved by the so-called social sciences, by mere research into the records of past activities, or by statistical and empirical studies of occurrences which have eventuated in the defeat from which society is seeking to extricate itself. Nor can the problem be stated and solved by reference to the ideologies developed in defense, offense, and justification during past conflicts of special interests, such as capital, labor, and agriculture, or their subdivisions. This seems to be a truism, for the reason that the problem and its solution imply the creation of a configuration of ideas and interests containing new elements to be summoned into being by thought and effort—elements differing, of necessity, from those of the past.

Therefore, the first step in proceeding to a consideration of national security conceived as economy is negative in character. It means clearing the intellectual atmosphere, emancipat-

---

[1] Although economic and military security are parts of the same thing, they are separated here for the purposes of convenience in treatment. Military defense is considered in the following chapter.

ing the mind from the clichés and tyrannical phrases of traditional economics, politics, sociology, and international diplomacy. The sweep must be clean, positive, and uncompromising, for not one of these so-called disciplines begins by positing a good life for the American nation defined in terms of producers' goods, permanent improvements, commodities, food, clothing, shelter, ways of industry, and economic institutions, and then proceeds resolutely, with the aid of applied science, to inquire into the best means of attaining the asserted ends. These alleged systems of thought and their tyrannical maxims must, accordingly, be put firmly aside in the quest for national security, and an entirely new approach made to the problem and its solution.

Equally necessary at the outset is a clean sweep of the maxims and verbiage of dominant practice. For more than three hundred years human energies and practical thought have been concentrated with increasing force on the selling of goods at a profit, as distinguished from the production, exchange, and consumption of useful, pleasurable, and beautiful goods in ways of life and labor conducive to virtue—the kind of virtue that is absolutely indispensable to the maintenance and continuance of a strong, cohesive, and secure society. Untold millions of men and women have been educated in the art of "making" money, of "drumming" and selling, as the supreme art of life as well as a way to personal riches; for almost two hundred years agriculture in the United States has been, in a large measure, a form of land speculation rather than a good way of life; and the governments of Western nations have been transformed into pushing and shoving agencies of salesmanship, with armies and navies to support their assertions of power. To this tyrannical conception of salesmanship, systems of education have been subjected and millions of the youth of the land have been trained in "the game" of selling and its associated operations. So far has this habit gone that even some who call themselves Christians are brazen enough to speak of "selling" the religion of Jesus to the multitude.

With respect to the international aspects of security, the same preliminary process of discarding maxims and ideologies created and employed by special interests—private and bureaucratic—is required by the nature of the problem before us. Fragments of thought, ideas, slogans, and catchwords, derived from classical, imperialist, and communist economics, must be stripped of their pretensions as alleged necessities and revealed in their true nature as the rationalizations and defense mechanisms of particular situations in the past projected into the present and future—class, national, and regional. Above all needs is emancipation from intellectual bondage to that form of international trade policy once conceived in the interest of the British manufacturing classes near the middle of the nineteenth century, known under various names but most commonly as "free international exchange"—a policy taken over by numerous economists and many communists as correctly representing some eternal and universal reality (above, p. 86).

AN EXPLORATION OF THE ECONOMY
OF NATIONAL SECURITY

With the intellectual climate cleared by the removal of historical assumptions and inappropriate traditions, the way is prepared for an examination of the economic part of the proposition (p. 210): The supreme national interest is the creation and maintenance of a high standard of life and ways of industry conducive to the promotion of individual and social virtues. This is, to repeat, a problem in ethics, esthetics, the domestic arts, and engineering rationality. It presents a simple, direct question: What consumers' and capital goods are necessary to overcome the crisis apparent in the poverty, misery, and insecurity all about us, and what are the resources and capacities of the American people for supplying these goods in the desired varieties and quantities?

It thus becomes the duty of the domestic arts, guided by ethics and esthetics, to disclose the physical requirements of a high standard of life in terms of food, clothing, shelter, comforts, and conveniences. This disclosure will reveal the needs of the nation, which must be supplied, if the crisis is to be overcome. Besides showing the material things needed, the report of the domestic arts will be accompanied by architects' designs of houses, homesteads, multiple-dwellings, city plans, and rural-region developments. It will include specifications for the diversified commodities and structures requisite to the standard of life, realistically conceived and presented statistically and graphically.[2] The cost of making such a report would probably not exceed the expenditure for a single battleship (of dubious utility for any war) or a political campaign between Tweedledee and Tweedledum.

At once it will be said, no doubt, that a standard of life is something vague, intangible, and fluctuating, that consumer psychology is utterly fickle, and that a standard-of-life budget is beyond the reach of hard and factual determination. This contention has merits. Even if it be admitted that the fickleness of consumer psychology is largely due to style changes feverishly introduced by private interests in the rush for quick and large profits, there are variables and intangibles in the standard-of-life area, which are beyond fixation for long periods. But granting all this, there are also invariables and tangibles within this area, and an effort to establish a national standard-of-life budget would start with fundamentals of food, clothing, and shelter, allowing for wide varieties of substance and taste, and then proceed to a consideration of objects of enjoyment and appreciation. For the overwhelming majority of American people the fundamentals are now poignant needs, inadequately supplied, where supplied at all. And domestic science even in its present stage of development, with its present knowledge, could present a fairly accurate standard-of-life budget for the nation—a composite budget for families, institutions, and individuals.

With the picture of national requirements in terms of food, clothing, and shelter prepared, engineering rationality will proceed to an analysis of the material resources of the United States and the powers of its technical arts, for the purpose of determining the extent to which American industry and agriculture can supply the stipulated requirements. Thus the domestic arts, aided by ethics and esthetics, will furnish specifications, and engineering rationality will provide information bearing on fulfillment.

[2] For a more detailed consideration, see Chapter XIII below.

When the standard-of-life budget for the nation has been prepared and engineering rationality has reported on the potentials of American industry, a balance sheet can be struck. Then it will be possible to determine with some exactness the requirements of the United States in the form of imports for the pre-established standard of life for the American nation. Then it will be possible to discuss the nature of foreign trade with reference to American needs as distinguished from the alleged intrinsic virtues and the profits of such trade.

Unfortunately for this exploration of engineering rationality necessary to the reduction of general policy to concrete terms, the scientific surveys and statistical materials now available are far from adequate. Some appropriate data have been assembled *for other purposes;* but it is not yet possible to answer from exact knowledge two questions of grand policy: What commodities can the United States produce efficiently in an abundance for domestic needs as measured by a high standard of national life? What commodities must the United States import to fill the gaps left by domestic production and in what quantities?

It is true that valuable surveys of national resources are at hand and since they are fairly objective in nature they can be readily employed by engineering rationality. But the resources of American technical arts, actual and potential, have never been minutely examined and are known in part only. Moreover, the statistics of production and foreign trade, though voluminous, are inadequate for the purposes here assumed and must be used with extreme caution besides. Unlike metallurgical statistics they do not represent natural and external facts, but, in a large measure, reflect results of past commercial *policies,* and are usually collected at the behest of, or with reference to, the demands of special interests concerned with raising or lowering the tariff. They show what has been done under given policies, not what can be done under other policies. Private compilations of production and foreign trade statistics must also be used with caution because they are generally taken from government sources, characterized above, and reflect in organization various ideologies of economics. Yes, despite these difficulties, engineering rationality must proceed to the collection, computation, and tabulation of the data required by the *purpose posited,* if national interest is to be transformed into public interest.

On the engineering side, the difficulties of making such a statistical and descriptive survey of American resources and technical arts are no doubt perplexing and admit of no easy disposal. What science and invention will and can do it is impossible to forecast with all-inclusive exactness. The national requirements of today may not be the same tomorrow. The degree of dependence upon foreign countries for raw materials and manufactured commodities changes with the progress of science and invention. There was a time, for example, when the iron industry in the United States did not need manganese; now this substance is fundamental and large quantities of it must be imported. The self-sufficiency of one day becomes dependence the next. Again, one generation of Americans relies heavily upon the importation of Chilean nitrate; the next generation, owing to science and invention, may declare its independence of the foreign market. In 1900 the outlook for copper ore reserves "was based on a requirement of five per cent metal content, but ten years later engineering advances brought into our reserves ore carrying only two per cent." [3]

Hence it may be argued that science and invention are unfathomable in their potentialities and that a description of national resources and technical arts is impossible. This may be taken to imply that the nation having once surrendered to blind acquisitive instincts and about to engage in a quest for control must now surrender to the demiurge of technology. All is afloat because no one can tell what will issue from the workshop or research laboratory. It is useless to formulate policies and make plans today because they may be destroyed to-

[3] George Otis Smith, *International Conciliation,* January, 1927, p. 9. It is the fashion of some "economic geologists" to treat varieties and quantities of imports as inexorable, whereas they are, in a large measure, the results of policy. For example, in the quest for profits, certain American manufacturers engage in exporting need certain raw material imports for the purpose of meeting competition in foreign markets. If it is inexorably in the national interest for American steel manufacturers to sell steel to Japan for use in constructing war vessels which may be employed against the United States, then the importation of manganese in given quantities is also inexorable. All hangs on the "if."

morrow by a chemist or engineer. Purposes must be dominated by hazard. The nation must stand paralyzed and hungry in the presence of the unknown potentialities of the microscope and test tube.

The truth of the major premise may be accepted without adopting the counsels of despair. The material resources and technical arts of the United States cannot be mathematically determined once and for all; and as Erich Zimmermann has precisely stated the case, it is impossible to present a picture of the resources of the United States until we have determined the kind of nation we want to create—made its standard-of-life budget. But enough can be known about the present resources and technical arts to make useful, if not absolute, computations respecting the amount and variety of commodities which can be produced efficiently in the United States. If statecraft waits for finality it becomes utopian and hence incompetent for its tasks. Furthermore technology can be made the servant of public purposes as well as of private interests and can be deliberately employed in discovering and inventing commodities calculated to increase the independence and security of the United States.

Although this is not the place to indicate more minutely, were the data available, the nature of the standard-of-life budget for the nation or the probable findings of engineering rationality with respect to national capacities to supply national needs, it is pertinent to say that enough is now known to support the assertion that a high standard of life for the American people is possible, if all imports of foreign commodities were cut off. To be sure, no mathematical demonstration is now possible, but partial findings of engineers sustain the contention. Moreover, actual experiences in American economic life, open to common-sense observation, afford proof of possibilities.

A single citation taken from the historical records of a single family may be used to illustrate, if not establish, the proposition. This family came to America in colonial times and began its career amid the primitive conditions then prevailing. By 1830 there were many descendants. All of them were farmers and artisans and owned homesteads of fair size. With agriculture they combined the crafts of shop and household. One of the men was a hatter, another was a tanner, a third was a smith and carriage maker, a fourth was a wood and metal worker who made spinning wheels, looms, barrels, furniture, and utensils, and a fifth was a distiller of brandy. The women of the household were equally versatile and skilled in the domestic arts—spinners, weavers, dyers, and conservers of foodstuffs; they made blankets, coverlets, sheets, rugs, and clothing, using wool, cotton, and flax, some of which, after the lapse of a century, are still in use!

Of food stuffs, this community of families produced wheat, rye, oats, and barley, chickens, ducks, geese, turkeys, pork, and beef, honey and sorghum molasses, cherries, peaches, plums, apples, raspberries, blackberries, and strawberries, potatoes, cabbage, peas, lettuce, onions, rhubarb, parsnips, turnips, melons, pumpkins, and squashes, pure wines and brandy. Wool, cotton, and linen supplied clothing, carpets, and bedding. Fuel came from the forests. Houses, all good and substantial, were made of brick and wood, the materials for which came from the farms. The only articles which the community required for a high standard of physical life were wrought iron, glass, and salt, with tea and coffee as luxuries. Furniture, hats, tools, and implements were made in the farm shops. The community supported an academy, housed in a building made of brick and wood supplied from forest and field and erected by community labor.

In colonial times and the early days of the Republic this community had no schools, but all members could read and write. All the branches of the family had books. In the middle years of the nineteenth century they received periodically the catalogues of booksellers from New York and Philadelphia and bought books with discrimination, if sparingly. The more intellectually alert among the family were acquainted with the main currents of thought then running throughout the Western world—religious, political, and scientific. None was rich; none was poor. No member of the community was ever uncertain as to possessing all the food, clothing, and shelter necessary for a comfortable life. All, men and women alike, were artisans and, judging by their surviving handicraft products, possessed an artistic skill which found joyful expression. This was not complete community autarchy, to be sure; such a thing is largely a fiction; but it was a high degree of self-sufficiency.

It is a matter of incontestable historical fact that these families had, largely as a result of their own labor without the boasted advantages of contemporary technology or foreign trade, an abundance and variety of food stuffs far beyond the budget of the overwhelming majority of American farming and laboring families today and they enjoyed a continuing security in economy vouchsafed to none of the one-crop farmers and industrial workers in the contemporary order of things, with its enormous technical resources. Furthermore the material conditions which made possible this type of individual, family, and community life still exist on a huge scale in the United States. In addition, science and invention have supplied new materials, products, and powers which are bewildering in variety and extent. When the whole area of the country is taken in view, with its variety of climate, soil, resources, products, and technical arts, it can be safely stated that a high standard of life for all families in the United States can be maintained, without any foreign imports whatever.

This is not to be taken to mean that, given the present set-up of American industry and enterprise, complete economic autonomy is possible, but that a high standard of life is attainable here and now. Nor does it mean that autonomy is desirable. It is simply the irreducible fact from which the quest for a policy founded on utmost security may proceed. Like other findings in economy it dictates nothing except to those who have the purpose, will, and power to make use of it.

Starting from the premise that security is the supreme national interest and given a balance sheet of productive potentialities on one side and consumer needs on the other, the next step is the adoption of means and policies calculated to keep the productive mechanism of the United States running at a high and even tempo. This leads into the very crux of the dilemma. It involves a large increase in the buying and consuming power of the American people and the elimination of the surpluses, real and so called, which cannot be sold at home or abroad. It means a flat rejection of the life and death formula offered to statecraft by exponents of imperialism, *laissez faire,* capitalism, and communism, namely, that, unless "surpluses" can be sold abroad or huge international commerce is kept going, the nation must sink to a low level of living, despite its enormous resources and unexcelled technical arts.

It substitutes for this formula of impossibilism and despair another interpretation of events: The so-called surpluses are not inexorable products of nature but are, with some exceptions, the outcome of the system of private property and wealth distribution now prevailing in the United States—a system of property and wealth distribution established before the advent of great technology and resting upon fundamental laws made by government. A corollary to this interpretation is an assertion: One of the hopes for resolving the crisis created by the alleged surpluses and for eliminating the perils to national security created by the outward thrusts of private interests seeking impossible markets for them lies in an *efficient* distribution of wealth within the United States.

Like all maxims and assertions, these are open to challenge, have been challenged in fact by many economists, who will seldom admit that they, too, are proceeding on assumptions and are making sheer assertions also. The propositions here advanced rest on the thesis that the primary element in each periodical panic is an unbalance between plant or productive capacity on the one side and consumer buying-power on the other, that the unbalance is due to the devotion of too much wealth to plant extension and too little to consumption, and that the disproportionate allocation of wealth to plant extension is owing in the main to the concentration of ownership which places too large a share of the annual wealth produced in the hands of a small number of people who simply cannot spend it on consumption goods but must pour it into the already overcrowded capital, or plant extension, market.

An efficient distribution of wealth, on the other hand, would hold the balance more even—by keeping the best possible equilibrium between capital extension and buying power. The question of justice in distribution, which troubles economists and philosophers, thus does not enter into consideration here. The issue is simply a problem of an *efficient* distribution which keeps the productive mechanism running under the impetus of adequate buying power. Should this interpretation be rejected, there remains the brute fact of the engineering finding: the United States has the material endowment and technical arts requisite to maintaining continuously a high standard of life for the American people and there is no *physical* reason why the productive mechanism cannot run uninterruptedly at a high tempo. What hinders the actual physical operation except inadequacy of knowledge, policy, will, purpose, and statecraft?

Stubbornly in the way of those who seek an escape from the economic crisis stands the fact of unbalance between plant capacity and buying or consumer power. Equally stubborn is the fact that there is an immense concentration of ownership in the United States which brings a large share of the annual wealth into relatively few hands, and forces increasing capital or plant extension for which efficient buying power is lacking. Although it is impossible to make an exact computation of wealth distribution, the income tax returns give some fairly precise figures. Tables compiled from those tax returns give, at least in rough outline, the number of taxpayers whose incomes run far beyond their power of consumption, the number who stand near or above a fair standard of buying power, and the immense number whose annual return is on or below the margin of the *vita beata, commoda et felix*.

It is this unbalanced accumulation of capital—overextension of plant capacity and the inefficiency of domestic buying power —which periodically slows down production to a ruinous pace, turns fiercer acquisitive energies into the quest for foreign outlets, sets armament industries in swifter motion, extends the American stake abroad, shifts the center of the nation's gravity from its geographical center toward the borders of the world markets, and makes the economy of the country depend upon the madness of world commercial operations utterly beyond any control on the part of the United States Government. Thus the uncertainty of the domestic market is intensified by the vagaries of foreign markets, fluctuating standards of life, wars, revolutions, political upheavals, tariffs, retaliations, regulations, prohibitions, and naval pressures abroad. So it is here contended that an efficient distribution of wealth within the United States would largely eliminate the unbalance between capital extension and consumption, provide domestic use for a considerable part of the so-called surplus, and reduce the pressures of the outward thrusts—thrusts which engender rivalries abroad, extend the interests of the country beyond the reaches of adequate defense, and lead to armament rivalries and their inevitable outcome—war.

This stabilization of the productive system in the interest of national security, which contemplates not a curtailment of production save, perhaps, in a few lines, but an expansion with growing buying power, as wealth is created, would lead to greater stability in the domestic market. As Karl Marx pointed out long ago, the market as it appears under the historic system is a riot, "a city without a plan." [4] Although in the office and factory, the capitalist and production engineer can proceed with rigorous rationality, determining the characteristics of their commodities, plant set-up, and speed of output, in the market they are subject to the vicissitudes of anarchy beyond rationality. Under the irrational tyranny of the market, in the best of circumstances, there must be guessing, efforts to forecast incalculable variables, espionage, great risks, and uncertain outcomes. Attempts to escape this madness have led to national combinations and international cartels; but these are unsuccessful expedients. A given monopoly, at the very height of its power, may be overthrown by a technical invention in the hands of a rival, which destroys at one fell swoop the value of its plant and throws its trained personnel into the streets. And international cartels cutting across the boundaries of countries and the jurisdictions of governments, with their various systems of law and their historic rivalries, never effect more than a brief breathing spell of order and profit-making for their organizers and sponsors. It is only by striking at the root of this unbalance or instability that a fair security for the domestic market can be attained: by establishing an efficient distribution of wealth within the United States—an adjustment of production and consumption and continuous control over the processes.

[4] Rühle, *Karl Marx*, pp. 352 ff.

It is not enough, however, to discuss the problem of economic security in terms of the distribution of wealth after the fashion of many contemporary economists, as if some mere manipulation of distribution could keep the economic machine running at high tempo. Goods must be produced before they are distributed and ways of distribution may break down and demoralize the productive mechanism itself. Conceivably a great deal of wealth can be transferred by taxation and other devices from unnecessary capital outlays to consumers eager for goods. Doles, pensions, allotments, and outright gifts may, for the time being, create an enlarged purchasing power; but a long continuance of such methods, however justified as temporary expedients, will doubtless create ways of life ruinous to productive industry and make millions of men and women wholly unemployable. Here the ethics of industry—the production of useful, pleasurable, and beautiful goods in ways conducive to social and individual virtues—enters into the considerations of statecraft. Rome once kept a large portion of her urban proletariat satisfied with bread and circuses, but as a long-run operation the experiment was disastrous.

Nor is there less peril to social coherence and the good way of life in efforts to resolve the crisis by establishing the four-hour day or the twenty-hour week in special industries. A four-hour day spent in industry amid unsatisfactory conditions of labor, with the rest of the time spent in homes and places of recreation degrading to manners and morals, might well undermine the very virtues essential to productive industry and social living. Labor is not a curse. It is ill-requited and despised labor in degrading conditions that is a curse. If it should be found, by engineering inquiry, that the mere necessities for a fair standard of life could be produced in a four-hour day, as industry is now set up, then the question would not be one of reducing hours alone but of improving the methods and techniques of industry and outside living conditions, with a view to giving the utmost comfort, convenience, and satisfaction in labor. To cut the work day to four or five hours and turn workers out into the living conditions now generally prevailing in the United States would be to menace the productive morale of industry.

As a matter of fact, to bring the standard of life for the entire population up to a fair minimum would require enormous efforts in the production of consumers' and capital goods over a long period of years. And should it be found that the production of basic necessities under machine technology would require only a three- or four-hour day, as often alleged, then it would be the duty of statecraft to increase the production of those goods which Professor Adelbert Ames calls non-consumable intangibles, such as education, science, music, and medicine, and non-consumable tangibles, such as parks, roads, and public services.[5] In the field of non-consumable goods, which give joy and satisfaction in life, there is no limit to the amount of production that is possible. It is in this field that capital and labor must be employed when any real overproduction occurs in the branches of industry engaged in producing consumable tangibles. For this reason, if for no other, ethics and esthetics are destined to acquire the recognition hitherto denied to them by a nation bent on selling rather than living.

With respect to the service activities which are to provide employment that does not compete with use industries, especially for men and women in their later years, there must be a closer organization of the arts, sciences, education, and medicine. Indeed, despite conflicts of interests and ideas within these several fields, a drawing together and an exploration of higher duties to American civilization are already apparent. This movement can be accelerated on a national scale. Here, as in the matter of planning the standard-of-life budget and providing the technological answer to national commodity needs, a grand survey of the nation's cultural resources is imperatively demanded by the necessity of expanding non-competitive service functions. What can education, adolescent and adult, offer to such a vision of civilization? What can the medical and nursing profession tender as the fullest possible realization of its splendid powers? What will be the nature of the social services required for the sick, defective, and dependent even in the best of circumstances?

[5] Adelbert Ames, "Progress and Prosperity," *Dartmouth Alumni Magazine*, January, 1932, pp. 5 ff.

What healthful activities are necessary to direct youth from the channels of crime in town and country? What have the arts to say about the creation, on an immense scale, of objects of beauty intended for delight and appreciation as distinguished (not sharply) from objects of sale and utility? Here is a challenge to vision and leadership more than Napoleonic in implication. And the latent and developing powers of America must answer it.

In this field of service activity, the intellectual, esthetic, and scientific forces of the nation must be employed—the artists, architects, teachers, doctors, nurses, and leaders in sports and recreation—employed not as derelicts out of jobs but as creative designers, directors, and servants of civilization. Already a vision of expansion in the domain of "service industries" is dawning in the consciousness of American thinkers, especially with the decline in the employment of children, the extension of the school age, the reduction of hours of work days, and the growing inability of men and women "over forty" to secure satisfactory occupations in high tension machine industry, with its stresses and strains. But it is not enough to speak of these occurrences as calling for "the right use of leisure" alone, at least considered in terms of dilettante dawdling, undirected "learning," or mere amusement. Education in the school years now so prolonged must not be confined to intellectual pursuits but must, from beginning to end, be geared into the use and service economy of the nation, allowing youths to participate in the activities of use and service under appropriate safeguards, while being prepared for full and competent discharge of adult duties in the later years. And provision must likewise be made for use and service activities adapted to men and women who have passed beyond the years of efficiency in high tension machine industry, blessing their later life with worthy and noble labors not beyond their strength and endurance. Perhaps this form of adult education may be closely related again to the school system where learning and the practice of the use and service arts are united under the cover of a concept of civilization.

Again it must be emphasized that this promotion of service functions is not to be conceived as dilettante and a side issue to the production of use commodities for sale. It is indispensable to the provision of that employment which great technology *cannot* provide in the use industries. It is indispensable to furnishing the physical stamina and emotional stability necessary to the perdurance of the very civilization in which the use industries function. It is required for the release of the powers of womanhood, so potent from primitive societies to the present, in the arts and sciences of life—powers which, if blocked and thwarted, lead to spiritual impoverishment and contribute, as in old Rome, to the decline of civilization. It is a condition precedent to the flowering of the arts in the grand style, as contrasted with precious and meretricious adornment —the kind of splendid presentation which can draw forth affection and admiration, exalt the spirit, and give distinction to a civilization. Any planning for the future which ignores the rôle of the arts and services will as certainly fail, as must any planning that neglects the powers of technology and the use industries. Too much stress cannot be laid on this potentiality in the quest for an escape from the dilemma in economy and thought. As Ruskin phrased the issue, life without industry is guilt, industry without art is brutality—and brutality cannot make an enduring civilization.

After the resources of the American nation and its technical arts have been surveyed, organized, and exploited with the utmost efficiency in the production of goods and services requisite to a high standard of life, there will yet remain raw materials and manufactured commodities which must be secured by import, if the highest possible standard of life is to be created and maintained. Here three questions arise. What varieties of commodities and in what amounts? How best can they be obtained, with the least risk to national security and of international friction? By what organs are imports and exports to be adjusted and controlled?

Tentative answers are offered. The varieties and amounts are not self-determined absolutes, but are relative to the standard of life which the nation sets for itself according to the degree of security, economic and defensive, deemed desirable. They cannot be fully determined by knowledge and thought until a complete survey of national resources, material and technical, has been made and the standard-of-life budget brought into conformity to its findings.

However, a preliminary classification of varieties of imports may be ventured: (1) products that cannot be produced in the United States owing to the absence of ores or non-metalliferous substances and to the lack of tropical climate; (2) products arising from differences in seasons; e.g., certain subtropical commodities which cannot be grown in the United States until Spring is far advanced; (3) products which cannot be provided in the United States in sufficient quantities; (4) commodities which can be produced in the United States but not efficiently; (5) commodities generically identical with American commodities but offering special varieties in taste; (6) commodities arising from certain skills and cultural qualities peculiar to other countries, both objects of economic utility and objects of taste and appreciation; (7) books, journals, instruments of pure science, and objects of pure art.

How can these commodities be obtained at the least risk? This question cannot be answered by reference to contemporary economic knowledge or the statistics of trade reflecting historic policies of governments. One negative reflection is possible: to secure these commodities or even a large part of them by employing force in seizing and holding distant places of the earth is an expensive process, as naval and army budgets indicate; and, in the present or any conceivable distribution of world power, a danger to national security in addition. On the positive side, it is evident that these imports can only be obtained in the course of trade by offering gold, goods, and services in exchange—in practice, mainly goods and services.

A survey of world resources and the technical arts of other nations is thus rendered necessary to discover the location of the desired imports, the posture of the nations offering them, and the American products likely to effect the greatest satisfaction in trade, either direct or triangular. This task is one in engineering rationality, not in theoretical economics, and will be undertaken with increasing thoroughness as the quest for national economic security proceeds.

Although it is beyond the scope of the present argument to provide a bill of particulars respecting agencies of operation for the attainment of the objectives posited, the foregoing line of argument points to the creation of a single national organ under the State Department for the adjustment and control of foreign trade.⁶ That organ might well be a public corporation, or Foreign Trade Authority with appropriate commodity divisions, equipped with technical agencies for studying the offerings and needs of other nations. It would have control over all foreign loans and credits and the conditions of their application; for loans and credits are at bottom and in the long run exports of American goods and services for which imports must be received. They are instrumentalities of exchange. The rôle of tariffs, quotas, licenses, and other means of exchange control in the operations of this foreign trade corporation cannot be closely determined in advance, but they would be subsidiary to the determination of exchange requirements.

Thus the United States would be equipped with a powerful agency for the negotiation and execution of trade agreements with other countries. It could combat foreign discriminations aimed at the advantages and profits of power as distinguished from the mutual benefits of commerce, and by its operations could contribute to the stabilization of trade—which is the essence of economic security for the nation. It could also help to emancipate the United States from the tyranny of instable currencies, whether based on gold or silver. Indeed, the currency problem in international trade, as in domestic affairs, would be incidental to the continuous operation of the productive and exchange mechanism on principles of engineering rationality.

In this adjustment of international exchange the issue of the carrying trade would have to be resolved. For years the governments of industrial nations have been straining every nerve to outstrip one another in merchant shipping, as an instrument of commerce and a naval auxiliary. They have poured billions into subsidies, with accompanying corruption, fraud, and inefficiency, and have brought about an overexpansion of shipping, with decreased earnings which have only augmented the clamor of private interests for more bounties from treasuries.

⁶ See below, pp. 286 ff.

At bottom, this marine rivalry is a part of naval rivalry and is involved in that issue. If naval rivalry cannot be positively restrained by international agreement, and competition in merchant shipping continues, they will exhaust public treasuries and culminate in the only possible outcome—the destructiveness of war, with results incalculable in terms of national security. If both can be regulated on the principle of ratios, then the merchant marines of the respective nations can be adjusted to the volumes of their exports and imports or on other principles (below, p. 280).

IN THE TREND OF INTERESTS AND IDEAS

Although the foregoing projections of policy admittedly contain ideal elements—desirable things deemed possible—and thus follow the example set by other works on statecraft, it is not conceded that they are mere abstractions or utopian hopes. On the contrary it is contended that they conform to positive trends in interests and ideas open to observation and knowledge in the Western world (above, p. 24). The dominant conception is that of Aristotle, not of Plato: policy must be the choice of the good, better, or best within the determinants and conditionalities set by the inexorable; and among these determinants and conditionalities is development—the movement of ideas and interests, knowledge, and thought.

The actual drift of domestic policy and practice is in the direction of the economic autonomy accepted in the preceding argument. For the United States this fact, on the import side, is illustrated in analytical detail by Alfred Rühl in his study *Zur Frage der internationalen Arbeitsteilung. Eine statistische Studie auf Grund der Einfuhr der Vereinigten Staaten von America*,[7] for the year 1927. In this classification and computation the imports of the United States fall into the following divisions and subdivisions:

I. Commodities supplementary to domestic production (non-competitive); percentage of total import, 89.3; following factors dominant:
   1. Impossibility of domestic production.
   2. Lack of domestic production in present conditions.

[7] Vierteljahrshefte zur Konjunkturforschung, Berlin, 1932.

3. Lack of definite kinds of product.
4. Lack of definite quality of product.
5. To meet demands of recent immigrants.
6. Differences in seasons of export and import countries.
7. Differences in technical arts of export and import countries.
8. Too limited domestic production in America.

II. Commodities imported despite domestic production (competitive); percentage of total import, 10.7; following factors dominant:
  1. Unfavorable domestic transport conditions (3.5%).
  2. Unfavorable domestic costs (7.2%).

Such was the degree of import autonomy attained under prevailing tariff policy and practice in the year 1927. No study has been made in the same detail of the economic effects of the Hawley-Smoot Tariff Act, but in the nature of things that Act has strengthened rather than weakened the tendency. And such is the posture of interests and ideas in the United States that to expect or hope for any drastic reversal of this tendency seems to be pure utopianism, despite powerful efforts to bring about a revulsion of feeling and conviction (above, p. 64). Changes may be made and probably will be made in matters of detail affecting unimportant interests, but a general reversal all along the line does not seem to be among the probabilities of the immediate future. This conclusion is fortified by the knowledge that other leading countries are moving in the direction of economic autonomy, for similar reasons —seeking an escape from the calamities and uncertainties in which historic policies and practices have eventuated.

Responding to changes in domestic economy reflected in the concentration of industries, the policies and practices introduced after the inauguration of Franklin D. Roosevelt in 1933 were in line with the conjectures just presented. Confronted by an almost total collapse of American banking under the historic conception of economy and morals, by falling markets, and by spreading social distress, President Roosevelt broke sharply with many traditions of his own party as well as the opposition, sought the security of greater domestic autonomy, and began operations on the assumption that American civilization does not inexorably depend upon any particular volume of foreign trade. The legislation and administrative acts of his régime, touching both foreign and domestic affairs, rest on the conviction that the United States can set its own house in order and keep it in a fair state of order with little dependence upon any volume of exports and imports. Although this is no place to review these laws and administrative acts, certain broad generalizations founded on their detailed analysis are relevant.[8]

1. The Roosevelt administration repudiates the long-dominant conception that the so-called surpluses of American industry and agriculture are inexorable surpluses for which export outlets must be found if the nation is not to sink down in the scale of civilization. Some of these surpluses it seeks to curtail by immediate measures and by long time planning of land utilization. Others it seeks to curtail by balancing industrial production and effecting a wider distribution through stimulated employment, both public and private, and through direct relief of the hungry and starving. This represents in policy and practice an abandonment of tradition and the development of new trends in ideas and interests.

2. The Recovery Program accepts the inexorable development of combinations in industry; abandons all faith in the healing power of dissolution and prosecution; and makes use of combinations in planning and fixing responsibility.

3. The Recovery Program recognizes the right of labor to organize, to be represented in industry, and to participate in the administration of the system established.

4. The Recovery Program calls upon millions of individuals in industry and agriculture, who have hitherto been pursuing their own interests at pleasure, to coöperate in adjusting production, setting prices, and maintaining standards—thus making imperative a new economic education on a colossal scale, an education founded on conceptions of collective duties and responsibilities.

5. The Recovery Program attacks the historic method of distributing wealth through the system of price and wage com-

[8] Beard and Smith, *The Future Comes* (1933).

petition, and substitutes, in part at least, price and wage fixing, haltingly and tentatively, but still positively.

6. In attacking the price system, administrators of the Recovery Program are coming to recognize that advance in this direction involves throwing daylight through the entire structure of industry and agriculture, illuminating the dark recesses where secrecy and manipulation accompany the struggle over the distribution of wealth, which arises from the conflict between private property and social needs.

7. In giving to agriculture an equality with industry in principle, the Recovery Program repudiates the whole classical doctrine of compensatory adjustment through the price system and its actual or tacit assumption that the maintenance of agricultural life is a matter of indifference to society. Thus the program recognizes the present inequality in the battle of agriculture against highly organized capitalism over prices and profits—inequality in organization, in wealth, in educational equipment, and in leadership—and concedes the incapacity of agriculture to defend itself against the cramping and draining effect of highly integrated machine industries. For years students of economy have been pointing out that agriculture is doomed in this deadly competition. Erich Zimmermann, in his excellent work on World Resources, has revealed the handwriting on the wall. Now the Government of the United States attacks the problem presented.

8. Implicit in all this is a call, in the Recovery Program, for a changed conception of economy and culture. For more than a hundred years American economy has been essentially speculative. Even agriculture has been a huge venture in land speculation rather than a way of life. The Stock Market has become a kind of national shrine. Not only the few but also the many have taken part in the grand gamble, and so widespread has been the disease that there is no way of knowing whether the nation actually has the powers of moral restraint requisite for the continuance of civilization. In insisting on stabilization, steady price levels, unrestricted competition in service only, and the elimination of market rigging, the Recovery Program runs counter to a powerful American tradition and demands for its realization a reversal of attitude in the

minds of millions who have had as their ideal the lucky wheat or stock speculator, with his town and country houses, his yachts and jewels, and his place in the affections of great newspapers.

9. The Recovery Program repudiates the idea, prominent in classical economy, that the misery of the unemployed is due to their improvidence, and provides government assurance of maintenance, at least, and government assistance in developing employment opportunities.

10. Through its banking, credit, public-corporation, process-taxing, and railroad measures, the Recovery Program is moving in the direction of a new economic sequence which subjects private interests to a broad nationalization, avowedly in a transcendent public interest.

11. In the sphere of foreign affairs, the Roosevelt administration also broke in some measure with traditional ideologies, without waiting for the London Economic Conference to defeat itself through the internal contradictions expressed in the hypotheses underlying its Agenda.[9] Those hypotheses embraced fragments of imperialist and *laissez faire* conceptions of national and international affairs, and assumed that unless "trade barriers" were lowered, unless some earlier state of international commerce was "recovered" or "restored," and unless the currencies of all nations were placed on a gold basis, no country could enjoy a high degree of prosperity and all countries must experience a fall in their standards of life (such as they were in the winter of 1933). Without waiting for the other members of the Conference to come to the deadlock of their own fundamental disagreement, either on the gold standard or lowering trade barriers, President Roosevelt boldly proclaimed the deadlock himself, broke with the traditions on which the Conference was presumed to operate, and announced that the United States would proceed to set its own economic house in order as far as possible by domestic measures and actions.

Yet the Roosevelt administration in breaking away from the tyranny of historic formulas in foreign affairs did not accept the full logic of its own professions and measures (below,

[9] Above, p. 113.

p. 316). It engaged in the old armament race with more avidity and abandonment than the Coolidge, Hoover, and Harding administrations—a race without meaning unless accompanying economic policies are to be pursued. Moreover, it yielded to the clamor of special interests or to the British theory of free trade by intimating the possibility of finding outlets for "surpluses" through some kind of reciprocity legerdemain. It did not, to be sure, and could not, indicate the precise reductions in duties or the exact commodities in respect of which such outlets might be obtained. It merely asked Congress for a blanket power to make changes in duties and prescriptions and to enter into negotiations with trading nations. If it did this solely with reference to the strategy of domestic politics, perhaps something may be said in defense; but if it assumed that such changes as it may bring about under the blanket authorization will be effective in providing adequate or even noteworthy outlets for the so-called "surpluses" of industry and agriculture—breaking the jam in economy—then it proceeded on the strength of discredited formulas and is destined to defeat.

It may be said that the domestic measures and policies of the Roosevelt administration have failed to set the productive mechanism of the United States in motion at high tempo and to establish a high standard of life for the nation and that they are bound to fail. The contention may be conceded. But those who make it usually jump to the conclusion that the way to raise the standard of life is to reduce the tariff barriers or engage in some other manipulations of foreign trade or politics. This is a beautiful *non-sequitur*. Granted, for the sake of argument, that economic autonomy will involve lowering the standard of life, it does not follow that the standard *can* be raised by any operation whatever in foreign commerce. The destruction of a proposition does not prove that its opposite is true. There is, in fact, no way of demonstrating that under any kind of foreign trade policies adequate outlets can be found for American commodities now produced in amounts beyond domestic requirements or buying power. If experience is any guide no such outlets can be discovered and obtained by any method (above, pp. 36 ff.). If a lower standard of life must result from failure to find such outlets, then it would be the better part of wisdom to adjust ourselves immediately to that lower standard rather than to delude ourselves longer by false hopes of accomplishing the impossible. Moreover, long time security accompanied by a lower standard of life is preferable to brief periods of fitful "prosperity" followed by disruptions, unemployment, and the degrading conditions of life and labor prevailing after the crash of 1929.

For many reasons it seems indisputable that foreign outlets for these alleged surpluses cannot be obtained by any process or policy of government or private enterprise. If so, it follows that hopes based on such an assumption are illusions, dangerous illusions, and that getting rid of them is one of our immediate tasks. Furthermore, there is ground for believing that if such outlets could be found temporarily the operation would be followed quickly by another devastating débâcle in domestic economy. In any event, it would be better for those who are indulging in false hopes about "adequate outlets for surpluses" to come down to earth at once and adjust themselves to a lower standard of life without cherishing any more feverish dreams.

But there is another alternative. Whether there is any such thing as "technological unemployment" may be left to those who enjoy intellectual jugglery. There can be no doubt, however, that there is an enormous amount of technology unemployed, to adopt Walter Polakov's phrasing, and that the efficient use of this technology in developing American resources can create the goods requisite for a decent standard of life in the United States. And if the industrialists who own or manage it cannot make it work, cannot avoid ruinous crashes periodically, cannot provide employment for the millions of idle who beg for a chance to live, then the Government of the United States can assume sovereignty over it, engage competent engineers to set it in motion with the aid of management and labor, and can distribute the output at home, with such compensation to the owners who have failed in their rôle as propriety may suggest in the circumstances. To accept the interpretation of an outstanding business leader, Gerard Swope, if industry cannot solve the problem, government will surely attempt to solve it.[10]

[10] "In the situation that confronts us at the present, the most disturbing aspect is that men who are able to work, who are competent workers, who above all things desire to work, cannot find work to do. . . . That industry must evolve and make ultimately effective those measures which will first ameliorate and ultimately eliminate these conditions must be the reaction of everyone who gives thought to what is taking place. I say that industry must do this thing, because it will surely be done. . . . Shall we wait for society to act through its legislatures, or shall industry recognize its obligation to its employees and to the public and undertake the task?" Gerard Swope, "Stabilization of Industry," *America Faces the Future* (ed., C. A. Beard), pp. 160-161.

CHAPTER XI

THE PROBLEM OF NATIONAL DEFENSE

ECONOMIC security being the supreme consideration, it follows that national defense is a prime element in every phase of policy—domestic and foreign. This is not hypothetical. All systems of political economy, even that of extreme *laissez faire,* posit national security and defense; and defense itself is deeply rooted in national emotions and interests. Obviously, a nation whose affairs are at the disposal of another power cannot develop its domestic resources to the fulness of their potentialities. On the other hand, if it is compelled to devote immense energies and a large part of its annual wealth production to wars, to preparations for wars, and to paying for past wars, then its civilian and cultural interests, like those of Sparta, will become the servants of military purposes and the military mind. In both cases, the results are similar in terms of economy and civilization: subordination to a foreign or domestic military machine or caste, with its inherent proclivities for making war on other countries out of lust and for self-preservation. Only on the assumption that war is a virtue in itself beyond all other virtues, that military culture is superior to civilian culture, and that the military mind can cope with the social and economic problems of the nation more successfully than the civilian mind can the supremacy of the military interest be defended. There is nothing in the experience of history to justify the assumption, and much to the contrary.

On the nature of defense and the rôle of war in history, however, there has always been and still is much confusion of theories and ideas. It is not going beyond the facts in the case to say that most American writings on defense and war consist of dubious assertions, untenable assumptions, and emotional outbursts. We have voluminous histories of wars, general and strategic, but not a single great treatise by a soldier or civilian on the nature and function of war. Mahan's writings on naval warfare are superficial as to historical facts, crowded with contradictions and confusions, and permeated with moral sentiments which vitiate any realism that exists in his thought. Yet Mahan is the only thorough-going systematist on war yet produced by American life. General Upton's work in military resources, though containing many pertinent and shrewd suggestions, must be characterized as the musings of a technician; narrowly concentrated on military preparation, it fails to grapple with the function of war. And the writings put forth by the American Navy League seldom rise above sophomoric levels of thought and knowledge. Debates in Congress and pronouncements of military and naval officers merely confound the confusion and lend color to the contention that only the special consideration of Providence has saved a badly prepared nation from destruction.

So in searching American thought on war we find mainly uncritical slogans. War is an evil—always wrong. War never settles anything. War is barbaric. Preparation for war leads to war. War is unnatural. War is the outcome of armaments. A million men will spring to the defense of the country over night, if need be. No nation will attack a disarmed and peaceful country. War is renounced as an instrument of national policy. War is a trade of professional interests, supported by munitions interests. War impoverishes and never enriches. War leads to the destruction of the fit and the survival of the unfit. War is an outcome of the capitalist system, with its greed for territory and trade.

On the other side are the military and naval mottoes. War tones up the morale of the nation. Adequate armaments are the best guarantee of peace. We can lick creation. The Navy must be strong enough to keep the seas open to American commerce, defend our interests everywhere, and protect the overseas possessions against all powers and combinations of powers. We may some time have to fight China's battles against Japan. Our military and naval forces must be strong enough to discharge our moral obligations to Spaniards, Indians, Negroes and mixed peoples in various places under the flag.

Our armaments are for defensive purposes only. The Army can "take charge of the nation" and cope with its "social and economic problems" in time of an emergency. The Army and Navy are the nurseries of honor and virtue. Our defensive forces must be adequate. Failure to build new ships imperils the nation's life. The Army is neglected by Congress and the country is thus put in jeopardy. Naval policy is a matter for naval experts. If the country had been "prepared" it would have taken Canada in 1812, secession would have been crushed in six months, and entanglement in the World War would not have occurred.

When these formulas out of which pacifist philosophy and American military science are constructed are subjected to the cold light of scrutiny, it will be found that they are all mere assertions. They are assertions of values and alleged facts. The former cannot be authenticated by any test. Whoever says war is evil or good does nothing more than declare that in his opinion it is evil or good. It is an opinion submitted to the judgment of mankind and nobody knows what that judgment will be in the long run. With equal ardor slavery was once proclaimed an evil and a good. Assertions of alleged facts can be tested by reference to historical knowledge; and few, if any, of the above aphorisms will stand any such trial verification.

An example or two will suffice to illustrate the process of scrutiny. War never settles anything. Now it is a matter of historical record that the War of American Revolution did establish political independence from Great Britain; the Mexican War clinched the annexation of Texas and added large areas of Mexican territory to the United States; the Civil War did put an end to the secession movement of 1861. Take, on the other hand, "Adequate preparation is the best guarantee of peace." Nobody knows what "adequate" preparation is in itself, but certainly Europe was heavily armed in 1914 and peace was not guaranteed. Whether armaments, however vast, are used in war depends upon the policies of governments, and policies are not determined entirely by armaments.

Again, take the proposition that adequate preparation would have added Canada to the United States, crushed secession in six months, and avoided entanglement in the World War. In one of these propositions war is held as a good—in its fruits, at least; Canada could have been seized. In the other two, peace is extolled as a good. Knowledge of history dispels all of them. Canada was not taken in 1812, principally for the reason that the interests dominant in the Madison administration were against it—irrespective of the size and power of American forces.[1] If the United States had possessed a large army in 1861 the major part of the leading officers and materials might have passed into the hands of the Confederates and secession triumphed in six months. At all events nobody knows what the result would have been. Everything hangs on unknown and unknowable forces and factors. What President Wilson would have done if the Army and Navy of the United States had been ten times as big in 1914-18 is unknown and unknowable. No disinterested seeker for the truth of the matter who spends years studying the official and private papers of the period can discover an answer. Still more relevant to national interest is the matter of desirability. Would it have been desirable to seize Canada in 1812 or to maintain neutrality in the World War? Desirable, from what point of view and with reference to what outcome? There is no way of securing an unequivocal answer to that question.

Writings on the subject of "defense" are as confused as writings on war. The line between aggression and defense has been, and can be, drawn in words only. In reality no dividing line exists. Nor do those who profusely and vociferously employ the term "defense" usually attempt to define the thing or things to be defended, the circumstances and policies which may give rise to the occasion for defense, and the limits to the capacity of defense, if any. It is true that President Coolidge and the Navy League of the United States once declared, in effect, that every American citizen and every American dollar abroad must be defended to the uttermost; but that is pure hyperbole. It must be evident even to Macaulay's schoolboy, that there are limits to the power of the United States to impose its will by victory on other great powers and combinations of powers. So, it is necessary, in a

[1] J. W. Pratt, *The Expansionists of 1812.*

search for a workable policy of security and defense of the national interest, to inquire into and clarify the conception of defense.

The conception of national defense is not separated from the conception of war in its broadest scope, either in the Constitution of the United States or in American thinking. The former contains confusions. The taxing power of Congress is for the purpose, among other things, of providing for "the common defense," and the militia may be called forth "to execute the laws of the Union, suppress insurrection, and repell invasions." It has been contended, and vigorously contended, especially during the War of 1812, that under the very terms of the Constitution the militia cannot be sent beyond the borders of the United States, cannot be used in wars on foreign soil, and must be confined in action to repelling invasions. The contention is now academic, in view of long practice, but the idea that military and naval establishments were intended by the framers of the Constitution to be dedicated solely to national defense is deeply imbedded in American popular psychology, and has a certain sanction in the supreme law. Indeed, the legislature of Connecticut resolved in 1812 that it was never intended that the militia "should be liable, upon demand of the President upon the Governor of the State, to be ordered into the service of the United States, to assist in carrying on an offensive war." [2]

Nevertheless, other sections of the Constitution, opinions of the framers, and practice support the view that unlimited power of war is conferred upon the Government of the United States. Congress is empowered to "declare war," not merely a war of defense, but war in the absolute sense, and the provisions relative to raising and supporting armies are without restrictions, save as to the period for which appropriations may run. The administrative divisions of the Government concerned with preparing for and waging war are called, respectively, the War Department and the Navy Department, not the Department of National Defense. And none of the foreign wars of the United States have been wars of defense in the strict sense of the term, that is, wars to repel invasions or threatened invasions. They have been wars in the execu-

[2] Ames, *State Documents on Federal Relations*, p. 18.

tion of national policy, for the protection and realization of certain rights, actual or alleged, outside the United States— on the high seas, in Mexico, and in Cuba and the Philippines. And the authors of the *Federalist,* as we have seen,[8] looked upon the war power as an instrument to be freely employed on the high seas in the promotion of American interests, especially in commerce. From that day to this there has been no clear distinction between war as an instrument of policy and war as an instrument of national defense. The Kellogg-Briand Peace Pact makes the distinction in words, but does not define either defense or aggression, that is, explain the difference between war as national policy to be renounced and any other kind of war as defense, presumably left permissible.

Judging by the climate of opinion at the time the Kellogg-Briand Pact was signed, war as an instrument of national policy meant war deliberately made for the purpose of seizing the territory and riches of another country or people. If this is the meaning of the Pact, then it is a work of supererogation, for no government of a civilized nation has officially proclaimed, confessed, or admitted, that it has been actuated by any such policy during the numerous international wars of the past half-century. In these wars, governments have declared with much vociferation that they have been actuated by the single desire of *defending* their territories or interests against the assaults of other governments. The fact that each belligerent has accused others of aggression does not alter the other fact that all have pretended to operate only on the principle of defense. Even in the case of the war against Spain, the United States, while emphasizing its concern for "humanity" and "civilization," brought the protection of American lives and property into consideration. All the belligerents in the World War were, by official profession, defending themselves against aggressors. And by collateral reservations the signatories of the Kellogg-Briand Pact have reserved for all time the right of defense. The United States has even withheld from the renunciation every interest covered by the Monroe Doctrine and has placed its

[8] *The Idea of National Interest,* Chapter II.

Latin American concerns, by implication, under the covering protection of defense.

Recognizing the fact that the Kellogg-Briand Pact left its fundamental terms undefined, certain advocates of peace, about the same time, proposed to define an "aggressor nation as one which, having agreed to submit international differences to conciliation, arbitration, or judicial settlement, begins hostilities without having done so." [4] This has the appearance, at least, of being clear-cut and offering a rule of classification. But it was impossible to win the adherence of any of the great powers to a proposition of this nature. Hence there seems to be full warrant for the statement that renunciation of war as an instrument of national policy leaves the problem of war and the practices of nations just where they were before the Kellogg-Briand Pact was signed. Later experiences in the Far East and in Latin America seem to confirm this view.

Amid all these confusions of ideas and interests, national policies and conceptions, and despite all pacts and agreements, war and preparations for war yet remain in the world of practice. The first question pertinent to the exploration here carried on is accordingly: Is war a primordial force, independent of national policy and will, an unknown and imponderable invariable of the future, for which utmost preparations must be made?

Although it may come as a surprise to readers unacquainted with military and naval literature, American as well as foreign, this question is answered in the affirmative by writers of undoubted intellectual acumen and wide influence. Any number of citations could be marshalled to show that war is widely considered as an absolute and unavoidable phenomenon of history; and it is highly probable that most military and naval men in the United States operate on a profound belief in that formula. They doubtless hold, with Georges Batault, that *la guerre est la loi la plus générale de l'évolution des sociétés humaines.*[5]

[4] For the Capper Resolution in the United States Senate, see Shotwell, *War As an Instrument of National Policy,* Chapter IX.

[5] Georges Batault, *La Guerre Absolue,* p. 237; Gerhart Lütkens, *Das Kriegsproblem und die Marxistische Theorie;* Archiv für Sozialwissenschaft, Vol. 49 (1922).

Can this proposition be proved by any knowledge or method open to the human mind? It cannot. It is a generalization presumed to rest on human experience. It is a belief, a conviction, a prophecy; it is not a statement that can be verified, as a generalized law in physics can be verified. It can be described and repeated endlessly, but it cannot be authenticated to the satisfaction of anybody who has respect for exactness of thought, for it is a fundamental finding of exact science that an invincible law can arise only where there is an isolated sequence of occurrences arranged in fact in a deterministic order. No sequence can be found in human affairs to support the proposition that war is a primordial force, independent of policy, operating under its own momentum as a process under its own law. The very idea does violence to all that is known of the nature of history.[6] It is an abstraction in words, satisfactory to those to whom it is satisfactory, but unsupported by knowledge of history as actual occurrences.

When attention is turned from war as an abstraction to wars as realities, it is found that they have always been associated with purpose and policy. It is true that minor conflicts, such as some Indian wars in the United States, have sprung from fits of temper, drunken brawls, or deep-hidden emotional centers. But the majority of wars known to history—all great wars—have been associated in origin with policy: with the more or less conscious purposes of the leaders, governments, or ruling classes that have precipitated them. The earliest of wars were wars of tribes and nations as robber bands—wars on neighboring tribes and nations for the bald purpose of seizing lands, property, cattle, and women; innumerable illustrations are furnished in the Old Testament and in the history of Europe. Other wars have been connected with the seizure of naval bases, backward places, centers of commerce, and natural resources, either openly or in the alleged protection of interests; these, too, have been associated with policy. Still other wars have sprung from domestic conflicts, from efforts of ruling classes to smooth domestic discord by foreign diversions. Innumerable variants could be cited, but no war is dis-

[6] Kurt Riezler, "Idee und Interesse in der politischen Geschichte," *Dioskuren* (1924).

associated from policy of some kind. Hence the assertion that war is an independent invariable subject to its own law, to which nations must succumb as victims, is without support in historical knowledge. If words have any meaning at all, then the characterization of wars as "natural phenomena," like earthquakes, independent of policy, is not an accurate description of the alleged facts covered by the assertion, declaration, or contention. If it were, then the idea of national interest and security as dominant considerations would be meaningless.

These conclusions are, in fact, supported by one of the greatest among modern writers on war, von Clausewitz. War, he says in effect, is simply the extension to the battlefield of conflicts of diplomacy which are not settled by compromises, concessions, and adjustments of policy. Then he goes on to add: "If war belongs to policy, it will naturally take its character from policy." According to this conception war belongs to policy; without policy it is senseless rage. And although senseless rage may move individuals and be a force in precipitating armed conflicts, war cannot be divorced from policy—rational purposes susceptible of visualization—especially modern wars which are the clear projections of diplomatic policies into the field of battle. So war turns on the issue of policy, not universal policy, but American policy, given the national heritage, geographical location, and economic system, and the postures and policies of other nations.

On this subject American thinking about war has been and still is utterly confused, and no clear-cut policy has yet emerged. It is true, one school of statecraft, which may be called dominant for practical purposes, has supported the vigorous pursuit of pecuniary interests by private persons and concerns in all parts of the world and favored the military and naval protection of those interests. This has the appearance of being realistic and hard-headed. It is an unlimited conception of policy; it is grand and powerful policy, leading in the direction of *la guerre absolue,* to war in its absolute form. This is the policy expressed by President Coolidge and Secretary of the Navy Wilbur when they declared American ships on the high seas and in foreign ports, American citizens, property and investments abroad, to be "a part of the national domain" and entitled to the armed protection of the United States. This is the official policy of the Navy Department expressed in its program—to support American commerce, protect overseas possessions, execute foreign policies, and to exercise ocean-wide economic pressure. This is the policy of the Navy League of the United States, and many individual admirals when they demand a navy strong enough to carry on (and presumably win) a major naval operation in the waters of Europe, Asia, and Africa, as well as the American hemisphere.[7]

The conception of unlimited policy leading to grand and unlimited war (*la guerre absolue*), though given official sanction and hammered into the minds of American citizens by a persistent, interested, and active propaganda, ignores the realities of the world: the distribution of nations, economic resources, zones of particular interests, the just claims of other nations which they will defend to the limit, and the probable outcomes and costs of such a policy pursued by arms. It is in flat contradiction to the treaties drawn up at the Washington and London conferences and duly ratified by the signatories. It is in flat contradiction to known facts in the contemporary concentration of the naval forces of France, Great Britain, Japan, and the United States on "home stations" and in the steady withdrawal of the naval powers into their respective "spheres" of influence and operation. It is true that the naval maps of all the powers overlap; since they cover lanes of commerce, they criss-cross one another in many areas; yet they do recognize that, owing to the distribution of naval bases and ships, zones of operation do exist in practice. Naval experts also know that a fleet "strong enough to operate in any part of either ocean" means predominance, if it means anything except disaster. To think of a major and successful operation by the United States Navy in the English Channel, the China Sea or the Inland Sea without thinking first of naval supremacy is to think without any sense for the realities of war, and to think dangerously for the United States.

[7] *Study of Naval Building Program;* Navy League publication, September 4, 1931; C. A. Beard, *The Navy: Defense or Portent?*

Any nation which is preparing for war and carrying on policies based on a conception of unlimited war—*la guerre absolue*—is disregarding realities as stubborn as mountain peaks. The paper pledges by which the United States agreed that it would not extend fortifications in the Philippines and that it would restrain its naval constructions in accordance with the 5-5-3 ratio may be cancelled, no doubt. Suppose they are cancelled and the United States starts to build a huge naval base in the Philippines and, in common with all the powers, begins unlimited construction of naval craft, what then? Is it probable that Great Britain, France, and Japan would stand idly by and see the United States become absolutely supreme on the seas—capable of carrying on a successful major operation against any rival or combination of rivals in any part of the Atlantic and Pacific (according to the official formula)?

If there is anything in human experience to guide us, especially in the fate of Wilhelminic Germany, they would not. War would break before the menace grew too great, and it would be a war of titans spreading around the world. But, assuming for the moment that the United States were permitted to build without limit by her rivals, and that in a world war the United States, at huge cost, became supreme on the seven seas, what national interest would be served? Who, what classes in the nation, would benefit and in what form? If considered in cold economic terms would the receipts exceed the operating costs and produce a favorable balance sheet? Those who propose and defend the policy of unlimited war for the United States know that they can make no precise calculations as to the outcome of that policy in battle, in economic terms, or in any terms of national interest. Facing realities, they refuse to see them and take refuge in words, dangerous words.

The confusion of American thought with respect to defense, to the objects to be defended, to the limited powers of defense which the United States will be allowed to possess in any case, and to the policies calculated to give the utmost economic security to the country is illustrated in the history of the Navy, the aphorisms of American admirals, and the *ex cathedra* pronouncements of Secretaries of the Navy presumably prepared by their technical subordinates. Apart from reference to the "philosophy of Mahan" there is nothing in the history of the Navy or its promoters to indicate in their thought any reasoned conception of war and defense in relation to the supreme consideration of national security, as distinguished from the profits of American traders, promoters, and speculators in various regions of the world. And as already indicated, the so-called philosophy of Mahan is no philosophy at all, but a collection of assertions and contradictions vitiated by sentiments, including acceptance of British naval supremacy as a moral good.[8] A search in naval literature discloses only a few fragments betraying any glimmer of insight into the purposes and rôle of war, by naval writers of professional competence. One of the fragments is an article by Lieutenant Commander Melvin F. Talbot, in *Current History* for April, 1933, and this article, after showing the irrelevant and thoughtless character of official naval policy, offers no clue to the problem left amid the ruins which it has created.

At no time when "the new Navy" was being built at the turn of the century was there any definition, in terms of public policy, of the functions which the Navy was expected to perform or could reasonably be expected to perform. There were pompous assertions about national prestige, world power, trade following the flag, the white man's burden, manifest destiny, spreading Christianity and civilization, and other more or less quixotic performances, imposed on the nation by "new duties." It was agreed that the Navy should be bigger, but how big was an issue neglected. It was to be "adequate," but no one asked: Adequate to what ends? No criteria were developed for determining its size. It was agreed, to be sure, that the Navy was not to be limited in size by the mere necessities of defending the continental domain of the United States—the home of the American nation and the center of gravity for

---

[8] *The Idea of National Interest*, pp. 337 ff. and 382 ff. Mahan was so sentimental about the British Navy and so oblivious to the proprieties of his profession that he once wrote privately to a British naval officer expressing regret that he would have to do his plain duty in case of a war between the United States and Great Britain: "If it [war] comes and I am in it, I think I shall have to request the Admiralty to hoist on your ships some other flag than the British—for, save our own, there is none other on which I should be so reluctant to fire." Taylor, *Life of Admiral Mahan*, p. 183.

security, but the matter of what was to be defended, where, and why, seemed too small for the consideration of naval statecraft.

Admiral William L. Rodgers, therefore, spoke truly when he declared in 1930, after fifty years of naval expansion, that nobody seemed to know what the Navy was for, and that for this reason the Navy Board felt moved to draw up a policy of its own. "All navies," he said, "relate to national policies. For many years the national platforms of both parties in this country have mentioned an adequate navy. They have not said 'adequate to what' so that the General Board, which has been charged since its inception with the general characteristics and size of the Navy, has been obliged to find out what the Navy is to be adequate to." [9] Thus the Government and taxpayers of the United States had been pouring hundreds of millions into a Navy; but no one knew why, and hence the General Board of the Navy had to explain to the muddled and blundering nation the purposes and requirements of the Navy. The idea would be amusing if it were not so expensive and fraught with such perilous consequences.

And what are the purposes of the United States Navy as defined by the Navy itself in the absence of any light from the civilian branches of the Government or any other quarter? First of all, the Navy is to defend, protect, and support the commerce of the United States—to guarantee the utmost security to American merchants, capitalists, and investments abroad. This sweeping statement means, if it means anything at all, preparation for unlimited supremacy over all other naval powers that refuse to accept the American view of the claims and rights asserted in connection with commerce and investments. The untutored citizen will say, perhaps, that it is the supreme duty of the Navy to protect American citizens and enterprise abroad, and that the American, like the proud Roman, must be able to say: *Civis Americanus sum*, and thus stay any hand that would interfere with his person or property in the most distant places.

But on analysis, it is evident that in time of peace the num-

[9] *Hearings before the Committee on Naval Affairs . . . on the London Naval Treaty of 1930*, p. 470.

ber of places in which the Navy can render such protection, if necessary, is small indeed: certain rivers and coastal waters in China, a few places in the eastern Mediterranean, and,some centers of disturbance in the Caribbean region. In Great Britain, France, Japan, and other countries which have established governments, the "rights" and "claims" of American citizens do not depend on the size of the American Navy. Piracy has been driven from the high seas. The protection, defense, and support of commerce in time of peace require only a few cruisers and patrol boats.

As Commander Talbot rightly says, the support of commerce "would seem at first sight a peace-time function, a rightful and merciful duty, to be performed without hostilities against, but rather in alliance with, other navies. In reality, however, it is hardly a naval function. Anti-pirate policing on the Yangtse, though assigned to naval ships, is essentially river-police duty. It necessitates especially designed gunboats. Were that our only problem, we could scrap all other types." Nor does protection against revolutions in Latin America, assuming its desirability, call for any considerable naval establishment. "Swift cruisers, however excellent they may be as emergency transports, are not built as such," continues Commander Talbot. "American traders in areas of chronic revolution are fortunate that these ships are ever ready to furnish them protection and support, but this duty is extraneous and essentially non-naval. It cannot be logically used as an argument for the maintenance of the present establishment. Let us make an end to half-truths. Battle fleets are not built to support commerce against banditry, piracy, or revolution; they are built to fight other battle fleets."

If by the support of commerce is meant the promotion of trade, as sometimes employed in arguments for larger naval appropriations, then, as Commander Talbot correctly contends, this is an economic function, not an operation connected with national defense. The opportunities for such trade promotion are small and the naval requirements for performing it, assuming desirability, are small also. There was a time, no doubt, when the British, Dutch, French, and Spanish employed war vessels freely in winning points of trade advantage and in seizing one another's posts and factories in various parts of the world, openly and in cold blood, but that age has passed. Similar conditions are not likely to exist again, for history never repeats itself in the same patterns. The old regions of trade contest have passed into the hands of strong nations, and unless the United States is determined to wrest these places from their present possessors, the Navy has no important function of this character.

Commander Talbot puts the case squarely: "The old conditions of monopoly and exploitation abroad have, for the most part, passed into history. Within the few remaining areas of continuous disturbance, the opportunity to buy, sell, and lend may still be more readily granted to nations that are strong at sea. Exactly how far the channels of trade are thus diverted from their normal course is a matter of opinion. It is far from certain that today 'trade follows the flag,' supported by a powerful navy, in preference to the salesman who offers the best bargains, sells the most cheaply, buys at the best price, and lends at the lowest interest rate. Not by interpreting support of commerce as its extension and encouragement shall we find a criterion of naval adequacy." If the Navy were so employed, the force required by its opportunities would be small, given the available area of operations of that nature.

In time of peace, therefore, the support, protection, and defense of commerce are functions of slight importance, calling for no extensive battleship or cruiser program. But what of war time? Should the United States be neutral in coming conflicts, then the question might become one of enforcing American conceptions of neutral rights against the interference of belligerents, of maintaining "the freedom of the seas" (below, p. 285). Here, immediately, the issue widens entirely beyond all precise calculations. Where will the war be? What powers will be engaged? What revolutions will be made by chemistry and mechanics in the technique of war?

No one can answer these questions. The World War dealt a death blow to the historic conceptions of contraband of war and "free goods." Despite the vigorous protests of the United States Government, the Allies defined contraband of war in their own interests and widened it to include innumerable ar-

ticles that had been regarded historically as "free." They interfered almost at will with American ships and goods destined
to neutrals and belligerents on the Continent, until scarcely
a shred of historic rights remained. How could the Navy of
the United States have "protected" American commerce
against this intervention? By defying the interdictions of the
Allies and convoying American merchant ships carrying forbidden goods to their respective destinations, or by waging
war on Great Britain and France and breaking their barriers
to trade? If it is the duty of the Government of the United
States to protect commerce, why was it not done then? It was
not done; and, moreover, after the United States entered the
war on the side of the powers which had interfered with its
commerce, it sanctioned and extended the practice of interference with neutral rights, destroyed in effect nearly all that
was left of "freedom of the seas," and set precedents utterly
ruinous to that commerce in war time—the commerce which
the American Navy is supposed to defend and protect.

The vindication of its neutral rights during a war to which
the United States is not a party is a function verging toward
war on the part of the United States (below, p. 285). The
alleged function furnishes no criterion for naval adequacy,
because no calculations of the situation can be made in advance—unless it is regarded as all-inclusive. Whether the
United States will push its claims to "rights of neutrals" to
the extreme of an ultimatum leading inevitably to war and
whether it will favor any belligerent in future conflicts will
depend upon circumstances beyond naval reckonings. American rights, historically considered, were flagrantly violated by
the Allies; the American Navy, though inferior to that of Great
Britain, in combination with the German navy might have
broken the blockade, destroyed the British supremacy on the
seas, protected American rights, vindicated them. If the protection of American commerce was the supreme consideration,
then a war on Great Britain would have been the inevitable
consequence. But other considerations entered into the formulation of policy and the opposite line of action was adopted.
Vindication of neutral rights in war time thus furnishes no
calculable scheme of sequences for determining the size and

character of the American Navy. Maps showing trade routes to be protected against the interference of belligerents, though mechanically drawn and beautifully colored, supply no intelligible data for estimating "adequate naval strength."

Next we may consider the duty "to guard the overseas possessions of the United States." So far as the Caribbean region and Hawaii are concerned, this is a function requiring little if any addition to the forces requisite for continental defense, but with respect to the Philippines and Samoa absolute supremacy in the Far Pacific is indispensable to the discharge of the "guarding" obligation. The Philippines are clearly within the Japanese zone of control, to say nothing of British and French potentialities in that region. Given the present distribution of naval power and the absence of an effectively fortified naval base in the Islands, they could be seized within a short time by the Japanese navy. They could be recovered only by an invasion of Japanese waters and victory over the Japanese navy, doubtless in the Inland Sea. Given the present naval ratios, such an invasion, after the American fleet had steamed across the Pacific, would be so hazardous for the United States as to be akin to suicide.

By general consent in naval circles the guarding of these overseas possessions would require an abolition of the naval ratios and the establishment of a powerful navy base in the Philippines. What Japan would do, while the United States was building up its Navy and constructing the base, is beyond calculation, although it would be a safe guess that she would strike while the iron was hot, before her doom was rung by American achievement. Safeguarding the Philippines is not, therefore, a function of the United States Navy and cannot be made a function without a complete reversal of the policies pursued since the acquisition of the Islands—a reversal highly improbable, and certainly one that could serve no national interest conceived in any terms involving the exercise of intelligence.

The function of "supporting the policies" of the United States is easily disposed of, if considered in specific terms. Among the policies of the United States is the Monroe Doctrine. The enforcement of that policy is relatively easy, adding

little if anything to the requirements for defending the continental possessions. No European power has challenged it
for many years. No European power has naval bases in the
region sufficiently developed to permit it to offer a serious
challenge with any degree of assurance. Not even the government of Germany in the Wilhelminic period contemplated
breaking the Monroe Doctrine, despite assertions and propaganda to the contrary, and Germany is now out of the race
as a sea power. The second formula, called a policy, is the
"open door," which Tyler Dennett has correctly characterized
as a "form of intervention in China." That doctrine cannot be
enforced for the same reason that the Philippines cannot be
"safeguarded." Enforcement means a war with Japan and
unlimited naval supremacy of the United States in Far Eastern
waters. The economic advantages that might flow from it
would be trivial in comparison with its cost, the political problems of government after victory would be baffling, and even
triumph would be a betrayal of the nation for the advantage
of private and material interests, if any interests at all.

With these criteria for naval adequacy ruled out, there
remains only one other—adequacy for victory in war. That
raises immediately the questions: War with whom, where, and
with reference to what national interest? At once all the imponderables and incalculables of the hidden future enter into
consideration. With whom is naval war possible, if not probable? With Great Britain or Japan. Now, victory in war,
according to naval reckonings, means not merely defensive
actions, but offensive actions, carrying combat into the waters
of the enemy, destroying his power, and breaking his will.
Yet, as Commander Talbot has said, and Naval War College
charts clearly indicate, there are "three definite naval spheres
where the controlling fleet is secure against any one of the
others." To be sure, these zones overlap in places and cannot
be mapped as positively as the territorial boundaries of the
various countries, but their central areas are indisputable. A
consideration of them is necessary to an elucidation of the
issue of naval adequacy for victory in war.

First of all, there is the zone of British preponderance in
the northeastern Atlantic, where, in a war with Great Britain,

the United States Navy would have to impose victory on the British Navy, after steaming many days through mine-strewn and submarine-infested waters. In that zone Great Britain is by no means as secure against all probable foes as is Japan in her waters, and the United States in her waters; yet the center of the power at which the United States would have to strike in a war with Great Britain is beyond effective reach. The British have open lines where French airplanes and submarines may work havoc. The England-Gibraltar-Suez-Aden-Singapore route is flanked by the French bases at Brest and Toulon, and by the Italian base at Taranto. Great Britain is not at the center of her trade routes and empire, but in a far corner, with open lines resting upon scattered bases. Although these lines might be raided by swift American cruisers and British commerce harassed by the American Navy in case of war, victory would require a fatal thrust home in British waters off domestic bases—a thrust impossible for the Navy of the United States.

In the American zone, the United States can be easily secure against either Japan or Great Britain. Within this area Great Britain maintains an unfortified dock-yard at Bermuda, some minor facilities at Trinidad, and a defended port with certain base facilities at Halifax. The North American squadron which Great Britain maintains in these waters, cruising from the Caribbean to Halifax and back between shore festivities, is small in size and in itself no threat whatever to American naval security. That some of these basis could be made formidable is certain, but since elaborate fortifications could only mean a thrust at the United States, the very beginning of work would imply a change of policy and serve as an advance warning to the United States. Such are the realities of receding rather than advancing British naval power within the American zone. In this area Japan has no possessions, no bases, no foothold. Even her uttermost outposts in the direction of the United States afford no support for striking at the United States with any hope of victory in a fight to the finish, given existing naval ratios, or even an American navy constructed primarily with a view to continental defense.

Within her zone Japan is equally secure. The British have

a base at Hong Kong, which they have agreed not to extend. The United States has a base in the Philippines, which it is bound not to develop by fortification. Both of these bases Japan might easily isolate or capture. The United States and Great Britain have "Asiatic fleets" which base at their southern ports in the winter and in Chinese waters in summer. They are not fleets which even in combination could impose victory on Japan in the Inland Sea. That they are utterly without weight in Oriental politics was abundantly demonstrated in the period which followed Japanese occupation of Manchuria beginning in 1931. Both British and American naval officers sometimes feel that their respective governments have "left China in the lurch," but that is a matter of sentiment, not of reasoned policy constructed in the national interest, conceived in any realistic terms. Neither navy exists for the purpose of playing the rôle of benevolent and sacrificial protector for China. This is well known by their respective home governments. And second thought reveals to them the actual position of Japan in her area, her security against victorious attack, given the present distribution of sea power, which is the only alternative to unlimited preparedness for war—*la guerre absolue.*

Although the existence of these three spheres of security is recognized by naval authorities and forms the center of all strategic considerations, fighting men can scarcely bring themselves to imagine a defensive war. Most naval officers, it seems, still think in conventional terms of conventional war at sea— bold and brave offensives driving into the heart of the enemy waters, searching out the foe, and administering a mortal thrust, at the risk of utter annihilation. The lessons of the World War have made little impression on them. Neither the British nor the German navy insistently sought out the enemy and staked everything on a single contest of power. There was talk in the British naval circles about "digging the Germans like rats out of their holes" but intelligence finally overcame emotion. No such effort was made. Both the British and the German grand fleets carefully avoided getting too close to each other's bases. There was only one great battle, at Jutland, and it was indecisive. Neither government was willing to risk everything on a single battle. Common sense suppressed historic sentiments. It might be heroics, in case of a war with Great Britain or Japan, to send a great battle fleet to the English Channel or the Inland Sea, to win a Pyrrhic victory, if won, or to suffer an irreparable loss, if defeated. Intelligence, however, held the British battle fleet in leash during the World War. It is hardly probable that the United States would sacrifice common sense to quixotism in a war with either one of the two possible enemies on the high seas.

§

1. Unless reason is surrendered to senseless rage, with corresponding imbecilities and perils of brute action, preparations for war and calculations for eliminating hazards will be based on policy, and the one policy that is possible under a conception which makes the American nation the center of interest and affection is *policy based on security of life for the American people in their present geographical home.*

The size of the Army and Navy should be determined with reference to the vindication of that policy and not with reference to any other criteria.

Since under the conception of national interest here posited the conquest and seizure of territories occupied by alien races are barred as flatly contrary to, and a betrayal of, national interest, military and naval preparations for such operations stand condemned on their face, a waste of national resources and a needless peril besides.

Since the business of the Army and Navy is to defend the American nation in its geographical home and, since the Army and Navy are or should be controlled by duty and not pecuniary considerations, it is a misuse and degradation of both to transform them into huckstering and drumming agencies for profit seekers, promoters, and speculators, in the name of "trade."

Effective defense of American trade and sea lanes beyond the American naval zone against any major power or combination of powers is impossible. It follows, therefore, that aggressive economic and diplomatic actions in distant regions,

based on the hypothesis that adequate defense will be forthcoming, merely create centers of friction which, in the supreme
test, cannot be controlled by American naval force; the existence of such centers of friction inexorably involves the perils
of war which, if it ended in victory, could not bring any
advantages to the nation comparable to the cost in blood and
treasure and, if it ended in defeat, would bring frightful losses
and humiliation, if not revolution and widespread ruin at home.

In claiming the right to be secure at home on condition of
non-interference with the affairs of other independent peoples,
the United States must, as a matter of hard fact and national
interest, concede similar rights of security to other great powers
outside the American zone.

2. So far as sea power is concerned, it is recognized both in
theory and practice by naval authorities, and by civil governments if they are informed on the subject, that Japan and the
United States are in truth secure within their respective zones
of defense, and that Great Britain is secure in her zone, subject
to the liabilities on her Continental flank.

3. This means that there are in fact three great zones of
naval power, in each of which outsiders must operate, if at
all, in mortal peril of defeat. These zones are not marked out
absolutely; their boundaries are somewhat uncertain; but their
respective areas of heavy gravity are definite and fixed.

4. Given this distribution of areas and powers, the possibility of absolute naval predominance is now excluded from
practical consideration. If any one of the three powers should
attempt to attain predominance by building two vessels for
each vessel laid down by its two nearest rivals, the outcome—
opposition and combination of the latter—could scarcely be
doubted.

5. Were naval predominance in the Atlantic and Pacific
possible for the United States, its desirability would have to
be predicated upon an assumption that such predominance
would bring commensurate economic returns from increased
trade, territorial possessions, and protectorates. Territorial
gains could be made only by seizing the possessions of economic rivals at the expense of incalculable wars. Should public
opinion in the United States sanction and support such im-

perialistic adventures, caution and economic accountancy would condemn them. The impossibility of enlarging trade indefinitely and materially by operations of this character has been demonstrated by experience.

6. No battleships are required for the defense of American citizens and property abroad in time of peace. A few cruisers and special police vessels can perform adequately all such duties. In other words, no navy of any consequence is needed for the effective discharge of this function.

7. The problem of upholding neutral rights when other countries are at war is assimilated to and is part of the problem of war itself—of commercial policy to be enforced by war (below, p. 285). In view of the coöperation of the United States with the Allies in the destruction of neutral rights in the World War and the probability that such rights will be completely destroyed by the technology of the next war, the United States could not, with a straight face, undertake to uphold the historic rights of neutrals in any coming conflict. Hence in the next war the problem for the United States will be one of entering or staying out of the struggle on grounds of policy conceived in the national interest as here defined.

8. If it be said that the above propositions indicate to Japan and Great Britain that the United States has surrendered its "sovereign rights" to enforce its own decisions in support of American citizens and property in all parts of the world, and is a confession of weakness, the answer is that Great Britain and Japan know the facts in the case, that the surrender (if this is the term to apply to something never possessed) has been made and is evident in the incidence of geography, the distribution of naval power, and treaty provisions confirming the realities of the situation. If advocates of unlimited "sovereignty" find this painful to contemplate, statecraft nevertheless takes account of the stark truth in the premises. Any other view is perilous quixotism—inimical to national interest.

9. The requirements of naval defense for the United States are thus determined by the technical issues of defending its zone of control, given the weight and disposition of the naval forces of Great Britain and Japan within their respective zones. Here is the true basis for defining "adequacy." In part it is

relative, not absolute; it depends upon the agreements which may be made with other powers. In part it is determined by the geographical configuration of the United States, the islands and waters of its zone and the state of military technology. The 5-5-3 ratio, on examination in the light of the above considerations, may be found appropriate or not. Conceivably the United States, by confining its naval and military measures to the realities of the situation, might materially reduce battleships and other expensive craft and concentrate on an extension of coast, air, and submarine defenses. At all events, when the illusions of *la guerre absolue*, of predominance, of promoting, protecting and supporting commerce at all hazards are at last realized in the councils of the nation and the issues of naval defense are clarified by the use of knowledge and reason, engines of war, for land and sea, will be altered and the forces of defense will be reorganized.

10. To give effect to such a policy, and to eliminate rivalry between the Army and the Navy, two consolidations should be effected. The War Department and the Navy Department should be combined in one Division of National Defense, and, along with all agencies and agents representing the United States abroad for any purpose, this Division should be placed directly under the supervision and control of the Department of State. The Committee of the House of Representatives on Foreign Affairs and the Senate Committee on Foreign Relations should be reduced in size and transformed into a joint working committee; likewise the military and naval committees. Among these consolidated agencies of the Federal Government close relations should be established, giving unity to councils and decisions and effecting adjustment of means to ends. In this way the reckless bickerings among them, resulting in weakness and indecision and discrediting the United States in its conduct of foreign relations, could be avoided, or at least minimized. In this way foreign policy and national defense, which are parts of the same thing, if rationally conducted, could attain the unity of purpose and will which is power. Policy would thus not go beyond the potentialities of defense and defense would be adjusted to policy.

But it will be said by military and naval experts that,

although they are constantly instructed by civil authorities in time of peace to confine their operations to the issue of defense, they are always in peril of being driven into offensive operations in distant places outside the continental domain. As a member of the General Staff of the United States Army once remarked to the writer of these pages, "We are told by Congress in times of peace to limit our estimates to defense, and then in the next breath we are ordered to take Canada (1812), to capture Mexico City (1846) to seize the Sultan of Sulu (1900), and to march on Berlin (1917)." In other words, civilians speak of "defense" and want to curtail expenditures in time of peace; then, without warning, they throw upon the Army and Navy obligations of distant offense for which no adequate preparations have been made. The paradox and irony of this situation are made clear in General Upton's classic work, *The Military Policy of the United States,* in which it is shown how much blood and treasure have been sacrificed by failure to prepare for the wars Congress has declared.

The confusions and contradictions involved in this issue cannot be entirely cleared away, for the reason that neither the civil nor the military authorities can penetrate the future and foresee the contingencies in which war may be waged. Such are the hazards and adventures of individual and national life. But hope for national security rests upon a unification of federal agencies concerned with foreign policy and war, and the deliberate and reasoned adoption of policies which will minimize the chances of collision with foreign powers, confine the necessary operations of American armed forces to the American zone, save as a possible ally of some formidable power, and diminish the dependence of the nation upon the caprices, interests, hatreds, and passions of other countries likely to be engaged in warfare. If the policy of the country is clarified and is founded on a conception of interest calling for the efficient use of the national resources in the development of a high standard of life for the American people, if adventures in sheer commercial promotion are firmly rejected and put down, if the people of the United States tend their own garden, if the Government ceases to be a trade drummer and investment collector, if efforts to force American goods and capital upon other peoples in bitter rivalry with other industrial nations are deliberately relaxed, then the United States will have a policy upon which military and naval authorities can make calculations adapted to clearly defined ends, adjusting their engines of war to exigencies that may be foreseen with some degree of assurance. Until this clarification of policy takes place, however, and until confusion in national councils is dissipated, it may be expected that military and navy men will demand every gun and ship they can get; and a nation that has no fixed frame of policy has little right to criticize them for their demands.

Nevertheless, American naval strategists in particular are under obligation to the nation as well as to themselves to relate their study of strategy and machines to the ends of rational policy. Up to the present about all they have done is to clamor for more ships, officers, men, and fighting equipment—more and more, forever. Owing to the enormous resources of prosperous capitalism they have managed to get an immense quantity of material instrumentalities and this has encouraged them to think of their art and responsibility in purely materialistic terms, sheer weight of men and metal. So far as they have considered policy in the large, they have committed themselves to an all-inclusive policy of trade promotion and defense in every part of the world. They have thus thought recklessly, adventurously, and dangerously for the American nation, and advocated taking about every gambler's chance open in the seven seas. Moreover they have carried on a propaganda to induce the nation to believe that some substantial interest or point of honor is involved in every such gambler's chance full of dangers. It is to be hoped, however, that they will come to recognize the necessary *limitations* on naval power and concentrate on effective limited policy, before they have involved the country in the kind of disastrous conflict which German navalists brought upon the German nation. As long as they can think of nothing except demanding more and more ships and men and raising more and more financial support for appropriations by the kind of propaganda they have been employing, they are a danger to national security rather than a guarantee of security.

All this points to one final imperative. A clarification and definition of national interest as a guide to policy is indispensable to national security. "If policy be grand and powerful," says von Clausewitz, "so will be war." If policy is grand and powerful with respect to national interest as distinguished from private and bureaucratic interests, then peace may be grand and powerful, not as an end in itself to which all must be sacrificed, but as a fruit of policy, as a means to a good life for the nation.

Fundamentally, this is a return to the conception of war and defense expressed by one of the wisest and shrewdest of the Founding Fathers, John Marshall. Speaking to the citizens of Richmond, Virginia, in the autumn of 1798, he said: "Terrible to her neighbors on the continent of *Europe,* as all must admit *France* to be, I believe that the *United States,* if indeed united, if awake to the impending danger, if capable of employing their whole, their undivided force—are so situated as to be able to preserve their independence. An immense ocean placed by a gracious Providence, which seems to watch over this rising empire, between us and the European world, opposes of itself such an obstacle to an invading ambition, must so diminish the force that can be brought to bear upon us, that our resources, if duly exerted, must be adequate to our protection, and we shall remain free if we do not deserve to be slaves." [10] To surrender this fortunate position for a mess of pottage in the form of profits on cotton goods, tobacco, petroleum, and automobiles, is to make grand policy subservient to special interests, betray the security of the American nation, and prove that we "deserve to be slaves."

[10] Beveridge, *The Life of John Marshall,* Vol. II, p. 572.

CHAPTER XII

INTERNATIONAL RELATIONS OF AN AMERICAN COMMONWEALTH

THE argument thus far advanced is directed to the proposition that an efficiently operated commonwealth offers the best escape from the crisis in economy and thought in which the American nation now flounders—is, indeed, both necessary and desirable, as a solution of the contradictions presented by the emergency. It is now in order to ask: What are the nature and forms of foreign policy and relations adapted to the conception and practice of such a commonwealth?

Broad Policies

When attention is turned from historical systems of thought about international relations—legalistic, economic, and diplomatic,[1] to the realities of objective occurrences, relations, and practices, what obtrusive relevances are found? They may be classified under six heads: technical, boundaries, culture, wars and revolutions, economics, and backward places.

Institutions and occurrences falling within some of these divisions are of such a nature as to raise few questions of national interest beyond fairly easy and rational adjustment by diplomacy, conciliation, and adjudication. Issues of technical relations, such as apportionment of the radio bands, international health regulations and ice patrol, for example, may be determined objectively with fair accuracy, and adjusted by experts without seriously disturbing domestic interests. The relations of governments arising from boundary problems, as between the United States and Canada, or the United States and Mexico, can, in the ordinary run of things, be handled by commissions and tribunals to the general satisfaction of the

[1] For an analysis of these systems, see above Chapters II-VI.

parties concerned, except where irrelevant quarrels are drawn into question. Likewise, the relations of governments and peoples arising from cultural exchanges—art, literature, science, travel—develop few conflicts in the regular course, although questions of propaganda may be involved in some circumstances. In other words, there are certain areas of international relations, in which grave conflicts can be avoided by the use of coöperative methods and without injury to national interests, however conceived. This is especially true of the United States, whose boundary lines may be regarded as fairly well established, and it is with the United States that we are concerned here.

Wars and revolutions, though associated with policy, are among the unpredictable occurrences of history, and the extent to which they may disturb the relations of the United States is incalculable. Though war may be started with certain purposes in view, those purposes cannot control the forces which are let loose by war, and like fires in a great city, wars may spread in directions wholly unforeseen. Here we are concerned with probabilities—those occurrences which in the physical world baffle mathematicians and in the world of human affairs are still more intractable to law. Yet a tentative law may be hazarded: The degree of the probability that the United States will become involved in any war arising anywhere in Europe or Asia bears a direct relation to the extent of the economic interests possessed by American nationals in the affected area, and in the fortunes of the respective belligerents. A conditionality is also involved in the law: The pressure of American nationals upon the Government of the United States for aid in realizing actual and potential interests in the zones of war on land and sea.

The constructive upshot is evident, given the law of probability and its conditionality. To encourage by State action American nationals to develop private interests in historic war zones beyond the effective control of American military and naval power is a betrayal of national interest conceived as supreme public interest. If, as proposed in a preceding chapter, all foreign trade is subjected to public control, and limited to the exchange of goods mutually beneficial to the participants, then powerful private interests in the United States will have no "stake abroad" to be defended by the blood of their fellow citizens. To this extent the perils of war will be diminished, not because they are evil in themselves, but because they endanger the supreme national interest—security. Thus the innumerable diplomatic conflicts over private rights, concessions and trade opportunities, which constitute the irritating substance of diplomacy, will be automatically curtailed. The pressures of these interests on the Government, personal and through party campaign funds and propaganda, will be materially reduced and ultimately eliminated. In the case of any war arising anywhere, the interests of the United States trading corporation (below, p. 287) in the conflict will be a matter of public record and common knowledge—as open as the budget of the Government; and the question whether the United States should participate in the war can be considered on its merits as a matter of public interest. Until this is done, the United States is likely to be drawn into every serious conflict in Europe or Asia without respect to national interest—indeed, to the peril of national interest.

Revolutions belong to the category of war. They are civil wars, even if more or less bloodless, and they may easily spread into international wars. The wars of the French Revolution, beginning in 1793, and the war of the Allied and Associated Powers on Russia after the November revolution of 1917 are examples. Here the law of probability with respect to wars in general may be applied. If the Government of the United States conceives national interest to be the sum of private interests in regions affected by revolutions, then recognition of revolutionary governments will be subjected to the demands of these private interests and the probability of being drawn into war will bear a direct relation to the strength of these interests in American politics. On the other hand, if national interest be considered in terms of the supreme public interest, security, the question of recognition will become formal and the question of making war on the revolutionary government will become a matter of estimating economic advantages—open and above board, calculated and deliberate. Whether wars would become more or less numerous cannot be predicted, but the likelihood of wars contrary to the national interest as public interest and perilous to national security, should certainly be reduced to the minimum.[2]

Now we come to a consideration of international relations as economics—the exchange of goods in time of peace. Under the system of economy and trade here contemplated few changes in American imports would probably take place, at least in the immediate future. What engineering rationality would disclose in an effort to enumerate the goods that can now be produced efficiently in the United States, given the resources and state of the technical arts, cannot be foreseen. However, the table of classified imports presented in Rühl's study of foreign trade (above, p. 233) doubtless gives an accurate general picture of the situation which would prevail under an ordered commonwealth, subject to many modifications in detail likely to occur after the pressure of private interests is relaxed and public interest substituted. At all events, the supreme question would be: What imports are necessary to the pre-established standard of life for the people of the United States? This question engineering rationality would seek to answer on the basis of private budgets brought into an aggregate national estimate.

With the import requirements determined by reference to the posited national standard of life, then the export problem would be attacked. Given these import requirements and the posture of the various foreign countries in the best position to supply them, what offerings can American industry make in exchange, considering the peculiar resources of this country and the state of its technical arts? In some cases the American goods offered in exchange would be genuine surpluses, that is, quantities actually in excess of the requirements of a high national standard of life; in other cases they might represent sacrifices of one element in the standard for other elements deemed more desirable. Here conceptions of utility and preference would rule.

Thus for the primary commodities of peaceful life inter-

---

[2] For emphasis, attention may be called again to the fact that war as such is not here regarded as a good or evil; the object is a reduction in the chances of wars perilous to national security—national security being posited as a good.

national exchange would be open and above board. The specifications and quantities of the goods offered would be known,
as public as a government budget, and laid before the other
nations with which exchange is to be effected. And on the
other side, the specifications and quantities of the goods tendered by other countries in exchange would be known also.
For the secrecy, subterfuge, and higgling of private merchandising would be substituted the operations of frank barter,
stripped of mystery and concealment, with both parties competent to pass judgment upon the properties and quantities of
the articles tendered and exchanged. Tenders of credit, if
any, would be based upon import requirements. Quantitative
measures of the necessities of production, not prices related to
fluctuating currencies, would provide the base for conditioning
the terms of exchange. The chicanery of misbranding, adul-
teration, and falsification, so common in private merchandising,
would be checked by engineers on both sides of the mutual
exchange for mutual benefit.

When the maximum economic independence for the United
States is under consideration, however, certain material facts
must be taken into account. Given the present forms of industrial and scientific operation in American economy, and assuming
no radical changes brought about by invention and discovery,
there are numerous commodities, necessary to the continuance of the present productive system in the United States,
which are not now available from resources under its jurisdiction. Some of them are essential to the technology of defense
and warfare. At least twenty-six "strategic products" have
been listed by the War Department as commodities produced
outside the United States and yet absolutely indispensable to
effective defense. Other foreign commodities are indispensable
to the production of goods which certainly support the present
level of civilization. Some of them may be cited as illustrations: manganese, chromium, antimony, nickel, silk, strychnine,
tin, camphor, rubber, quinine, coffee, shellac, tungsten, and
platinum. The list could be easily extended and without much
difficulty it could be shown how deeply these commodities enter
into important phases of our material civilization—medicines
to cure disease and assuage pain, substances essential to pho-

tography, aviation and motorization. With great eloquence a picture of American dependence has been painted by pacifists who long for world peace, and militarists who demand the use of imperialist methods to seize lands bearing such resources or a navy big enough to keep the sea lanes free at all times and all hazards.

There can be no solution of this problem by any world-wide verbal arrangement, or by the attempt to build up a physical and moral force large enough to impose victory everywhere, at any time, on any and all possible foes. There may be no solution at all. But the policy here offered, based upon the desirability of maximum self-sufficiency and minimum hazard, presents an approach on which statecraft can act. By domestic control over all foreign trade, by the relaxation of the capitalistic pressure of the United States on world markets in standardized manufactures and commercial investments, by concentrating national energies on the development of national resources and the efficient distribution of wealth at home, by deliberately withdrawing from the rivalries of imperialist nations, the United States would take its official nose out of a thousand affairs of no vital concern to the people of the United States, would draw back its defense lines upon zones that can be defended with the greatest probability of victory in case of war, and would thus have a minimum dependence on the "strategic products" indispensable to war. And by multiplying many fold its outlays for scientific research in analytic and synthetic chemistry, it could steadily decrease its dependence on world markets for the essentials indispensable to our material civilization in time of peace.

In short, by cultivating its own garden, by setting an example of national self-restraint (which is certainly easier than restraining fifty other nations in an international conference, or beating them in war), by making no commitments that cannot be readily enforced by arms, by adopting toward other nations a policy of fair and open commodity exchange, by refraining from giving them any moral advice on any subject, and by providing a military and naval machine as adequate as possible to the defense of this policy, the United States may realize maximum security, attain minimum dependence upon governments and conditions beyond its control, and develop its own resources to the utmost. Besides offering the most realistic approach to the dilemma and conforming in a high degree to the necessities presented by the posture of nations, it is a more promising way of life for the people of the United States.

Such a policy does not preclude constant and sympathetic collaboration and coöperation with other nations so minded. On the contrary, it can be most fully realized when other nations have put their own houses in order, repressed predatory interests within their own borders, renounced war in practice as well as in the theory of the Kellogg-Briand Pact, and organized their domestic economy in such a way that exchange on the new basis of mutuality of benefit is possible. Hence the immediate and future attitude of the United States toward the World Court and the League of Nations would not be that of passionate hostility (often interested hostility), or of undiscriminating friendship. Adherence to the World Court is already hedged about with sufficient reservations to protect the policy here advocated, and the question of joining the League would turn on modifications in the Covenant and the practices of nations designed to safeguard the interests of the United States as defined in the preceding pages.

When the various nations have developed their internal efficiencies, renounced commerce of pressure and violence, and prepared themselves by organization and change of acquisitive spirit for commodity exchange as mutuality of benefit, then the League of Nations can be developed into a coöperative organ for building something approximating "a world order," and facilitating the appropriate international transactions. Until then the United States will have a care for its interests conceived as security and commonweal.

SPECIFIC ISSUES OF POLICY

From the broad principles laid down as points of reference for designing and controlling policies and actions in detail, we turn to a consideration of the chief among the specific issues appearing as immediate exigencies. These issues include settlement of the intergovernmental debts, policies with respect to American investments abroad, the merchant marine, the munitions trade, so-called neutral rights in war time, practical institutions and procedure, the adjustment of domestic-interest conflicts arising out of past economic practices and export trade policies, and the organization of government to effect policy. These are stubborn realities which American statecraft cannot escape in the here and now, must deal with under some conception of national interest, either hit-and-miss or deliberately formulated and pursued.

Let us face first the intergovernmental debt issue. Like all problems of foreign policy this is also a problem of domestic-interest conflict between the broad public-interest and specific group interests. In the public-interest view, the debts owed to the Government of the United States rose out of funds provided by American taxpayers—direct and indirect—and payment of these debts will relieve American taxpayers of burdens, while non-payment will increase such burdens to some appreciable degree. On the other side is the special interest view. If these debts are paid they must be paid in goods and services, and the import of such goods and services for sale in the United States will conflict with or disarrange those domestic enterprises—industrial and agricultural—which supply similar or identical goods and services in the domestic market. If these debts are not paid, then domestic-interest groups affected will be relieved of the competition at home arising out of this import of goods and services. Moreover, non-payment of debts offers a promise of increased exports for certain domestic-interest groups, for the reason that payment for new exports in new imports will be facilitated. Likewise non-payment of debts to the Government of the United States will facilitate payment of debts owed to American private interests by foreign governments and enterprises, now in parlous condition, and make additional lending abroad easier for private interests.

Such, baldly stated, is the economics of the intergovernmental debt politics in the United States. There is no way of *proving* that the triumph of one or more large domestic-interest groups over the public interest of taxpayers will increase the real opulence of the American people. Nor can the contrary proposition be *proved*. Any conclusion on the matter is an *opinion* and nothing more.

How, then, does the issue appear within the above frame of policy? The essential element in policy conceived as commonweal is an economic organization at home which provides the greatest possible insulation of internal economy from the disruptions of uncontrolled international transactions. This does not necessarily mean "a closed economy," or less foreign trade. It means a more efficient control over the international transactions of the United States than is allowed under existing economic theories and practices, and for this very reason offers a wider range of methods for the liquidation of intergovernmental debts. It may employ all the devices available under existing conditions, and at the same time it renders new methods practicable. In fact, judging from the impasse of the past, there is every reason for believing that unless new methods are employed, the irritating controversy may drag on indefinitely, adding nothing to opulence and disturbing domestic economy and international exchanges.

To the policy of centralized control the old methods are available: cancellation, scaling, refunding at lower interest rates, and liquidation through formal lump-sum payments. But these operations would bring benefits to certain private interests, and the conception of public interest would, in that case, require a shift of some domestic tax burden to these private beneficiaries. If some such shift is not coupled with reduction or cancellation, it is likely that the pressures of the general taxpayers represented in Congress will not permit scaling operations to occur.

Among the newer methods which a commonwealth could employ, the following appear appropriate to that system of policy. Intergovernmental debts could be used to cover the expenditures for the maintenance of American embassies, legations, consular offices, and other agencies abroad—in better style than current congressional appropriations allow. They could be substituted for domestic capital exports, or employed in the development of raw-material supply sources in foreign countries, thus reducing the costs of necessary raw-material imports for American industries. They could be diverted in whole or part to a scheme for the establishment of a stable international monetary system separate from the national monetary system.

Since under the conception of national defense adapted to security (Chapter X) armament is a relative matter and every reduction in the burden of armament is a gain for opulence considered as an abundant life, intergovernmental debts could be applied in pressing for a general reduction of armaments, especially on the sea and in the air; for example, governments willing to cut armaments paralleling in costs cuts made by the United States could be allotted, as credits on account, the amounts saved to the American Treasury through reductions as against previous actual outlays. Inasmuch as the supreme aim in international affairs is security with peace, policy as commonweal would not cancel these debts in a sentimental gesture, on the false assumption that the forgiven debtors would increase their affections for the United States or surrender the pursuit of their interests in dealing with the United States, but would hold them as instruments subservient to the high cause of security.

Other specific measures are available in dealing with intergovernmental debts. Policy as commonweal proposes not only that "no American citizen shall starve," but also that a high standard of domestic life shall prevail. Now into this prevention of starvation and maintenance of a high standard two kinds of goods enter. The first are material goods—consumable commodities. And policy could allow foreign governments to discharge obligations to the United States in the form of material goods to supplement the doles, gifts, and other subventions made to millions unemployed or poorly employed. Domestic manufacturers, farmers, and merchants now supplying goods for which taxpayers must provide payment would be undisturbed by these imports, which would otherwise increase competition and close domestic outlets. They would continue as before, but supplementary supplies derived from debt-payment imports would raise the standard of life for the recipients of public relief. According to the recent trend the number of such recipients is likely to be large for an indefinite period.

No less important is the second class of goods—non-consumable intangibles, goods and services. These are objects of appreciation, delight, enjoyment, and intellectual concern. They include pictures, books, sculptures, maps, artistic and architectural designs, and services supplementary to those already created or which can be created in the United States. Under a commonweal policy, the United States Government could import from debtor countries immense quantities of such non-consumable, non-competitive goods and services, and distribute them freely to American museums, galleries, schools, colleges, and other institutions for the promotion of spiritual and intellectual life. Thus the country would be enriched in the truest and noblest sense of the term by the possession of goods and services available in the enlargement of its esthetic and intellectual appreciation and enjoyment. Moreover, the wide prevalence of such goods and services in America should form intangible connections with the countries of origin so powerful in the development of good will among peoples; and it might in the long run immensely enlarge the regular market in the United States for non-consumable goods of foreign creation. Doubtless practical persons will imagine that a barrel of gunpowder for exchange purposes in blowing up neighbors is valuable, while a beautiful picture hanging in a public gallery is not valuable because it brings no revenue and is not offered for sale; but the conception of national wealth pressed in these pages includes as wealth goods and services not sold or employed for profit-making.

Under the head of investments abroad, centralized control confronts two issues, one pertaining to existing investments and the other to future investments. In connection with the first, the essential problem, as in relation to intergovernmental debts, is one of transfer of payments to American security holders. It involves the question: How is the income from American foreign investments to be converted into purchasing power for the use of Americans at home and abroad? Only some technique which can meet adequately the transfer riddle can meet the situation already created by American investments abroad.

Clearly the solution of the transfer problem lies somewhere

in the field of foreign trade, and consolidated control of that trade in the national interest is the only technique that seems adequate to deal with the problem. Such a procedure will relax the pressure of American nationals and the American Government on the trade of other countries, and withdraw them from commercial warfare as carried on under historic conceptions. American direct investments in those countries, in the shape of mines, plantations, factories, and commercial services, will thus have a greater area of economic activity accessible to them in various parts of the world. Their expanded trade will enable them to translate income originating in each specific country in which investment exists into purchasing power for American investors to use in other countries. Increased trade activity among foreign countries will improve their situation, thus assuring Americans a better opportunity to realize on their "portfolio" investments in the public securities of those countries.

There now remains for consideration the transfer of earnings abroad into purchasing power expendable in the United States. Here again a single organization for trade offers a positive method of attack. With the rationalization of its trade, the United States can deliberately mark out broad areas for import which may be utilized to convert income from abroad into buying power within the country. It can correlate both its trade and foreign financing operations with the definite purpose of affording permanent conduits through which income from foreign investments may flow into the United States. This is a technique which is not now possible, on account of the constant fluctuations in international trade and the consequent uncertainty in international balances of payments. With American economy insulated from international economic disruptions, the possibilities of working out investment and credit problems would be indefinitely increased; while at present such operations are constrained to narrow channels and the historic methods which have so often and so miserably failed.

If, in the case of past investments, such are the lines projected by policy, what will be the rôle of future foreign investments in the scheme of things? First of all, a distinction must be made between investments and the financing of foreign trade. Although they have had a close connection in the past, they are by no means identical; and the assumption that they are in substance identical is responsible for no small part of the disturbances and dislocations of recent years.

Under the proposed plan investments abroad will be of two kinds. The one will supplement the controls in the trade technique. Indeed, the regular financing of trade relations will be a part of that technique. It will perform a temporary function such as serving as the medium for bridging the gap between existing producing enterprises and the markets, as trade acceptances now function in domestic economy. That part of foreign investments, such as "portfolio" and "direct" investments, which comes within the long term scope and has little if any immediate connection with trading operations, will tend to decrease. The financing of foreign industries which, in virtue of low living standards, will tend to thrust themselves into the sphere of American domestic economy and foreign trade operations will be prohibited. Loans for "cultural" purposes, such as building gilt-domed capitols and political boulevards, will certainly be closely controlled, if not forbidden. In time all foreign investments will be brought within the range of a single objective: safeguarding the integrated economy of the national life. Until this objective is established, all discussions of foreign investments are bound to be confused and contradictory, indeed largely unprofitable, if not futile.

Especially difficult will be adjustments in merchant shipping in the realization of projected policy and emerging practice. That activity is not purely economic in the contemporary world. It is connected with national defense, armament rivalries, and the warlike propensities of mankind. It is involved in the conflicts of army, navy, and aviation interests—so involved that the intellectual climate is full of fog and confusion. If all the forces of the American nation were concentrated on the problem of national defense adequate to the requirements of the posited zone and plans of the country, if the conflicts of the shipbuilding and aviation interests could be kept out of pressure politics, and if the rivalries of the Army and Navy for appropriations could be subdued to a genuine conception of national defense (above, Chapter X), then the merchant shipping issue could be handled on its merits, principally as a branch of foreign trade economy.

In that case, transportation of luxury, skill, cultural, and pure surplus goods (above, p. 214) could be left, at least in a large measure, to foreign shipping, and the credits applied to foreign debts due to the United States. Thus, by giving foreign shipping a real interest in a trade function not vital to American domestic economy, the Government would be in a position to exert pressure on the home country of any transportation concern whenever it discriminated against American interests or abused American confidence in the fairness of its commodity offerings in commercial exchange.

With those nations willing to put aside chicane and adopt the open and above board methods of international commerce herein described, the United States could enter into conference for the purpose of working out routes, cargo allocations, and transport conditions on a world or regional basis. But, as in the matter of investments, this cannot be done while world trade is regarded as internecine commercial warfare, that is, until participating nations have evolved and put into practice conceptions of domestic economy that are compatible with international trade as mutuality of interest, rather than as mutuality of distrust, cut-throat competition, and deception. As long as efforts are made to reconcile two irreconcilables, confusions of councils are bound to prevail.

Far more difficult of adjustment than the ordinary exchange of commodities is trade in munitions of war, and in goods intimately related to the uses of armed conflict. That this traffic, besides being essential to war, is a powerful force in stimulating preparations for war and stirring up the international hatreds from which wars spring is well known; and the thesis is abundantly documented in many studies, particularly in the elaborate work of Ralph H. Stimson, as yet unpublished. Certain facts are established beyond dispute. Munition enterprises in private hands are highly profitable, especially during war scares and actual conflict. Powerful personalities, including ex-officers, are associated with them. These concerns are international in their operations. In time of peace, and occasionally in time of war, they sell munitions to foe as well as to friend. Leaders among them have been implicated in propaganda, corruption of the press, and opposition to the policies of their own governments. They constantly seek new inventions for the purpose of rendering obsolete old equipment, and bring pressures on governments with a view to increasing outlays for armaments. It is not too much to say that munitions makers are among the most powerful, sinister, and corrupt influences in modern civilization, whatever may be the private virtues of individual manufacturers.

This situation is recognized in many official works and in Article VIII of the Covenant of the League of Nations. But the usual proposal for the solution of the problem, namely, government manufacture of munitions, does not dispose of the chief questions involved. As Ralph H. Stimson shows, it is impossible to draw a sharp line between munitions industries and other industries, between commodities useful for war alone and commodities useful for war and peace. As he also points out, government ownership does not escape the pressure of powerful private interests—such as organized labor insisting upon continuous employment at high wages in munitions plants, purveyors who sell materials to such plants, and military and political personalities interested in prestige, power, and politics. It is impossible to separate munitions manufacture from manufacture in general; and government ownership of munition plants, while theoretically eliminating the profit motive, introduces other pressures likely to be interested and also sinister. The rivalries of governments to sell to other countries might be more intense and irritating than the manipulations of private parties.

Since all industries now operate on the profit motive, and munitions industries are related to other branches of manufacturing, and since, as Mr. Stimson's statistical tables indicate, a rising pressure of munitions manufacturers for an increased export accompanies declines in the domestic market and depressions in general, it follows that something more fundamental than government ownership of munitions plants is necessary to eliminate and restrain this private interest in death and destruction. If all industries were fairly stabilized, as here contemplated, the pressure of munitions makers for outlets in time of depression would be reduced. If all industry were planned and controlled with reference to the national security and standard of life, then the munitions industries, direct and indirect, would come under this system of accounting. The Government might own and operate outright plants devoted to the manufacture of the leading munitions of war, such as warships, ordnance, and armored tanks. Other related industries could be keyed into these industrial operations, and all their accounts, profits, and expenditures could be made matters of record open to members of Congress and public officials. The pressure of private propaganda and corruption could thus be relaxed and with it the international tension arising from profit-making munition industries engaged in selling at home and abroad.

A vital question would yet remain: According to what principle should the Government of the United States control the export of munitions and related products? It would be the conception of national defense limited to its zone of interest. The Government would enter into general and regional agreements for the curtailment of armaments, with a view to reducing this burden of national waste, and in time of war it would place an embargo on, or release, munitions for export, with reference to its defensive interests as above defined. It would recognize the fact that an embargo on the export of munitions or a release of munitions for export is in substance an act of policy which is warlike in nature and a measure short of war. Thus the Government of the United States would control the munitions trade with reference to the perils to national defense offered by the actions of other governments, engaged in war and preparing for war. It would cast off the delusion that the export of munitions is a private matter to which national defense can be indifferent, at any time, in war or peace, and would make the munitions business an open adjunct to its war policy, that is, the defense of the national zone of interest.

Entirely apart from any grand conception of national policy, the munitions business deserves special consideration. Taking the democratic tradition at face value and in commonly accepted terms, there are reasons for singling out the munitions industry for particular treatment. According to the democratic theory, the interest of the majority must govern in political affairs, unless the arbitrament of force is to be relied upon. Under capitalistic ideology of the classical type, however, industry was long conceived as a war of all against all—*bellum omnium contra omnes*—a merciless conflict in which the strongest and most cunning survived. Yet even those who took this extreme position did not, openly at least, contend that participants in this internecine economic warfare should be permitted to make their own laws in utter defiance of public or State interest. The most ruthless among them conceded in principle if not in practice that certain forms of competition and activity had to be restrained, at least in the face of foreign enemies and in time of war. They recognized that industry had an obligation to effect a certain solidarity and mutuality of interests under the pressure of international rivalries and conflicts involving the life of the State. In these circumstances the right of each industry to do exactly as it pleased, without respect to other industries and the fate of the national interest, came under some imputation of restraint.

Nevertheless, industry has not yet fully developed the concept of majority and minority interests, and asserted the right of the majority to protect itself against the machinations of special interests, aside from all issues of State. It does not see clearly that a minority interest, such as the munitions industry, may bring ruin upon the majority of industries, or at all events, contribute to a disruption of their ordinary transactions, and burden them with ruinous taxes. Only now and then does an American industrialist betray any recognition of this fact and proclaim the right of the majority in industry to control the minority and establish self-protection against particular munitions industries engaged in waging their war for profits against all. It seems, from an examination of newspaper files, that Henry Ford, alone among outstanding industrialists, issued a vigorous protest against the machinations of munitions industries in 1934 when a widespread discussion of the subject was opened in the forum and press.[3] Other leading industrialists apparently either are unaware of the existence of this inner war of industries, or are linked with munitions purveyors, or are indifferent to their own fate. Here again, as was said with respect to the domestic economic crisis (above, p. 239), if industry can put no effective restraints on the most dangerous business in the United States, then the Government, unless it is to be enslaved to that special business, must develop and enforce such restraints.

Assimilated to the munitions business is the right of private interests to trade with belligerents in war time. To assume that this is a purely private operation to which policies of State can be indifferent is to ignore obvious facts in the case. Historic neutral rights, based on a possible classification of goods into contraband of war and non-contraband, have been destroyed by the technology of modern warfare and the accepted practices of nations, as illustrated in the World War. Historic neutral rights are now a mere fiction. To treat them as real rights which the Government is bound to support is to foster a dangerous delusion. Hence, in the program here proposed, control over foreign trade in time of war will be directed by the same principle as control over munitions. It involves warlike policy and will be shaped with reference to the perils to national defense raised by the foreign belligerents who seek to buy American goods in time of war. To speak concretely, the challenge of possible implication in war will be openly accepted by the Government of the United States in each case at the outbreak of a foreign war and the consequences of embargoes and control will be calculated with reference to the strategy and possible outcomes of that war, whether the United States enters it immediately and directly, or later, or not at all. The defense of so-called neutral rights in war time is a

[3] New York *Times,* March 8, 1934. An ironical illustration of interest-conflict appeared in connection with the Chaco war in 1934. Munitions makers in the United States were selling munitions to Bolivia, presumably for cash, while American investors could not get payments on the defaulted Bolivian bonds which they held. Here is another case of the survival of the "fittest" under the law of the capitalistic jungle.

warlike measure, however characterized in the polite language of diplomacy, and in the future will be adjusted to and controlled by the defensive policy of the United States.

Since insistence on historic neutral rights in the next general war, and on the right to sell supplies and munitions to belligerents, will, as sure as fate, involve the United States in that war, the only way to avoid being drawn into the holocaust is to establish positive restraints on such rights now by legislation. The nature of the restraints is indicated with compelling cogency by Charles Warren, a man competent through training and bitter experience to speak with authority.[4] Such measures would include (1) absolute ban on the sale of munitions as specified in minute detail, and on their shipment in American vessels; (2) exclusion from American ports of all armed ships of belligerents; (3) closure of American ports to the ships of all belligerents which permit their vessels to fly the American flag for purposes of deceiving the enemy; (4) exclusion of all belligerent prize ships from American ports; (5) exclusion of belligerent submarines and aircraft from waters and territory under American jurisdiction; (6) seizure of all vessels belonging to belligerents, which are not removed from American waters within a brief period of time; (7) prohibition of loans to belligerents; (8) prohibition of the recruiting of soldiers in the United States by belligerents; (9) forbidding the enlistment of American citizens in belligerent armies; (10) forbidding American citizens to travel on supply ships of belligerents. With such restraints on the operations of private interests clearly and firmly established in advance, the Government of the United States could then decide, on the merits of the issue as public interest, whether to enter or stay out of the war.

PRACTICAL INSTITUTIONS AND PROCEDURE

What would be the rules and instrumentalities required to give effect to the general program of foreign trade control just outlined?

The question certainly is in order, and the task of answer-

[4] *Foreign Affairs*, April, 1934, pp. 377 ff.

ing it, though involving hazards, will not be avoided, even at the expense of appearing amusing to the wise. Here is the answer ventured, or rather two answers. The first contemplates a thoroughgoing attack by a single federal agency on the whole problem of foreign commerce as related to an effort to build a decent civilization in the United States—a policy that may be forced upon the Government of the United States before the present crisis is mitigated, or at all events in the next general calamity of the kind. The second, more moderate, calls for a minimum of intellectual and moral effort, and is based on a manipulation of the tariff mechanism, so cherished by traditional politicians.

1. Control of Commerce by a Foreign Trade Authority

First. There will be established in the State Department a Foreign Trade Corporation, or Foreign Trade Authority, equipped with competent specialists in the physics and chemistry of commodities, in the distribution of the world's resources and industries, and in the present commodity movements of foreign exchange. It will have full power to control exports and imports into the United States directly and through licenses, with checks on performance provided by customs offices and shipping manifests.

The fact basis for its operations will be: (1) the import needs of the United States as determined by the domestic-arts budget and the reports of American technology; (2) the data of the world's resources and industries, indicating countries and regions from which import needs can be best derived in exchange for such goods as the United States has to offer; and (3) the reports of American technology on the goods which the United States can best afford to offer in exchange for the satisfaction of its import needs.

Second. The technique of operation in foreign trade. Trade agreements will be entered into with selected nations, on the basis of the best satisfaction of American needs. These selected nations will be asked to permit the entry into their territories, for fixed periods of time, of specified quantities of American goods, on a free trade, a revenue, or a predetermined tariff level. In return the United States will agree to receive specified quantities of foreign goods on determinate conditions of entry. The foreign nations in question need not, as nations, receive American goods on government account, nor will it be necessary for the United States Government to conduct trading operations through an official bureaucracy. In other words, the trade itself need not be carried on as a government enterprise. All that the participating governments need to do is to sanction the entry of specific quantities of goods as a practical political proposition. Bickering, quarrelling, threatening, and the operations of haggling would be eliminated at the outset. The position of the Foreign Trade Authority would be: "Here are the commodities which the United States desires to import. Here is the list of commodities we are prepared to offer in exchange. Here are the physical and chemical specifications for proposed imports and exports. We are prepared to do business with any country offering us the best basis of exchange."

How would the Foreign Trade Authority secure goods from American producers to be employed as exports in the payment for imports? It would invite domestic producers to make bids on supplying it with certain quantities of goods, as determined by foreign marketing agreements, at certain prices. The bid offering the largest desired quantity at the lowest domestic price would be accepted by the Trade Authority, and the producers paid in domestic currency or purchasing power, less the costs of exchange. Then, in the adjustment, the domestic price of the imports will be fixed on the basis of what it costs in the United States to produce the values delivered abroad in exchange.[5] In this way it will be possible to stabilize the whole area of the American market, domestic and foreign, for long periods of time on the basis of trade agreements. In this way real "surpluses" can be discovered and cut to a minimum, reducing the wastes and tragedies of over-expansion, contraction, and explosion. It would permit the establishment in each

[5] Triangular trade would be carried on by the same technique and agency, without losing national interest in the maze. In exchange for imports, where the United States cannot offer proper exports, the Authority can tender bills on other countries having such exports—bills acquired by direct trading operations with the latter.

country of labor standards, return on capital, and costs of production, without subjecting them to the upsetting influence of world-wide disturbances, as at present. The doctrine of comparative costs, which is now often a mere fiction in practice, would have a chance to function along the lines envisaged by Adam Smith.

Third. The question of values, or "prices," will immediately arise. For a time, given the disorder of national economies and their long servitude to the fetich of the price system, values in foreign exchange would doubtless be more or less arbitrary—the outcome of higgle and barter; but such a system would flounder in a psychological morass of abuse, deceit, and confusion. In due course a more rational and objective method would be developed.

On its part, the United States, having decided upon policy, would be equipped for exchange by a *knowledge* of the values of its commodities in terms of labor time, capital outlay, material cost, and general standard of living. It would also possess considerable knowledge of the values of proposed imports offered by other countries in terms of their labor time, capital outlay, material cost, and standard of living. If those nations should organize their economics on similar principles, this knowledge would become extensive and common property. If other nations exercise similar control, the values of their commodities tendered can be computed along similar lines, and thus the task of bringing exchange values into adjustment would not be an insuperable, even a difficult, performance. Where other nations do not exercise such control, the United States will advertise its list of wants and offerings and invite other countries to make bids on American goods proffered and indicate quantities tendered in exchange. Then the United States will trade with the lowest bidders offering comparable qualities, deliveries, and other benefits.

Fourth. The above paragraphs deal with the import of commodities deemed necessary to American economy, as circumscribed by the principle of security. Now we must consider articles of luxury, skill, and culture, and goods and services entering into pure surplus, so far as the essentials of the standard of life are concerned. The exchange values of products falling within this category may be established in either one of two ways: (1) the process of offering and bidding may be carried on in accordance with the technique applied to commodities deemed necessary to American economy, with present tariff practice harmonized with the procedure or not, as the importance of this branch of international commerce might dictate; (2) the exchange of such commodities may be left to complete freedom of individuals with values meeting in an international exchange market—the central banks of the several countries acting in unison to stabilize monetary factors, all subject to tariff restrictions, or none at all. In either case the volume of this business would bear a small proportion to the total volume of business and the stabilization of exchange would be made easier. Experience would indicate the extent to which the exchange of luxury and cultural goods would have to be controlled in the interest of stability and balance for the principal operations of foreign commerce.

Throughout the total process of international exchange, a prime consideration would be the utmost insulation of internal price levels from the disrupting influence of international trade activities—wars, dumping, revolutions, and price-cutting conflicts. Dumping would be ruled out entirely. The irresponsible exchange of goods as now carried on solely for the largest possible profits would likewise be ruled out, so that international trade would not become a savage competition in the reduction of standards of living. It is possible, indeed very probable, that two price levels would emerge: an internal or domestic price level sustaining the economy within the country, and an international price level at which commodities would exchange between the nationals or public agencies of one country, and those of another. Some such adjustment may be necessary to avoid the anarchy of world trade and maintain internal security.

2. Trade Control Through Tariff Mechanism

A second method of handling the flow of goods into and out of the United States, in line with the policy presented above, may be developed out of the tariff mechanism, with which

American politicians are so familiar. This method would involve the creation of a Public Corporation, or Foreign Trade Authority, charged with the duty of developing and systematizing the findings of engineering rationality with respect to the import needs and export potentials of the United States; but the Trade Authority would not actually control, through its own decisions, the movement of goods in international exchange.

In the processes of this second method—tariff manipulation—trade agreements need not be a part; nor would it be necessary to alter the existing channels and operations of trade as such to any considerable extent. Control would be exercised through the tariff mechanism itself.

Under this scheme the tariff mechanism will be employed to control effectively both price and quantities—price through duty levies and quantity through import and licensing features.

In the case of imports deemed necessary to American economy, as determined by the standard-of-life budget and engineering rationality, quantitative methods of importation will be dominant. Shifts in tariff schedules and classifications will gradually move imports of this character over to the free list, but with positive limits on the total quantities imported over any specified period of time.

In the case of luxury, skill, cultural, and pure surplus goods, as determined and specified by domestic action, price control through duty levies will dominate, with maximum quantities fixed in relation to the levels of domestic purchasing power, or in accordance with the calculated and probable effect of importations of this class on American economy.

Under such a policy many shifts of tariff schedules and classifications will be necessary to make the requisite adjustments. Many items on the dutiable list will be transferred to the free list, and *vice versa*, since the present schedules follow no conception of domestic economy whatever, but merely reflect the jostle and pressure of special and conflicting interests.

Such transfers will be effected by the Foreign Trade Authority on the basis of the findings established by the determination of the domestic living standard and the domestic facilities available to support such a standard of living in the most efficient way. With these positive mathematical determinations in hand, the Trade Authority will reorganize tariff schedules and classifications and set quantitative limits. Since the procedure presumes the utmost use of domestic productive equipment and capacities, and the application of engineering rationality in making determinations, the usual scramble for special favors should be reduced to a minimum. The data of determination will be open and above board. Imports will have to conform to the established plan of American economy according to standards as accurate as physics and chemistry can make them. When this conformity is assured, goods will be admitted for a term of years in spite of the objections of any special interests that remain unsatisfied under the national plan. Commodities not included in the list of permissible imports will be barred wholly or partly as the Trade Authority may provide.

In this program, prices will be determined much as they are now, by individual producers under the terms of industrial codes. The exchange process will operate much as it does now, with the exception that currency conversions will have to be stabilized as far as possible by international action. Stabilization, however, would not be as difficult as at present under the régime of private propulsions and determinations, because the interaction of the domestic price levels with international price levels will be adjusted and smoothed out by national control over the flow of commodities into and out of the country.

It is this interaction which in the past has operated to disrupt, intermittently if not almost constantly, prices and trade, both in the domestic and international markets. It is a regular accompaniment of "the normal course of trade" as historically conceived and practiced. Such schemes as the British Equalization Fund, the American Stabilization Fund, blocked marks, and other exchange controls represent efforts to overcome its disruptive effects and point in the direction of a separation of domestic from international price levels through monetary manipulations. Although viewed in some quarters as temporary expedients intervening in "normal freedom" it is highly probable that they are mere forerunners of a permanent mechanism for insulating domestic economy, in a large measure, from the shocks and vicissitudes of international commercial operations, and reducing both to more stable and complementary functioning.

Between the two plans of foreign trade control thus presented there is an important difference. That lies in the degree to which the Government takes part in the trading process. In the first plan (pp. 287-290), the Government is an agent, and its corporate authority the instrument through which and by which foreign trade is actually conducted. In the process that employs the tariff mechanism, the Government is not an actual participant in trading operations. Here the Government marks out the broad areas of trade and establishes the conditions according to which trade must be carried on; but within these broad limits individual nationals act in their own discretion, and for their own interest and account. They create obligations and settle them in ways similar to those historically pursued. The fact that the Government may enter into executive agreements with other nations for the adjustment of tariff rates, as contemplated under so-called "bargaining" tariff legislation, would not alter this relationship of the Government to private enterprise. Such agreements merely assist in defining and establishing the conditions in which trade is carried on among private individuals.

Of the two methods proposed, the one most likely to emerge immediately from the present confusion is the latter, that is, control through the tariff mechanism. That this will be so may be ascribed to the enormous "lag" which habit, tradition, interest, and institutional practices produce in social adjustments. But the process will be quite distinct from past tariff legislation and operations. The influences of government action upon the flow of trade will tend to shift the character of trade, and alter the channels of trade through the establishment of positive circumscriptions, conditioning commercial processes. In time, however, it is likely, new abuses will appear and dislocations will occur under tariff-mechanism manipulations, and the first of the two methods will be brought into action. In this case there may be a merger of the two methods: trade basically necessary and responsive to American economy will be conducted by the Foreign Trade Authority; while trade in luxury, skill, cultural, and true surplus goods will come under the technique of a tariff mechanism as described, or some modification of it.

DOMESTIC INTEREST ADJUSTMENTS [6]

It will be said on every hand, of course, that the policy here urged, and its subsidiary implications, will mean a serious readjustment of domestic interests; and as a rule those who advance this contention really hope to effect a realization of already vested private rights built up on past policies and methods—such as the right of an automobile manufacturer to sell abroad profitably the same number or a larger number of automobiles than in past years, or the right of a wheat farmer to sell profitably the same amount of, or more, wheat abroad. At bottom, this is what is meant by those who oppose the conception of policy as commonweal. And they paint dire pictures of the future under such a cultural polity. Henry A. Wallace presents their argument when he says: "If we continue toward nationalism we must be prepared to make permanent the withdrawal from cultivation of over 50 million acres of good farmland, and face the consequences of all the social and economic dislocations which are bound to ensue."

But those who think in such terms cannot thus avoid the issue of domestic dislocations and adjustments. At bottom they are thinking in terms of rights once historically vested and realized, and they are in fact divided into two interest-schools, agrarian and industrial. Each is seeking to protect its vested rights, often knowing full well that such protection or realization means dislocations and adjustments for the other. Mr. Wallace sees this clearly and advances boldly. His program of protection and realization for agriculture is to force dislocations and readjustments in industry, by reducing the tariff, by destroying rights vested under previous tariff policy, and importing an additional $500,000,000 worth of industrial commodities, in the hope of saving twenty-five million acres of farmland for their possessors. Likewise, on their side,

[6] For fuller treatment see above, Chapter IX, Interest as National Economy.

industrialists have shown themselves willing, and are still willing, to dislocate historic agriculture and force readjustments there. In other words, policy is to be special interest. There is no ambiguity about that. Politics is to continue as an open struggle among special interests, with what long term outcome for the nation no one knows, although the present impasse in which such a struggle has eventuated is well known.

That the control of foreign trade here contemplated will force domestic readjustments is beyond question. So will any modification of foreign trade policy worthy of notice. And if it comes to an unequivocal conflict of domestic interests, it is highly probable that the industrial interests will emerge triumphant, unless a schism should occur in their ranks (above, p. 64). Their tariff policy has not been touched under the administration of Franklin D. Roosevelt, and the adoption of the bargaining or reciprocity tariff measure is not likely to unhorse them. Certainly those divisions of American agriculture now strongly entrenched behind protective walls will swing to the industrialists in any severe struggle. And in the end, if experience is any guide at all, the present deadlock will be continued, under that conception of policy, bringing more ruinous "readjustments" in agriculture, industry, and labor, such as the country has suffered since 1920, to go no further back in time. This is more of the same kind of defeat (above, Chapters III and IV).

In final analysis, there is no choice in the matter of adjustments, if the crisis is to be overcome for more than a brief breathing spell. Neither the industrialist nor the agrarian policy can prevail when a real attack is made on the problem presented by the emergency. A commonwealth based upon the efficient use of national resources and talents and an efficient distribution of wealth is the only alternative to the continuance of the interest-conflict hitherto dominant, and to the acceptance of the waste, discouragement, social distress, and ruin which, tested by its fruits, flow out of that system of policy. Assuming a desire and will to overthrow the crisis, there is no choice before the American nation, save among the minor techniques which may be employed in attacking the problem of the efficient use of national resources. That drift and muddle may continue, will continue, is possible, nay, highly probable; that drift and muddle require the exercise of less intelligence and will than powerful constructive effort, may be granted, but such concessions to human weakness do not invalidate the thesis that the efficient use of national resources is a fundamental line of attack on the crisis.

Even if it were demonstrated that the policy of domestic concentration here advocated would be accompanied by lower standards of life in the United States, besides forcing painful domestic readjustments, it does not follow that a lowering of standards can be avoided by the continuance of the interest-conflict conception of policy. Such a reduction may be fated in the very trends of modern economy. But some things seem certain. Proof that the utmost self-sufficiency would actually lower the general standard of American life would not of itself demonstrate that it is more desirable for the United States to pursue a course of heavy reliance on world trade— followed, for example, by Great Britain—sink its agriculture into peonage, transform its population into an urban proletariat, jeopardize national security by incurring the hazards of world-war disruptions and wars of commercial defense in addition. Nor would it demonstrate that, in the long run, this reliance on external and uncontrollable chances would uphold even the present standards of life, such as they are for millions of the American people. On the other hand, it appears that policy as commonweal could make the lowering of standards, if necessary in view of world economy, more equitable to the American people and less perilous to the social order.

In any case, now that technology has established the fact that a high standard of life is physically possible, is within the grasp of our powers and resources, there is certainly more hope of approximate achievement in an open, avowed, direct attack on the domestic crisis with the instruments at hand than in any resort to the manipulation of currency and trade according to the policies and processes which have eventuated in calamitous results. And after all has been said for economics pure and simple, the issue of policy can be debated in terms of national ideals—the greatest possibilities of security, peace, and social order. In terms of civilization it is not the richest person who is greatest, but the one who makes the noblest and most effective use of his resources and talents.

ORGANIZATION OF GOVERNMENT TO EFFECT POLICY

If the unified and consistent policy thus proposed, or in fact any unified and consistent policy, is to be realized, then it follows that there must be a concentration of the departments, divisions, branches, agencies, and establishments in Washington which deal with foreign relations of every form and nature. To have the State Department pursuing one line, the Department of Commerce another, while the War Department and the Navy Department make policies of their own, and the Senate is at loggerheads with all, is not conducive to unity and supremacy of policy. On the contrary, the result is a divided and distracted government, which is no government, but a collection of competing agencies, bureaucracies, and politicians —one that multiplies rather than diminishes perils of conflicts and wars. It makes for vacillation and uncertainty, stirs up both enmities and false hopes abroad, and tends to the befuddlement of the nation in practice.

In order to give effect to the policy proposed above, a reorganization of federal administration would be imperative; and the following suggestions are offered: the abolition of foreign trade agencies and activities in the Department of Commerce; the concentration of all agencies having to do with foreign trade and relations in the Department of State; the consolidation of the Departments of War and Navy into one Division of National Defense, with two bureaus—Army and Navy; the abolition of the practice of giving Cabinet positions to the chiefs of War and Navy; the substitution of technicians for civilian politicians as heads of the bureaus of Army and Navy; the subordination of the Division of National Defense to the State Department; the establishment of a Public Corporation, or Authority, for Foreign Trade in the State Department; and the establishment of a Council for Foreign Affairs, including trade, to be composed of the President of the United States, the Secretary of State, the head of the Division of National Defense, the heads of the Bureaus of Army and

Navy, delegates from the Corporation or Authority for Foreign Trade, and representatives chosen by the Senate and House committees dealing with foreign affairs. Coupled with this reorganization would be a provision of law forbidding civil, military, and naval subordinates—active or retired—to write articles for the press, to make public addresses, and to give out statements on the foreign policies of the United States, likely to pass as official in nature. This would place no limitations on freedom of speech for members of Congress, but it would suggest the impropriety of wild and indiscriminate addresses on foreign affairs likely to stir up unnecessary enmities, launch quixotic enterprises, and endanger national security as disclosed by the policy of public interest.

Supplementing this concentration of establishments concerned with foreign affairs should be an amendment of the provision of the Constitution which makes it possible for one-third of the Senators plus one to defeat at will any treaty proposed by the Executive Department. The existing provision surrenders the control of treaty relations to partisan and factional groups. The disadvantages of the system have long been recognized and various expedients have been offered as substitutes. Perhaps the most appropriate proposal is that of requiring the ratification of treaties by a simple majority of both houses of Congress. Although this may not be an ideal solution, it seems more calculated to secure a representation of national interest than the present arrangement. In this case, a joint committee of the two houses on foreign affairs should be established and represented in the Council on Foreign Affairs suggested above. At all events, the ratification of treaties by the two houses would couple responsibility with power in the lower chamber and might tend to reduce the amount of undiscriminating discussion of foreign affairs in that body.

It may be said, perhaps in tones of horror, that the concentration of forces proposed above would mean the creation of an agency of substantially unlimited power over foreign relations. The contention is conceded. The answer to objections is that found in the *Federalist*. Since the United States is in no position to limit the powers of other nations, it should set no limits to the powers of its Government to deal with them, save that of ultimate responsibility to the nation from which its authority is derived. It will be said, also, that such power may raise great perils in foreign relations. The answer is that more perils are created by divided, confused, and irresponsible powers, variously directed and often controlled by private interests contrary to the supreme public interest. If power adequate to defining public interest and enforcing it cannot be entrusted to any public body, then national interest is a meaningless shibboleth and the maintenance of national economic security as public interest is impossible. Objections are, in fact, largely academic. There is good reason for believing that the autarchic tendencies of other governments will force such a concentration of policy and power in the United States, despite all theoretical objections that ingenuity can devise and offer. Again, it is a question of a correct interpretation of trends in the world realities of the living present.

Objections will be raised also against the "perils of bureaucracy" and the overburdening of the State Department. That there are perils in a bureaucracy cannot be denied, but it is easier to cope with the shortcomings of a bureaucracy than with the perils of economic crises and the wars engendered by the passionate quest for unattainable markets and for distant and dangerous points of naval support for commerce. With respect to burdening the State Department, it may be said in reply that this is necessary to maintaining the original principle of American Government, namely, the supremacy of civil policy and authority over military policy and authority. The concentration here proposed simply makes it easier for the President, who possesses authority and is burdened with authority, to discharge his obligations and exert control more effectively than is now possible, owing to the division and conflict of interests in the several departments and establishments of the Government.

THE NATIONALISM AND INTERNATIONALISM OF COMMONWEAL

The broad principles of policy for the United States and its implications in detail, as presented above, rest upon the assumed validity and authenticity of the following propositions:

1. The competition of capitalists, entrepreneurs, and merchants in the various markets of the world is economic warfare, however veiled, is a prime source of naval competition, and forms a large part of the substance of diplomacy, of which physical combat is a manifestation when issues of conflict cannot be adjusted by diplomacy.

2. A large part of modern commerce—how large has not been estimated—is not the exchange of commodities reciprocally useful to the participants, but is competition—effort to undersell, oust, and destroy competitors.

3. The export of capital on a large scale develops, in many, if not most, cases, competition with home industries, curtails the export of manufactures, and, to meet interest and amortization charges, demands imports which call for no balancing exports.

4. If American foreign trade were limited principally to the import of commodities necessary to the maintenance of a determined standard of life and to the export of commodities of which there is a genuine surplus, then the pressure of the United States in the world market would be relaxed and America would be viewed as a benefactor, rather than a belligerent competitor. Americans would be attending to their own business in most matters, serving as benefactors in others, and acting as competitors in none. Such a state of affairs would do more for peaceful relations with foreign countries than all the formulas of peace which could be devised, accompanied by increasing bitterness of trade rivalry.

5. With little or no dependence on other countries for the fundamentals of a standard of life, the United States would thus be less affected by European and Oriental wars and could more readily stand aside in the conflicts that may arise.

6. By attending to its own business, exerting no competitive pressure in international economic rivalries, standing ready to trade on a rational basis, capable of defending its zone of interest, the United States can command more respect and affection in other countries than by intermeddling with its neighbors' affairs, whether under the formulas of *Machtpolitik* or those of democracy, beneficence, and world peace. The expressions of gratitude received from European governments in

exchange for participation in the World War may serve as illustrations of the principle.

7. The United States can do nothing whatever to assuage the long racial, national, and economic bitternesses and rivalries of Europe by offering moral advice. It may do something by setting a living example, without seeking to set an example.

This type of policy may be branded as "nationalism," but, as Walter Lippmann has repeatedly pointed out, there is nationalism and nationalism. There is the nationalistic philosophy which assumes that a given "race" is endowed with superior qualities and is the agent of Almighty God, privileged and instructed to ride booted and spurred over "inferior races," to subdue, exploit, and "civilize" them, to impose "culture" upon them, whether it be the culture of England, Germany, France, or the Declaration of Independence. Under this philosophy, the nation which pursues it thrusts its navy and army outward against other countries, penetrates their boundaries, dictates to them, proclaims its sovereignty everywhere, asserts its "historic rights," and refuses arbitration and collaboration when its interests are challenged or infringed.

This is the nationalism, sometimes called predatory, against which historic internationalism is directed; but that internationalism does not come to grips with the dynamic and acquisitive thrusts of such nationalism. On the contrary, it neglects or ignores them, or assumes that their effects can be overcome by "modifying trade barriers," or by verbal agreements made in diplomatic language at international conferences. If the history of the past fifty years, the history of the past ten years, and the present state of international relations do not convince the advocates of traditional internationalism that they are on the wrong track and indulging in delusive hopes, then they are beyond the reach of knowledge based on experience.

In contradistinction to previous schemes of thought respecting international affairs, the type of thought urged throughout this work is not that of traditional internationalism or traditional isolation. It assumes that foreign policy and domestic policy are aspects of the same thing, that nations are governed by their interests as their statesmen conceive these interests, and that control over international relations can begin most effectively with control over domestic policies and forces at home, where each government does possess a high degree of power. So far as international affairs likely to be dangerous are concerned, these domestic policies and forces are essentially economic in character, public and private. If they are inexorable and determine the policies of State, then international relations are determined by them also. If, on the other hand, as here assumed, the State may destroy some of these forces, control and direct others, then the State, by fashioning domestic economy, may control foreign relations, in a large measure, by improving domestic conditions.

The nationalism of the commonweal, which is not nationalism in the generally accepted sense, while acknowledging the reality of politically organized societies, proposes positive control over the domestic forces responsible for outward thrusts of power which interfere with and sometimes dominate the affairs of other nations and backward peoples. It turns in upon itself so far as may be necessary to make the most effective use of its own natural resources and technical talents, and offers to the outside world honest goods at a just price in exchange for commodities not efficiently produced at home. Its diplomatic agents become diplomatic agents, not hucksters of trade, sneaking and snooping, twisting and turning to beat rivals, win concessions, and undersell competitors. Instead of wasting its energies and talents in vain efforts to impose its culture on other races, it channels and concentrates them on the building of its own civilization, offering to mankind an example in the use of talents and opportunities instead of trade artifices and bayonets and guns.

The chief operating base for the attainment of commonweal is not in an international conference, but in the council of the nation itself. And the character and force of the domestic energies and requirements which are to involve the economies of other countries are to be shaped with reference to domestic security, to the domestic standard of life adjusted to the hazards of international trade, and to the development of American nationality in its continental domain.

If the United States should continue and develop the policy

of economic security, limited defense, rational control, and reciprocal exchange here outlined, European nations would have before them more constants and fewer variables in American policy by which to shape their course. The United States thus would not attempt to play the rôle of philanthropist by advising European countries, or intervening in their historic quarrels. It would take care of its interests on principles and terms open and known to the world by acting within its own jurisdiction, namely, its limited defensive zone.

The policy proposed as within the sphere of positive action by the Government of the United States does not, as may be hastily supposed, run counter to "prudent and generous international collaboration." It attacks the problem at a point where it may be attacked effectively with some prospect of success, namely, within the United States. It is based upon the conviction that the conflicts and controversies of nations do not arise outside the respective nations, but spring from outward thrusts originating in domestic economies and forces.

Far from excluding collaboration with other nationalities, the policy here expounded demands a domestic practice which makes collaboration possible and transforms it from efforts to overreach and outdo rivals in chicanery into efforts to exchange openly given quantities of goods at just prices, and to live on fair terms with neighbors so ordered and so minded. It is not pacifism proposing peace at any price. It does not put aside the conception of defense. On the contrary, it arranges its commitments and responsibilities in such a fashion that they may be actually defended with a maximum possibility of victory in case of war. It does not make world-wide claims and then withhold from its soldiers and sailors the power necessary to defend them in fact. It is cautious but not cowardly; circumspect, but not supine. It is pacific but not pacifist. It does not assume that the arts of war are superior to those of peace, but makes them servants of a clarified national purpose in which the utmost development of the peaceful arts in security will be the goal of statecraft. It does not reject the World Court, but accepts adherence to the tribunal under reservations already made. It does not rule out of consideration the League of Nations, but proposes the conditions on which the League can be brought into harmony with national interests conceived as security and commonweal. It does not exclude any noble sentiments associated with historic internationalism. Quite the contrary; it gives them positive content and treats them as precious values—precious, that is, to a conception of nations as civilizations set over against predatory barbarisms.

CHAPTER XIII

IN THE SPHERE OF PRACTICAL ACTION

A THEORIST may present a conception, a system of economy, or a utopia without thought of any practical outcome, with a gesture of take it or leave it; and it cannot be said that such speculative philosophers are without their use or influence in the general run of life. But throughout this work the crisis is treated as one in thought and action, and this union of the two in consideration calls for an examination of ways and means to be employed at once in an effort at realization. It is thus necessary to face the hard question: How are you proposing to start on transforming program as necessity and ideal into realization?

Various interest groups dominated by fixed ideas, imagining themselves to know the sure, one thing to think, say, and do will bring forth their formulas. It is contrary to the Bible, or the Constitution, or the Great American Tradition, or the Euclidian inexorabilities of Karl Marx, or the demonstrations of the New Deal. On the right it will be asserted that all we have to do is to do nothing. "Nature" will take her course, and recovery or restoration, on a bigger and grander scale than ever, will come from "around the corner" like blessing in the night. On the left it will be said that only the proletariat can conceive a commonwealth, can plan and execute plans, can bring international peace, and that before the proletariat can function it must "overthrow" the capitalist system by violence, spreading the wreck and ruin of inherited ideas and practice in all directions. In the middle, fascism is proclaimed as the inevitable outcome of the conflict, as the one and only gospel of salvation—fascism as irresponsible, dictatorial force.

Such are the responses which those who are *sure* that they *know* make, amid the thunders of their own Sinais, to all other quests for the shape of things to come and to be made. Anyone who accepts the one is damned by the others. Anyone who suspects that history may not take, in fact, the course they severally prophesy, and that other alternatives are open to choice, receives the unanimous condemnation of all three courts of assurance. In short, it is held that thought outside the fixed categories of these faiths is trivial and irrelevant, the acquisition of fundamentally new knowledge by the processes of research is impossible, and the exploration of new ways of accomplishing ends is a form of treason to sovereignties that *know* history and clothe their policies in the guise of the historical necessity which they have manufactured for their purposes.

As a matter of fact, however, any student fairly well acquainted with multitudinous facts of history and the history of systems of closed omniscience can turn historical weapons against them. No one can *know* history as it actually was, is, and will be, for to know it is to possess the attributes ascribed by the theologians to God. Moreover, enough facts of history are established to demonstrate the proposition that the exact patterns of past institutions, practices, and conduct, once dissolved, have never yet been "restored" or "recovered," thus making highly improbable any restoration or recovery of any past order in the years to come. As for communists, they may be reminded, in their reliance on the violence of the proletariat as the guarantee of victory, that their chief engineer, Marx, had no such faith, but believed that the ruin of the contestants was also a probable outcome of any class struggle. And fascism is also an answer of violence to the despised "liberalism" and "democracy" inherited from the nineteenth century—an answer which leaves unsolved the essential problem of putting technology and the industrial arts to work, even unapproached, if the history of fascism in Italy and Germany is any guide to knowledge.

That violence, widespread, revolutionary, and international, may intervene in efforts to bring into being an economy of abundance and security is certainly among the possibilities of the immediate or distant future. That it will, or will not, is not, and cannot be, *known*, as the coming of tomorrow's sun is known. But whether it does intervene or not, violence leaves unsolved and untouched the fundamental problem of giving effect to the potentialities of the industrial arts, technology, and resources in the United States. Before violence begins, the issue presents itself as a problem in engineering rationality and social conduct. After violence ends, if any reason is left and the possibility of orderly social conduct has not been drowned in rage and hatred, the issue will still remain as a problem in applied engineering rationality and social conduct. In the science of probability, as it now stands in contemporary thought, there is no assurance that prolonged and extensive violence, communist or fascist or international, will not make the employment of social and engineering rationality out of the question for a thousand years. Those who think they are sure are mere guessers.

If anything is known, however, it is that certain operations are requisite to bringing technology and the industrial arts into full use in the United States, whatever concomitants of conflict and violence may appear in coming history. The requirements of a standard-of-life budget must be known. The resources of nature, technology, and the industrial arts for supplying these requirements must be known. Coöperation on the part of practically the whole population of the United States will be necessary to bringing these resources into efficient use, and knowledge of the terms, conditions, and fruits of that coöperation must be deeply impressed upon the mind of every man, woman, and child in the United States. Surely all who are concerned with resolving the crisis in economy and thought, as distinguished from their personal interests and propensities for rage, will admit that this knowledge of demand and powers, needs and resources is indispensable to efficient action. They will likewise agree that, so far as common action in the field of rational conduct is necessary to applying resources to needs, a nation-wide spread of relevant knowledge is indispensable to effective action, whatever techniques of emotional appeal may be engaged in promoting knowledge and stimulating action.

If this is so, then statecraft, as contrasted with the politics of attaining and retaining power for its own sake, is under obligation to see that the requisite knowledge is acquired, that it is universally distributed, and that agencies of application are called into being. It is by neglecting this function and following the policy of drift and muddle that statecraft increases the probabilities of collapse and violence, perhaps postponing indefinitely opportunities of constructive achievement. Hence by the necessities which must accompany the establishment of security and functioning economy, statecraft as action is compelled to proceed along certain lines clearly indicated by the requirements of the problem and efforts at solution.

In starting and carrying on this procedure is it necessary to change the Constitution of the United States? Owing to the fact that special interests opposed to the national interest, conceived as commonweal, often employ that venerable document as a shield and defense mechanism, it is frequently assumed that nothing can be done until the Constitution has been fundamentally modified or supplanted by some other plan of government. Seldom do those who wage verbal battles over this theme take a realistic and historical view of the supreme law of the land. Generally they treat it in an animistic fashion as a beneficent or maleficent spook or fetich which, of its own motion, will effect the desired good or impose on fate the hated evil; whereas the Constitution is, as the great commentator Cooley said long ago, just what the American people in their thought and practice believe that it is. Within its ample folds, or under its elastic language, the United States has had, at certain times, loose and highly individualistic anarchy and, at other times, closed and omnipotent dictatorships. And such polar oppositions have been entirely within the letter and spirit of the Constitution as indicated by the debates in the constitutional convention of 1787 and the *Federalist* written as an appeal to the voters for support.[1]

To be sure, opposition parties and factions have usually assailed the concentration of leadership and energy in the executive as Cæsarism, tyranny, and dictatorship and as "the abject surrender of Congress to the President," but in point of fact all parties and factions have employed executive concentration or have been willing to employ it as their interests have directed. Hence those who are concerned with the substance

[1] Especially Number LXIX.

of things, as distinguished from the verbalism of debate, give no thought to such lucubrations but accept them as the froth that always accompanies great action in the forum.

The enormous concentration of powers in the hands of President Franklin D. Roosevelt by the congressional legislation of 1933 was entirely within the letter and spirit of the Constitution as indicated by historical practice and the development of judicial opinion. The power of Congress to recall, modify, and cashier was not surrendered, but remained potential as before. To characterize such a convergence of authority a dictatorship is to employ words without any respect to historical or practical usage. A dictatorship means the possession of irresponsible power beyond recall or modification except through physical violence. No such institution was established by the legislation of 1933; nor need it be established to accomplish the program presented in the preceding pages. On the contrary, since the coöperation of the masses of the people is required, the continuance of representative government, as expression and control, is indispensable to the long time functioning of the domestic economy projected.

Perhaps equally verbalistic are most discussions of popular demand, opinion, compulsion, consent, and acquiescence in politics. That the essence of government in final analysis is compulsion cannot be denied; but compulsion without a high degree of desire, consent, and coöperation on the part of large groups and classes is out of the question. At no point is it possible to separate opinion as demand from opinion as consent and acquiescence. As G. D. H. Cole has pointed out, a great deal that goes under the head of liberty is compulsion, social or governmental. The millions of unemployed seeking work or relief have the appearance of being free persons with liberty of choice in the present order of things. How much, in truth, do they choose their channels of conduct or voluntarily acquiesce in the state of affairs by which they are constrained? It would take more than a philosopher to answer that question. Governments create demand or opinion, as well as respond to it, and they have always discharged this function with more or less effect. Opinion, consent, acquiescence, and compulsion are all interwoven in a single emotional complex to which ap-

peals are made by statesmen and by those who would oust or
supplant rulers actually in power.

In any system of politics, whether dictatorial or democratic,
initial motive forces come from individuals and groups of individuals who present or submit proposed programs of action.
Not even a Hitler or Mussolini when actually in power declares
baldly that the sword put him in power and that the sword
alone will keep him there; as an American writer once remarked even the Grand Turk must truck and huckster in order
to hold his authority. Still more in American society, where
literacy is widespread and the right to turn out elective officers
retained, is it necessary for leadership in politics to operate
through the popular appeal. No other course is open to it,
whatever instrumentalities or ends are actually proposed. And
under the Constitution of the United States, as expounded by
the *Federalist* and revealed in practice, the task of leadership
may appropriately be assumed by the President. It has been
assumed in times past and may be assumed in the present and
future.

In assuming leadership the President, naturally, incurs the
risk of being baffled if not defeated by groups and interests
opposed to him. This truth may be illustrated by innumerable
references to past and current history. The same fate may
befall those who aspire to dictatorship either by appeal to the
middle classes or the proletariat. The assumption of fascist or
communist leaders that their appeal cannot fail is likewise without warrant in history. To be sure, Karl Marx declared that
change in the direction toward which he pointed his proposals
was inevitable and that the technique of revolution by the proletariat was the unequivocal instrument for bringing about the
climax. But this is sheer assumption beyond any possible
verification of knowledge. For all anybody knows, communist
agitations and appeals may be the chief forces in bringing
about the utter defeat of all working class movements, their ex-
tirpation root and branch, and the establishment of middle-
class dictatorships, as in Italy and Germany, equipped with
tanks, poison gas, bombing planes, and other instruments of
destruction. The contrary may be asserted, but it cannot be
proved by reference to knowledge as distinguished from hopes

and faiths, notwithstanding the "necessity" and "determinism" so freely and confidently employed by Marxians. Nor, on the other side, can fascists be certain that the very forces of passion and hysteria which they evoke will not in the long or short run shatter their authoritarian and totalitarian state, if they fail to deliver the promised utopia—their absolute.

It is, then, always with the prospect of defeat before him that the President of the United States assumes leadership on a petty or grand scale; but owing to the magnitude of the crisis in which the nation is now struggling and the evident necessity of action on large policy, there is more likelihood of defeat and oblivion in caution, timidity, and indecision than in the bold stroke that brings pivotal issues to a focus. It may be that the nation would on a solemn referendum declare in favor of another gambler's chance, like that of 1929, but if the nation is "sound at heart," as proclaimed by statesmen of all schools, then the prospect of victory for commonweal would be enhanced by a central drive aiming at nothing less than resolving the crisis in economy and thought by bringing the resources and technology of the United States into efficient use in maintaining a posited standard of life. What would be the initial procedure?

The first step would be to create, perhaps under powers already enjoyed, a single national authority, with two divisions: (1) a division charged with the responsibility of fixing a national standard-of-life budget with quantities, qualities, and specifications expressed in the most exact and scientific terms; (2) a division of production specialists empowered to show in how far, and by what methods, the resources and industrial arts of the United States can supply the requisite goods and materials. As a matter of course women expert in both fields would be included in both divisions. This would not be another fact-finding commission to heap up tons of meaningless statistics for the bewilderment of the nation. The business of the authority would be to indicate just what must be done to establish a national standard of life, and the resources and powers to be employed in creating and maintaining it. It would not be a vague declaration in favor of "the abundant life"; it would be a statement showing the shoes, coats, hats, houses, electrical apparatus, and the thousand or more additional things requisite to an abundant life, and a bill of particulars describing the nature and applications of resources and industrial arts necessary to the continuous provisions of the enumerated commodities, including imports needed.

In essence the report of the standard-of-life authority would be a realistic picture of the American nation in terms of things and processes appropriate and indispensable to the highest possible standard of life—a picture as realistic as the domestic arts and engineering rationality *can* make it. It would not be a utopia, beyond attainment, but a forecast of reality actually possible. It would be accompanied by maps, pictures, and other forms of graphic presentation dramatizing the whole conception and by engineering specifications of technological ways and means of attaining the posited ends. At the center of the graphic presentation would be illustrations of scattered and fragmentary accomplishments already effected in the United States—in homes, arts, sciences, and industries—contrasted with graphic presentation of the shanties, miseries, and degradation so evident in the American scene. In the engineering specifications current achievements in production would be included, as well as the specifications of new performances required by the national standard-of-life budget. In short this report would be the most stupendous and superb presentation of accomplishments, possibilities, and projects ever made in the whole history of civilization.

Before the report is finally submitted to the nation it would be presented to the representatives of interests opposed to any such conception of policy and they would be called upon to indicate why and how, in their opinion, it cannot or should not become the program for America. Thus would be disclosed the chief interests and methods standing in the path of realization. In this open way would be made clearer the measures and practical steps necessary to proceed with the program.

On completion, the President of the United States would present the report to the nation, by messages, addresses, and radio. Either the whole document or condensed outlines of it would be sent to every newspaper, every family, and every single individual in the country. It would be made the prime document of policy to which all partial measures would be referred for consideration and testing. It would become the center of discussion wherever and whenever the affairs of the nation are under review and debate. It would give immediate guidance to individuals and communities, indicating how each may begin immediately on some phase of realization. For the loose language of current politics and economics, it would substitute positive indications of *things which may be done,* objectives that *can* be attained.

By presenting ordered knowledge and vision, the program for America would give direction to public education, now so rudderless. If it is the business of education to indicate things that may be done, powers that may be developed and applied, then the program would become the supreme document for all makers of curricula, in the social studies, sciences, and arts. At the very center of contemporary educational activities, now so bewildered, mechanical, and contradictory in aims and hopes, it would place a solid core of known things that can be accomplished by the employment of rational and imaginative faculties in appropriate ways. In its terms, neither too rigid to admit of free discussion nor too vague and flabby for profitable consideration, the program would provide guidance for perplexed educators tossing to and fro in their efforts to find a scheme of instruction that will command the affection and energy of youth and indicate outlets for imaginative and creative activities.

In these and other ways, knowledge and comprehension of what may be done to bring the powers of America into full use would be spread abroad throughout the land from one end to the other, thus making possible and providing conditions of realization. In such ways approval, consent, acquiescence, knowledge, and coöperation must be attained, whatever violences of power politics may intervene, if the full potentialities of American resources, industrial arts, technology, and skills are to be brought into action in the creation of a standard of life and a civilization worthy of the best that is known and dreamed.

Is all this chimerical, that is, outside the thought of practitioners in politics and the realm of "practical politics"? The answer is that some such stupendous intellectual and moral effort has already been sanctioned by the words of Franklin D. Roosevelt, President of the United States. The broad view of history as movement of necessities and ideas he has made his own. With evident pleasure, in speaking of "so-called economics," he quotes the following passage from "that father of economists, John Stuart Mill": "History shows that great economic and social forces flow like a tide over communities half conscious of what is befalling them. Wise statesmen foresee what time is thus bringing and try to shape institutions and mold men's thoughts and purposes in accordance with the change that is silently coming on. The unwise are those who bring nothing constructive to the process, and who greatly imperil the future of mankind, by leaving great questions to be fought out between ignorant change on one hand, and ignorant opposition to change on the other." [2]

In his writings and speeches, President Roosevelt has also made it clear that he has made a study of, and given thought to, the rise and growth of city planning, regional planning, state planning, and national planning in idea and practice. While he was governor of New York he manifested interest, recommended measures, and took certain steps in line with that movement. Between his election and his inauguration he studied and sifted innumerable plans that had been presented to public consideration and employed his findings and conclusions as a broad basis for operations after he took office. "As far back as the autumn of 1930," he says, "I had begun to discuss ways and means for the relief of unemployment and for the reconstituting of our economic machinery. This involved, of course, a complete survey not only of agriculture and industry and finance, but also of the social needs of the whole Nation." [3] Thus, as he adds, he began "to apply to industry a concept new in our history." There was to be a social inventory of the whole nation and of industry and agriculture in relation to those needs. Here is certainly a break with the traditions of industrialist and agrarian statecraft.

Although compelled to act immediately with reference to

[2] *On Our Way*, p. 189.   [3] *On Our Way*, p. 84.

the banking collapse, unemployment, starvation, and misery, using many expedients at hand, the President continued to lay emphasis in his thought, and in certain striking measures, on the conception of a grand national plan. This he brings out in connection with the Tennessee Valley Development. The plans for this region, he says, "contemplated the creation of a public authority to direct the development of a region comprising thousands of square miles. . . . By controlling every river and creek and rivulet in this vast watershed, and by planning for a highly civilized use of the land by the population of the whole area, we believed that we could make a lasting contribution to American life." [4]

Though a single enterprise, the Tennessee Valley Development was regarded as a real beginning in applying the principles of survey and planning to the entire nation. Speaking later of the work in the Tennessee Valley, President Roosevelt said: "I look forward to the time in the not distant future, when annual appropriations, wholly covered by current revenue, will enable the work to proceed with a national plan. Such a national plan will, in a generation or two, return many times the money spent on it; more important, it will eliminate the use of inefficient tools, conserve and increase natural resources, prevent waste, and enable millions of our people to take better advantage of the opportunities which God has given to our country." [5] Moreover, the President is conscious that there is an "amazing and universal increase of the intelligent interest which the people of the United States are taking in the whole subject of government. In cities, in hamlets and on farms men and women in their daily contacts are discussing as never before except in time of war, the methods by which community and national problems are ordered." [6]

Here, then, is indisputable evidence that the conception of an attack on the crisis in economy and thought on a national scale through a survey of needs and an application of technical powers and skills appears in the frame of reference of President Roosevelt who, tested by the canons of practical politicians, is not lacking in practical sense. The broad philosophy of the controlling thesis presented in the pages of the present

[4] *On Our Way*, p. 54.   [5] *Ibid.*, p. 205.   [6] *Ibid.*, p. 244.

work has thus been officially anticipated. What is urged here is a swift speeding up of the process, a courageous whole-sale advance on the entire front, a dramatization of the task before the nation, a deliberate preparation of the people through all instrumentalities of education for a comprehension of the problems involved and for effective coöperation, and finally the formulation and execution of measures designed with a view to realization. The movement of acknowledged necessities compels action and the movement of ideas indicates the lines of constructive effort ahead. To concede that con-fusion, set-backs, reactions, and shortcomings will accompany the processes is merely to admit the truism that in human affairs only some rough approximation to the ideal is possible to thought and labor.

But a caveat must be entered now. Although President Roosevelt has more or less clearly envisaged the issues involved in creating a "sound internal economic system" for the United States, he has not yet brought the foreign policy of the United States entirely into line with his domestic theory. Nor will it be easy for him to accomplish this task on account of the en-tanglements which previous policies have created in all parts of the world and the pressures of powerful interests still bent on realizing on their properties and risks. He has, it is true, professed his devotion to peace, declared against single-handed intervention in Latin America, announced a new canon of recognition for Central America, approved the Senate investi-gation into the munitions manufacture and traffic, recognized the munitions business as "a serious source of international discord and strife," urged the ratification of the international convention for controlling the arms traffic signed at Geneva in 1925, recognized Soviet Russia, presented for consideration another non-aggression pact, suggested a willingness to abstain from interfering in collective actions taken by other nations against aggressors, approved the abolition of control over Cuba by the partial repeal of the Platt Amendment, supported Phil-ippine independence, and joined the International Labor Organization. The significance of these measures is not to be overlooked or minimized.

Over against them are to be placed, however, other considerations. The profession of peace is made by all contemporary statesmen, no matter how aggressive their foreign policies may be. Action in Cuba will speak louder than words. The recognition of Russia may properly be conceived, among other things, as an implement of traditional *Machtpolitik* in the Far East. The Roosevelt administration has, perhaps inevitably, reasserted the policy of the open door in the Orient, which is a form of American intervention in China against other powers. At the same time, President Roosevelt has displayed an apparent hope that substantial outlets for the "surpluses" of American industry and agriculture can actually be found in the manipulations of tariffs and trade agreements in the old style. Finally, and still more important, is the fact that he has contributed materially to the recent acceleration of the armament race by allocating nearly three hundred million dollars from public relief funds to naval construction and sanctioned congressional action authorizing additional construction to the amount of more than a billion dollars. If, therefore, President Roosevelt has a foreign policy appropriate to the trend of his domestic policy, he has not yet revealed it. It may be that he is waiting the opportune hour or that he really hopes to avoid the issue and reconcile two opposites which are beyond the possibility of reconciliation. Only the future can disclose the truth of this matter.

AMERICA'S HOUR OF DECISION

Such then is the posture of the American Republic amid the world of nations. Its past is closed and determined for all time. That past can never be restored, recovered, or repeated. The great trends or tendencies of the living present are stubborn and irreducible: multiplication of government functions and responsibilities, increasing centralization of control in private economic life, expanding quest for social and economic security, growing industrialization of nations, intensification of the struggle for markets, multiplying controls of governments over international trade, amplification of armaments and preparations for war, and the spreading revolt against the systems of thought and practice which have eventuated in the crisis of economic and moral life.

Over against these tendencies is contemporary knowledge of powers that can be unfolded and possibilities that can be achieved by plan, will, and effort. The science of engineering has demonstrated that the full use of our national resources, technical arts, and managerial skills *can* provide a high standard of life and security for the American people. The tragic issue of the conflict between the ideal (in homes, farms, factories, transportation systems, and objects of beauty and inspiration) on the one side, and the real (the ugliness, wastes, inefficiencies, miseries, and degradation) on the other, *can* be resolved by the application of our arts and sciences; and the real thus brought within a fair approximation of the ideal. Like Mount Rainier this central fact, known and subject to authentication, lifts itself up on the American horizon, high above the dust and pettiness of personal and political controversies. It catches the imagination and hopes of youth; even old age trying to warm itself by chill embers of reminiscence admits its challenge.

Already the vision of things that can be achieved by the talents and energies of the Republic applied to its natural resources is caught by millions of the American people. Already the fateful spell of dream nothing, hope nothing, do nothing, and grasp at the false shadow of easy fortune is breaking. Even now, on the verge of the impending future, thought and practice advance on the work to be done, haltingly and amid futile conflicts, but surely and resolutely. Set-backs may come, will come, as between 1850 and 1865 or 1893 and 1900, the timidity of leaders will baffle and bewilder, wars may intervene; but the lines of advance are plotted, and unless science, technology, the domestic arts, and the American spirit are to be defeated, no other course seems to be open.

Enthroned between two oceans, with no historic enemies on the north or south, the Republic can be defended against any foes which such a policy might raise up against it. By withdrawing from the war of trade and huckstering, by avoiding the hateful conflicts of passionate acquisition in Europe and the Orient, by offering to exchange honest goods for honest goods without employing any engines of coercion, by using its own endowment wisely and efficiently, it could really make its diplomacy the diplomacy of "the good neighbor," as distinguished from the diplomacy of the dollar, the navy, and the marines. Nations choosing the predatory course could continue fighting like cats and dogs over crumbs of trade, burn down their houses, drench their peoples with bombs and poison gas, and exhaust their powers in senseless rage. The American Republic would have no part in it, would sell no munitions to belligerents, would lend them no money, would sit in no diplomatic game played in the old style for old ends. It would surrender forever the imbecilic belief that it should or could "defend" every dollar invested everywhere and every acquisitive merchant seeking his private interests everywhere. It would engage in no race for naval supremacy but would provide an army, a navy, an aviation force, and coast defenses adequate to the protection of the continental domain. Having adopted this program and established its own security, it would tender coöperation and collaboration to nations willing to surrender predatory conceptions of power and to devote themselves to the development of their own resources and talents to the uttermost. Offering to the world the strange sight of a national garden well tended, the United States would teach the most effective lesson—a lesson without words.

In due time the American Republic must adopt and pursue deliberately this course, if it is to avoid costly and bloody entanglements in the historic quarrels of Europe and Asia. If, as H. G. Wells forecasts in his *Shape of Things to Come,* wars and revolutions do lay the earth in ruins, this course will remain the only way open to builders, after berserker destructionists have burnt out their wrath and folly. Should those who now direct the domestic and foreign policies of the United States play the old game in the old way, despite plain evidences of its inexorable outcomes, and seek to escape the domestic crisis by diplomatic fulminations, war scares, and war itself, a new crisis would come upon the Republic in forms and aspects more terrible to contemplate. The policy adopted by Grover Cleveland in the panic of 1893-97 (above, p. 101).

can no longer be carried on covertly and without effective public protest. The policy forced upon the Republican party and
the United States by Alfred Thayer Mahan, Theodore Roosevelt, John Hay, and Henry Cabot Lodge is buried under the
ruins of economic defeat (above, pp. 47 ff.). Another course
is plotted by the trend of things and an hour of decision has
come.

INDEX

Agadir, 172

Agrarian statecraft, especially concerned with outlets for farm produce, 36; subjected to test of historical experience, 70; its center of interest, 70; is intra-national and anti-imperialist, 70; its program most fully applied 1897-1933, 71

Agrarian thesis examined, 71; elements embraced by, 71, 72; analysis and criticism of, 72; tariff barriers, 73-75 (see also Free trade); item two in, challenged, 84-86; item three, once a prophecy, now an assertion of possibility, 87; trend reversed, 87; can nations in future be induced to reverse trend? 87, 88; summary of, 89, 90

Allies, during World War, definition of, of contraband of war, 255, 256; interference of, with American ships and goods, 256

American nation, and its interest, two elements in the problem, 179; the society with which American statesmen and citizens are concerned primarily, 179; immediate manifestations of crisis within jurisdiction of U. S., 179; focus of power, Government of U. S., 179; what American statesman confronts, 179; what concretely is the, 179; a summary, 208, 209

American nationality, racial elements in, 187, 188; nationalism of European type impossible in U. S., 188; a cultural polity, possessing objective and subjective characteristics, 188; a significant fact bearing on immigration, 188, 189; rise of organized labor a force directed against influx of cheap labor, 189; view rejecting racial interpretation of immigration bill of 1924, 190; comment of N. Y. *Times* on this measure, 190; psychological tests to determine desirability of immigrants, 190, 191; findings attacked, 191; report of eugenics expert still more important in shaping determinations of Congress, 191; what report seemed to show, 192; on the point of unassimilable immigration, 194; white population as of 1920 according to findings of Bureau of Census, 194, 195; brought under analysis as a social composition, 195; may be classified as objective and subjective, 195; in the first category, the geographical setting, 195; no State Church, military caste, or landed aristocracy, 196; no ruling family, 196; lines between classes not sharp, 196; theoretically only one class, 197; American social ideal, 197; methods employed giving distinct characteristics to institutions and sentiments of, 197; on the industrial side, 197; agricultural phase of, 198, 199; American political institutions objectively considered, 199; on the subjective side, traditions of human equality, 199, 200; the idea of progress, 200, 201; common conceptions of right and wrong must be developed, 202; in terms of policy, no more conquest of territory of subject races, 203; the quota rule for immigration involved, 203; interests should be balanced, 204; terms in which issues may be stated, 204

American Navy League, 242

American Republic, posture of, amid world of nations, 317; great trends at present time, 317, 318; Republic can be defended against any foes such policy might raise against it, 318; its diplomacy as that of the "good neighbor," 319; course which must be adopted in order to avoid entanglements, 319

American Revolution, what it accomplished, 243

American Stabilization Fund, 292

American stake abroad, 225; see *also* Stake abroad

Ames, Professor Adelbert, "Progress